THE EMOTIONAL INTELLIGENCE ACTIVITY KIT

THE EMOTIONAL INTELLIGENCE ACTIVITY KIT

50 Easy and Effective Exercises for Building EQ

ADELE B. LYNN and JANELE R. LYNN

ΔMACOM

American Management Association

New York | Atlanta | Brussels | Chicago | Mexico City | San Francisco

Shanghai | Tokyo | Toronto | Washington, D. C.

Bulk discounts available. For details visit:
www.amacombooks.org/go/specialsales
Or contact special sales:
Phone: 800-250-5308
Email: specialsls@amanet.org
View all the AMACOM titles at: www.amacombooks.org
American Management Association: www.amanet.org

This publication is designed to provide accurate and authoritative information in regard to the subject matter covered. It is sold with the understanding that the publisher is not engaged in rendering legal, accounting, or other professional service. If legal advice or other expert assistance is required, the services of a competent professional person should be sought.

Library of Congress Cataloging-in-Publication Data

Lynn, Adele B.
    The emotional intelligence activity kit : 50 easy and effective exercises for building EQ / Adele B. Lynn and Janele R. Lynn. — First Edition.
        pages cm
    Revised edition of: The emotional intelligence activity book, c2002.
    Includes bibliographical references and index.
    ISBN 978-0-8144-4923-3 (pbk.) — ISBN 978-0-8144-4924-0 (ebook) 1. Emotional intelligence—Problems, exercises, etc. 2. Success in business—Problems, exercises, etc. I. Lynn, Janele R. II. Lynn, Adele B. The emotional intelligence activity book. III. Title.
    BF576.3.L96 2015
    152.4076—dc23   2015010337

About AMA

American Management Association (www.amanet.org) is a world leader in talent development, advancing the skills of individuals to drive business success. Our mission is to support the goals of individuals and organizations through a complete range of products and services, including classroom and virtual seminars, webcasts, webinars, podcasts, conferences, corporate and government solutions, business books, and research. AMA's approach to improving performance combines experiential learning—learning through doing—with opportunities for ongoing professional growth at every step of one's career journey.

Printing number

10 9 8 7 6 5 4 3 2 1

CONTENTS

PDF files for the handouts are available to purchasers of this book at:

www.amacombooks.org/go/EmotionalActivityKit

ACKNOWLEDGMENTS

We would like to express our deepest thanks to our community of colleagues, friends, clients, and family who helped write this book. There simply would be no book without them. We have also received tremendous support from AMACOM, as well as from Earl McDaniel, who continues to try to make us better writers.

Janele would like to thank those who helped inspire these activities: Jennifer Kudla, Tahsin Alam, and my HR partner in crime and best friend, Candace Hassinger. I'd also like to thank my husband, James Tuttle, for his endless patience with this project and his willingness to take notes when I was brainstorming, and Sherman and O'Brien for keeping me warm and laughing. Finally, to those who are no longer with us, thank you for providing a guiding light when we needed it. Especially to Dad, who I know was cheering for us.

## CHAPTER 1

EMOTIONAL INTELLIGENCE—THE FRAMEWORK FOR GREAT PERFORMANCE

You've probably witnessed people in organizations who display great skill beyond traditional cognitive ability. More than likely, you have also witnessed people who, despite great cognitive capacity, demonstrate gaping deficiencies at work. These deficiencies could be attributed to a variety of factors, one of which is a lack of emotional intelligence. The theory that multiple types of intelligence exists has been recognized since 1983, when Howard Gardner published *Frames of Mind: The Theory of Multiple Intelligences*. Along the way, the term "emotional intelligence" was coined to describe competencies related to managing oneself and one's interactions with others. Thirty years of research and ongoing debate have ensued about the definition of emotional intelligence and whether it even exists. Still, if you are a coach, trainer, or organizational development practitioner, your job comes down to helping people become more effective in their roles. In addition, you've come to appreciate that something other than cognitive skills is at play. In the learning and development field, emotional intelligence is widely accepted as a desirable element beyond cognitive skills for success in the workplace. This book is designed to give you practical ways to help others improve their emotional intelligence.

Studies show emotional intelligence competencies as a distinguishing factor in functions as diverse as sales, service, healthcare, productivity, profit, and even ethical decision making. Research that demonstrates the link between emotional intelligence and increased organizational performance are not hard to find. One study found that executives who scored high on Emotional Quotient (EQ) scales were more profitable than their peers and had a greater ability to express empathy and self awareness than their peers, who stood lower on the EQ scale.[1] Another study showed that businesses whose owners had a higher EQ earned greater revenues and experienced higher growth. The owners used their EQ to positively shape company culture.[2] As a predictor of performance, Druskat found that emotional intelligence is two times more accurate as a predictor of performance than cognitive intelligence, and it predicts success beyond an employee's skill, knowledge, or ability.[3] Her work examined how teams and leaders effectively manage complex interpersonal and coordination challenges in cross-functional, cross-cultural, and self-managing work environments. Emotionally intelligent managers are responsible for a 34 percent greater annual profit growth, increased customer satisfaction, and higher retention, according to a 2003 study by Reuven BarOn and Geetu Orme.[4] Even ethical decisions, critical to the long-term success of any organization, were linked to emotional intelligence in a study of physicians and nurses. Higher EQ scores translated into decisions that were more ethical.[5] And, the more senior the leader, the more emotional intelligence matters. In a study of officers in the British Royal Navy, EQ competencies predicted overall performance and leadership better than any other predictive measures. This was especially true as the officer obtained higher rank.[6] For a comprehensive understanding of the research behind emotional intelligence, visit the Consortium for Research of Emotional Intelligence in Organizations.

A Lack of EQ—What Are the Challenges and How Do They Affect the Organization?

Lack of emotional intelligence can limit a person's ability to get results. This inability can limit, derail, or halt careers. Here are some examples of how a lack of emotional intelligence can interfere with a person's ability to deliver results:

- One leader was known for always telling people what to do. He had all the answers to all the questions all the time. He second guessed his executives' decisions and freely told them what they were doing wrong. Besides annoying people with his arrogance, he eventually found himself inundated with details as others learned that if they didn't involve him in a decision, he would find fault with it. His approach also cost him loyalty and turnover when several of his key executives left the company for other positions.

- Another leader was promoted to president of a large division, in which a key role was to maintain positive relationships with employees. Her predecessor had done this by constantly demonstrating his appreciation to employees. He had strong bonds with people at all levels of the organization, knew everyone by name, and engendered a genuine sense of caring and engagement. The new leader struggled. In fact, she avoided people. She even figured out which path to take to the ladies room so that she could see the fewest colleagues. Several months later, the employee engagement scores had tanked and turnover was at an all-time high.

- Another senior executive had an intense need to compete and win. He always wanted the biggest budget, the greatest span of control, and the last word. It actually cost him dearly in his relationships with his peers. Not until the CEO told him that these behaviors were the reason he was not considered for promotion did he pay attention to the cost and consequences of this behavior.

- A senior leader continually created tension among her peers by always reacting with skepticism to new ideas. Although contrary opinions and evidence are useful in decision making, someone who constantly reacts with skepticism will find it is draining and damaging to relationships. It also gives the person a label that she may not want to have.

- A leader lost his job when his new boss became tired of hearing him make excuses. His favorite excuse was, "We can't control business conditions." The new boss's favorite expression was, "We create our own business conditions by steering the business in the direction of opportunity."

The leaders in these examples are real. Each failure can be traced back to an emotional intelligence-related competency. Each leader suffered a career consequence because of a lack of emotional intelligence. More importantly, each leader had the ability to successfully recognize and overcome his or her failure and increase emotional intelligence competency.

However, leaders are not the only ones who suffer career consequences related to limited emotional intelligence. Everyday people are inadvertently sabotaging their careers with these types of behaviors:

- The IT person who, once again, has offended the customer.

- The call center worker who rarely can deescalate the conflict and, so, requires the supervisor's time and effort.

- The engineers who intensify the never-ending email battles for the sake of proving themselves right.

- The coworkers who are so involved in the daily cat fight that they miss the fact that they are actually being paid to work.

- The healthcare worker who is so caught up in the daily "who should be doing what" argument that important health details are not communicated.

And, no doubt, each of these persons may be right about something. However, their methods of interaction may be flawed. It's the methods that encompass the emotional intelligence failure. Although all of these actions may invoke an individual career penalty, ultimately, the organization suffers the consequence. Moreover, the consequences can be costly. Lost customers, lost time, the best solution giving way to ego, or even medical mistakes, can all result from EQ failures. Otherwise talented individuals misdirect their time and expertise, and the businesses and individuals both lose. The challenge of EQ failures begs for a solution. Coaching and training offer part of that solution.

Development professionals can provide an essential service to the organization by enhancing the emotional intelligence of the workforce. This book offers the "how."

A Working Definition of Emotional Intelligence

The definition of emotional intelligence is "the ability to manage ourselves and our relationships with others so that we can live our intentions and reach our goals."[7] This definition, and the competencies that follow, offer a practical model for emotional intelligence. In addition, the activities in this book make the definition and competencies actionable for adults in the workplace, which is the focus of this book.

The first part of the definition ("the ability to manage ourselves") clearly centers on with the individual. Common language requires people who are emotionally intelligent to be aware of their emotions and be able to self-manage, self-regulate, or exercise self-control. The second part of the definition ("the ability to manage our relationships with others") requires that people be aware of the impact they have on others, so that they can productively manage the relationships that life requires. In the world of work, those relationships are with employees, peers, customers, vendors, supervisors, and other people with whom we interact. If those relationships do not function successfully, productivity, morale, retention, and costs will be negatively affected. The definition continues with "live our intentions and reach our goals." From the point of view of an organization, living with intention equates to acting in alignment with the organization's values. Finally, an organization sets goals to be achieved. Of course,

the definition can be applied outside of the organizational context. If so, living our intentions and reaching our goals would imply living and exercising our personal values and reaching the goals/purpose that we have set for our lives.

Five Areas of Emotional Intelligence

Our model for emotional intelligence includes five areas: self-awareness and control, empathy, social expertness, personal influence, and mastery of purpose and vision (see Figure 1-1).[8] Within these five areas, several specific competencies emerge (see Figure 1-2). Definitions and competency descriptions of the five areas follow.

1. **Self-Awareness and Control.** The ability to fully understand ourselves and use that information to manage emotions productively. This area includes the competencies of accurate understanding of our emotions and the impact emotions have on performance, accurate assessment of strengths and weaknesses, understanding our impact on others, and self-management or control, including managing anger, disappointment or failure (resulting in resilience), and fear (resulting in courage).

2. **Empathy.** The ability to understand the perspective of others. This area includes the competencies of listening to others, understanding others' points of view, understanding how our words and actions affect others, and wanting to be of service to others.

FIGURE 1-1 Five Areas of Emotional Intelligence

Self-Awareness and Control

Empathy

Social Expertness

Personal Influence

Mastery of Purpose and Vision

Inward   Inward   Outward

FIGURE 1-2 Emotional Intelligence Table of Competencies

AREA OF EMOTIONAL INTELLIGENCE	DEFINITION	COMPETENCIES
Self-Awareness and Control	Ability to fully understand myself and my impact on others and use that information to manage myself productively.	**Self-Awareness** • Impact on Others—Accurate understanding of how our behavior or words affects others. • Emotional and Inner Awareness—Accurate understanding of our emotions and thoughts affect behaviors. • Accurate Self-Assessment—An honest assessment of strengths and weaknesses. **Self-Control** • Emotional Expression—The ability to manage anger, stress, excitement, and frustration. • Courage—The ability to manage fear. • Resilience—The ability to manage disappointment or failure.
Empathy	Ability to understand the perspectives of others.	• Respectful Listening—Listening respectfully to others to develop a deep understanding of their points of view. • Feels Impact—Ability to assess and determine how situations, as well as our words and actions, affect others. • Service Orientation—Desire to help others.
Social Expertness	Ability to build genuine relationships and bonds, as well as to express caring, concern, and conflict in healthy ways.	• Building Relationships—The ability to build social bonds. • Collaboration—The ability to invite others in and value their thoughts related to ideas, projects, and work. • Conflict Resolution—The ability to resolve differences. • Organizational Savvy—The ability to understand and maneuver within organizations.
Personal Influence	Ability to positively lead and inspire others as well as myself.	**Influencing Others** • Leading Others—The ability to have others follow us. • Creating a Positive Work Climate—The ability to creating an inspiring culture. • Getting Results Through Others—The ability to achieve goals through others.

AREA OF EMOTIONAL INTELLIGENCE	DEFINITION	COMPETENCIES
		Influencing Self • Self-Confidence—Appropriately believing in our skills and abilities. • Initiative—Being internally guided to take steps or actions. • Goal orientation—Setting goals for ourselves and living and working toward achieving them. • Optimism—Having a tendency to look at the bright side of things and to be hopeful of the best. • Flexibility—The ability to adapt and bend to the needs of others or situations as appropriate.
Mastery of Purpose and Vision	Ability to bring authenticity to my life and live out my intentions and values.	• Understanding Our Purpose and Values—When we have a clearly defined purpose and values. • Taking Actions Toward Our Purpose—When we take actions to advance our purpose. • Authenticity—When our motives, actions, intentions, values, and purpose are aligned and transparent.

3. **Social Expertness.** The ability to build genuine relationships and bonds and express caring, concern, and conflict in healthy ways. The competencies of relationship building, organizational savvy, collaboration, and conflict resolution are included in this area.

4. **Personal Influence.** The ability to positively lead and inspire others, as well as ourselves. Leading others, creating a positive work climate, and getting results from others are the components of influence. It also includes self-confidence, initiative and motivation, optimism, and flexibility.

5. **Mastery of Purpose and Vision.** The ability to bring authenticity to our lives and live out our intentions and values. This includes competencies of understanding our purpose, taking actions toward our purpose, and being authentic.

As the model in Figure 1-1 depicts, three of the components relate to our internal world (self-awareness and control, empathy, and mastery of

purpose and vision). The other two form our relations to the external world (social expertness and personal influence). However, it is important to recognize they are interrelated and one component builds on the next. Without self-awareness and control, it is difficult, if not impossible, to improve our relationships with the outside world. For example, if I am not aware of my actions, thoughts, and words, I have no basis for self-understanding. If I have some awareness and self-understanding, then I can ask, "What is my impact on others, in my current state?" If I find that impact to be negative and detracting from my life goals, I may choose to change my actions, thoughts, or words. However, some people understand their negative impact on others or that their actions, words, or thoughts detract from their life goals, yet still either choose not to change or find change too difficult. In emotional intelligence, this change is what we call self-control. It is about knowing and then deciding on the appropriate volume level and expression of our emotions. How do these emotions enhance or detract from our relationships with others and our life goals? Thus, self-awareness and self-control are intertwined, as self-awareness alone will be of little service without self-control. Leaders, teammates, and others in the workplace are interdependent, so it behooves everyone to improve self-understanding and then to act upon this knowledge.

Beyond self-awareness and control is empathy, which is also listed as an internal function on our model. Empathy must be felt inside before it can be reflected in our relationships with people in our external world. Therefore, empathy is a turning point or transition in our emotional intelligence, as it plays out in the outside world. Further, without empathy, we are incapable of comprehending the impact our actions or words have on others. We may have been told that a particular behavior or word affects others in a negative way, but empathy enables us to experience it. It also drives us to want to be helpful or of service to others.

Next in our model is social expertness. Few of us can work or live in isolation. People are generally a part of the equation. Social expertness allows us to build genuine social bonds with others, to know them beyond name, rank, and serial number, and to connect with them honorably. It's not about the number of people in your contact list, but rather the reaction those people have when you're on the other end of the phone. Are they delighted that you called or would they rather be talking to the long-distance carrier trying to sell phone services? Beyond honorable social bonds, social expertness calls on us to invite those within our social bonds to collaborate in achieving our intentions. How well are we able to collaborate with others and blend thoughts and ideas to achieve goals or life intentions? But, once we have invited people to collaborate, conflict is inevitable, as different ideas will emerge. How will we resolve those differences? Social expertness demands high levels of conflict resolution skills that work to preserve social bonds and trust. Social expertness also requires us to have organizational savvy to move ideas and goals forward while maintaining positive relationships.

Personal influence is the next area in our model for emotional intelligence. It also reflects our interactions with others. Personal influence is where true leadership emerges. Before this, we are peer to peer; it is here that we intend to influence others toward goals or missions. However, we cannot influence if we have not created strong bonds and invited others to collaborate or if we lack the ability to resolve conflict in healthy ways. Leadership, however, is not reserved for positional leaders; all people are leaders. Even if we think about leadership in terms of influencing our children, this area of emotional intelligence is essential for a rich life and calls on us to influence others. That ability to influence ourselves is equally important. It is within the walls of our own souls that the most work must be done. As we influence ourselves to change, we can be an instrument of influence to others. Influencing ourselves requires our ability to take initiative, stay motivated, display confidence and optimism, and be flexible.

Finally, the model includes mastery of purpose and vision. It is the most internally seated of all the aspects of emotional intelligence, and it serves as a foundation on which to build a more emotionally intelligent life. It is, in essence, both the reason we strive for emotional intelligence and the driver that keeps us anchored. If we can identify our purpose, it is much easier to determine what type of emotional reactions will serve our purpose and which will defeat it. Mastery of purpose makes it easy to know why we should even bother. We place it last because it is sometimes the most difficult to know and conceptualize. Although it is certainly possible to excel in all other areas of emotional intelligence without yet discovering true purpose, once we discover true purpose, we can more easily improve emotional intelligence.

The activities and exercises that follow in this book give trainers and coaches concrete ways to address the deficiencies mentioned earlier in this chapter that can derail careers and cause havoc in organizations. Coaches and trainers can select activities that cover all five areas of emotional intelligence or zero in on specific competencies. When coaches and trainers combine these activities with astute application to the organization, tremendous progress and development can occur for the individuals in all areas of emotional intelligence. Both the individual and the organization can benefit and avoid the pitfalls that can extinguish careers and affect organizational success.

Notes

1. Stein, S.J., Papadogiannis, P., Yip, J.A., & Sitarenios, G. (2008). "Emotional Intelligence of Leaders: A Profile of Top Executives," *Leadership and Organization Development Journal,* 20(1), 87–103.

2. Ozcelik, H., Langton, N., & Aldrich, H. (2008) "Doing Well and Doing Good: The Relationship Between Leadership Practices That Facilitate a Positive Emotional Climate and Organizational Performance," *Journal of Managerial Psychology,* 23(2),186–203.

3. Druskat, V., Sala, F., &Mount. G. (Eds.), Linking Emotional Intelligence and Performance at Work (pp. 97–124). Mahwah, NJ:Lawrence Erlbaum Associates, 2006.

4. BarOn, R., & Orme, G. (2003). In Orme and Langhorn, "Lessons Learned from Implementing EI Programs," *Competency & Emotional Intelligence,* 10,32–39.

5. Deshpande, S.P. (2009). "A Study of Ethical Decision Making by Physicians and Nurses in Hospitals," *Journal of Business Ethics,* 90, 387–397.

6. Dulewicz, C. , Young, M., & Dulewicz, V. (2005). "The Relevance of Emotional Intelligence for Leadership Performance," *Journal of General Management,* 30 (3), 71–86.

7. Lynn, A., *The EQ Difference; A Powerful Plan to Putting Emotional Intelligence to Work.* New York: AMACOM Books, 2004.

8. Lynn, A. *The EQ Interview.* New York: AMACOM Books, 2008.

## CHAPTER 2

HOW TO USE THIS BOOK

Before the Activity

Activities are tools. As with any tool, it is helpful to know when and how to use it. Of course, each activity in this book will have specific directions for use. Just as a hammer is used to drive nails and a screwdriver is used to insert screws, activities also have specific purposes. Every activity is different and every learner is different. It is your responsibility as the coach/trainer to pause and consider the needs of the organization and the individual learners. As the coach/trainer, you must also consider your location, the interests of the group, challenges, and quirks. There is no simple formula for selecting an activity or scripts to tell you exactly what to say to introduce or debrief an activity. It is your responsibility as the coach/trainer to consider your learners' needs. However, by following just a few steps here and having a willingness to improve, you can definitely succeed at facilitating these activities. Here are some thoughts to help you prepare before the activity.

➤ Needs Analysis

- It's important to consider the needs of the individual learners and the organization. Not all activities support all needs, so it is important to first identify what exactly you would like the activity to accomplish.
- Some questions to consider
  - What are the current challenges?
  - Is there conflict?
  - Do the individuals know each other?
  - What level of awareness of the need do the participants possess?

➤ Competency Analysis and Activity Selection

- Activities are grouped based on the EQ competency and general content areas they support, as well as the audience with which they work best. The EQ competencies are described in Chapter 1, and exercises are ordered by competency, audience, and content area in the tables contained in Chapter 6.
- Some questions to consider
  - What EQ competency best matches the needs of the learner/organization?
  - What type of audience will I be working with? Is this a one-on-one coaching engagement or a classroom setting? Consider the number of participants and the amount of time you will have for the exercise.
  - What personalities will I be working with? Will an activity that requires quiet reflection meet their needs or would an activity that requires movement or problem solving work better?
  - Is this level of disclosure appropriate? Exercises that are lower disclosure can be fun and engaging and provide learning opportunities, but a higher disclosure exercise might create interesting learning opportunities for your participants to grow and stretch their understanding of themselves. Choosing the appropriate level of disclosure for your learners is a critical task. For more information on choosing an appropriate level of disclosure, see Chapter 3.

➤ Visualize the Activity

- It's important to make sure you are well prepared to use the activity. If you do not fully understand the purpose of the activity or understand what should happen next, the activity will fall flat. An unprepared activity is like a joke without a punchline.
- Some questions to consider:
  - Have you read the activity several times?
  - Can you visualize what is supposed to occur?
  - Can you anticipate questions?
  - Can you anticipate what the responses to the debrief will be and how you can redirect those responses to match the needs of the group?

➤ Personalize the Activity

- You should consider how you will personalize the activity based on your own experiences and with examples that will help make the activity relevant. Use the information included in the exercise to ensure that the learning is accurate and includes personal examples that explain why the activity is important. Remember, when using personal examples, **never** point out problems between team members as an example of why this activity is important or what the activity can accomplish.
- Some questions to consider
  - When in my life has this competency been important/impactful?
  - What do I still struggle with in regard to this competency?
  - Can I use examples that will help the participants better understand based on their perspectives? What examples will the participants find relevant?

➤ Identify Roles

- Think about what role in the activity you as the facilitator or coach must play. For some exercises, you'll be a motivating force; for others you'll be a timekeeper or enforcer. For the activity to be a success, you must commit to these aspects of the role so that the learning will be most effective.
- Some questions to consider
  - What role will the activity require of you?
  - What should I say to clarify that role?
  - What will my tone be? Kind? Supportive? Firm? Direct?

➤ Gather Materials

- Materials needed for each activity are listed in the materials section of the activity.
- Some questions to consider:
  - Do I have everything I need to complete this exercise?
  - Do I have proper equipment to play videos or music or display images?
  - Have I confirmed that any audiovisual components are working?
  - Do I have enough handouts for everyone in class?

➤ Consider Room Setup

- This is most important for classroom learning, but it can also have an impact during one-on-one coaching sessions and with web-based learning.
- Some questions to consider
  - For coaching, is the space comfortable? Is the positioning of the chairs intimidating?
  - For web-based learning, how will learners participate? How will I cover the ground rules of participation? For example, when will microphones be muted to ensure clear sound and how will questions/comments be received?
  - For classroom training
    - How will the chairs be arranged?
    - Will you need a flip chart? If the instructions are lengthy, it will save time and confusion if you write them on the flip chart in advance of the meeting.
    - Is there enough space in the room for the activity, or will I need an alternate location?
    - Is there ample room for groups to move around or for me to create smaller breakout groups?

➤ Anticipate Problems

- There is a chance with any learning activity that problems will occur. Participants may not fully grasp the concepts at hand, they may be unwilling to participate, or they may direct the conversation away from the learning points you wish to make.
- Some questions to consider
    - What problems are most likely to occur with this activity?
    - What problems are most likely to occur with these participants?
    - What else could go wrong?
    - How can I address these issues in the moment?

During the Activity

The role of the coach/trainer is to act as a facilitator for the learners. It is sometimes easy to be critical of participants' learning, but you need to work instead to facilitate the learning. The participants who are most likely to benefit from the activities are those who come to the learning freely.

➤ Use Words Carefully

- The way you introduce and position an exercise can be critical. It is important to set the stage to provide the correct context for the participants to experience the activity and grasp the learning. Be open with the objective (unless instructed in the activity not to) and explain why the activity is important.

➤ Watch Your Mood

- Are you excited about the activity? Confident that it will work? The mood and emotion that you bring to the activity will be interpreted by your group and will impact the experience of its members.

➤ Be Clear

- Give clear instructions for the activity. If necessary, display the instructions or pass them out. Unclear instructions can quickly create an unwillingness to participate.

➤ Check Twice

- After you have given clear activity instructions, check for understanding with the group. Ask if the group members have any questions. Volunteer to demonstrate the activity.

➤ Facilitate the Activity

- Your main role during the activity is to help the participants learn, not to participate or influence the activity. If the exercise requires you to be an enforcer or timekeeper or to play another role, make sure you do so, but in a way that is as unobtrusive to the learning as possible.

➤ Watch the Group

- Watch the verbal and nonverbal behaviors of the group as the activity unfolds, and make note of your observations. These observations can be useful additions to the debrief of the exercise.

➤ Correct Instructions

- If the participants misunderstand the instructions, you may need to correct the problem (unless a level of confusion is necessary to achieve the desired outcome, which will be noted in the activity). If you need to make a correction, don't place blame; just pause the activity and restate the instructions.

➤ Practice Safe Activities

- Some participants may not feel comfortable participating in an activity because of the nature of the activity or the other participants in the room. Don't force anyone to participate in an activity, especially in a group session. Coaches with a one-on-one relationship can reiterate the safety of the space if the learning is critical.

➤ Inappropriate Comments

- During an exercise, if someone makes an inappropriate comment, redirect it immediately, and ask that the group speak respectfully.

> Stay Flexible

  • At times, even after careful planning and appropriate clarification attempts, the activity still may not go as planned. If so, listen to the conversation that comes up in the debrief. You may gather valuable information that will help you connect the learning point or will address a later learning point. As the facilitator, it's best that you remain flexible.

After the Activity

As the facilitator, the debrief period after the activity requires you to be at your most flexible. Generally, it is during the debrief period that learning actually takes place. The questions you use to debrief the activity are the most important piece of the exercise. The best way to think about the debrief period is that it is a reflective time to generate learning. It is a fantastic time to learn from one another, too, because everyone sees and experiences things differently.

> Ask for Reflection

  • Start by asking the participants to reflect on the activity. Build their curiosity about what others might have experienced.

> Use Questions

  • Use questions to drive their learning. The debrief questions in the activity will provide a place to start. Add questions based on your own experiences or to direct the participants to a particular learning need.

> Celebrate

  • It can be hard to share learnings from the activity, especially in a group setting.

Thank people for their comments, and celebrate the comments you receive by being generous and sincere. This celebration helps reinforce the internalization of the learning to help them apply the concepts to the job.

> Encourage

  • Encourage all members to comment. Some people will be more reticent, but ensure that it is useful for all points of view to be heard.

> Silence the Dominators

  • If one person is dominating the discussion, sincerely thank the person and say, "What do others think about Joe's comment?"

> Be Silent

  • One mistake some facilitators make is that they try to fill the silence after a question. Allow some quiet time so that the group members can ponder their answers. As the facilitator, you already know the answers, and if you speak too quickly, you will inadvertently send the message that the others are not required to participate.

> Clarify, Don't Judge

  • Make sure you stick to the role of facilitator when someone answers a question. Facilitators ask for clarification, for examples, for the individual to elaborate, and for agreement or disagreement with the group. If you judge the response as being right or wrong, there is suddenly a penalty for communication.

## CHAPTER 3

WHAT YOU'LL SEE FOR EACH ACTIVITY

Each activity is organized consistently so that you can easily follow and compare them. Each activity includes the following categories, which will help you understand and effectively implement the activities.

Prerequisite and Companion Activities

Some activities have the graphic shown in Figure 3-1 to designate that it must be paired with a prerequisite activity. Other activities pair particularly well, even though there is no requirement to use them together. For activities that complement one another, the trainer or coach will see the graphic shown in Figure 3-2 at the header. Most activities do not have pre-requisite or companion designation.

EQ Area and Competency

The EQ Area and Competency section shows which of the five areas of emotional intelligence and which of the 26 competencies the exercise supports. For a description of the five areas of emotional intelligence and the 26 competencies, see Figure 1-2. The charts in Chapter 6 will allow you to quickly reference the EQ competencies addressed in each activity. As the facilitator, if you wish to use the exercise to highlight one particular competency over another, you can select debrief questions that highlight the lessons learned specifically for that competency. You should select competencies based on the needs identified for your learners and the needs of the organization.

How to Use This Activity

The How to Use this Activity section explains the purpose of the activity. The intention of the exercise will help you decide whether the activity is the best one for achieving the desired objective and meeting the specified need of the group. This section provides a brief understanding of the basic concepts learned in the activity and will allow you to quickly determine if this activity will support the group's needs. Once you have determined that the activity is appropriate for your group, you can use this summary to help explain to the participants what the activity is intended to accomplish.

Applicable Content Area

Certain activities are appropriate for different content areas, such as communication skills, conflict resolution, customer service, interpersonal skills, leadership development, or teamwork. Content areas that fit each activity are listed in this section, and the charts in Chapter 6 will also help you locate an activity that focuses on a particular content area. All activities can fit with a general emotional intelligence curriculum, but certain activities highlight particular issues in those content areas.

Audience

These activities have been designed to work with various learning modules: in person, group-based classroom training, one-on-one coaching, and web-based learning. You can find a list indicating which activities fit each type of audience in Chapter 6. This section will also describe the type of audience this activity will best serve. Most activities have been written from the perspective of classroom training, but you can make simple modifications to adapt them to coaching or web-

FIGURE 3-1

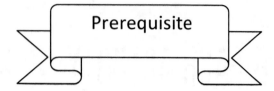

FIGURE 3-2

based learning. For example, in a one-on-one coaching environment, you may need to insert yourself in the activity as a partner to discuss self-reflection. Another example of a simple modification for web-based training would be to send specific instructions to one individual in the group via a private conversation or to send handouts to the entire group via email prior to the exercise.

Estimated Time

A time estimation is included with each activity. As experienced coaches/facilitators, you understand that such estimates depend on a number of factors, including the number of participants, the chattiness or reticence of each participant, and the amount of thought and time spent completing reflection worksheets. Therefore, our time estimates are based on an average class of 15 to 25 participants. Obviously, the fewer the participants, the less time will be required, and vice versa. As a facilitator who is cognizant of time, you can find many ways to modify the exercises to allow for more participants or to ensure you stay on schedule. For example, you can always ask individuals to partner up to share learnings and then ask for a few contributions from the group as a whole to save time.

Level of Disclosure/Difficulty

The Level of Disclosure/Difficulty section will show a "High, Medium, or Low" designation to allow you to quickly determine the level of difficulty of the activity. By "level of disclosure," we mean the level of discomfort the participant may feel when completing the activity, based mostly on the level of self-disclosure or difficult reflection that the activity requires. Some activities require very little self-disclosure; others require much more, and some individuals will feel greater

discomfort with more self-disclosure. When designing your course or coaching assignment, we recommend that you first work with exercises that are of low difficulty and require little self-disclosure. This allows the coach/facilitator to build a level of trust with the learners and will help create a safe space for sharing thoughts and ideas. Once that level of trust has been established, you can introduce higher disclosure activities. Each team is different, and disclosure factors can change depending on team dynamics, but we have assigned a level of disclosure based on our experience with most groups. You as the facilitator will need to use your discretion to determine your own group's comfort level and select or adapt the activities to match it. It is important to note that just because activities are high disclosure, they shouldn't be avoided. Some activities with the most impact may be ones in which participants are asked to think about difficult concepts or challenging topics. It is important for you as the coach or facilitator to create a safe environment, so your group can address those concepts and topics. Also, it is very difficult for a facilitator to read the emotional climate of a web-based training group and, therefore, to determine the level of safety the participants will feel. So facilitators should use caution in selecting high-disclosure activities for web-based training.

Materials

This section lists materials that will be needed to successfully execute the activity. Some activities require few materials; others require more. If a handout or instructions are required, they are provided at the end of the activity. It's always useful to have a flip chart and markers handy. Web-based activities may require a different execution of materials, such as a platform that allows a presenter to add items to a screen so all can view their contributions.

Purpose/Why This Is Important

This section provides insight to the facilitator/coach on why the particular competency matters and why it is important for individuals and organizations to develop it. You can use this section to provide examples and information to explain the concept to the participants. It is particularly helpful for adult learners to understand the big picture and why the activity is important. For more background information, consult *The EQ Difference* by Adele Lynn.

Set the Stage

The coach/facilitator needs to introduce the concept of the activity to the participants. At this point, unless otherwise instructed in the activity, you should do more than explain the purpose of the emotional intelligence competency and why the concept is important; you should also provide more depth about the concept of the specific activity and why these concepts relate to work. This can require that you provide examples, ask questions, or, at times, just explain the concept or terminology. Occasionally, for the exercise to have impact, the "setting the stage" step can be deliberately misleading to the audience. This may be designed, for example, to cause frustration during the exercise to specifically create lessons about dealing with those frustrations. In those cases, it is important that you, as coach/facilitator, stay on message, so that the activity has the desired impact. For other activities, though, it is important to ensure that the activity is framed in the context of the required learning so the maximum benefit can occur.

The Activity

This section gives a detailed step-by-step description of the activity for the facilitator/coach. It explains what you should do during the activity to ensure it progresses smoothly.

Key Debrief Questions

The key debrief questions are essential for the success of the activity. These questions will spark learning and help link that learning to the participants' jobs so that the activity is practical. As coach/facilitator, focus your debriefs specifically on the outcomes you wish to achieve for maximum success. For example, some debrief questions may be more applicable to teamwork than to leadership development. You should focus your debrief on the questions specific to the learners' needs. Several important debrief questions have been captured in this section, but you do not need to pose all of the questions on the list nor is it necessary to only ask those questions. As coach/facilitator, you should feel free to create specific debrief questions to your audience's needs and to tailor these questions to the group and the discussions that have already occurred.

Key Learning Points

In addition to Key Debrief Questions, Key Learning Points are also included in each activity. Depending on the savvy of each individual, more or fewer debrief questions may be required to ensure that your participants have learned from the activities. For example, if you as the coach/facilitator ask a simple initial question in the debrief that causes an in-depth discussion on the key learning points of the activity, it may not be necessary, and could in fact seem redundant, to continue to ask debrief questions. Alternatively, you may find that the individuals are just not quite able to articulate the key learnings during your debrief questioning. In that case, you may want to reiterate some of the key learning points to help clarify their thinking. The key learning points have been provided so that you have a method to ensure that the debrief discussion can be directed in the appropriate way.

## CHAPTER 4

A GUIDE TO THE 50 ACTIVITIES

Figure 4-1 is a quick reference guide that provides an overview of the activities, including the competencies they address and the purpose, disclosure level, and estimated time for each.

FIGURE 4-1 A Guide to the 50 Activities

ACTIVITY NUMBER	ACTIVITY NAME	ALL COMPETENCIES EXHIBITED	PURPOSE	SUMMARY	LEVEL OF DISCLOSURE	ESTIMATED TIME
1	The Critic	Organizational Savvy, Feeling Impact on Others, Getting Results Through Others, Creating a Positive Work Climate	Read the climate and observe and respond to influencers in a group setting.	A group leader's behavior is deliberately showing favoritism toward one group member and others must determine how to navigate the situation.	Low	30 minutes
2	Know a Guy	Building Relationships	Demonstrate the importance of building and nurturing relationships in the workplace.	Ask participants to search their networks for access to particular skills or resources; discuss the value of networks.	Low	30 minutes
3	Cups and Ice	Initiative and Accountability, Flexibility, Emotional and Inner Awareness	Explore one's attitude and approach to mundane tasks, and recognize that others form opinions based on attitude.	Show video clip and process specific questions.	Low	30 minutes
4	Fifteen Minutes	Emotional and Inner Awareness, Resilience	Explores perspective and resiliency related to one's skills and also one's failures.	Worksheet provides thought provoking questions around success and failure in one's life.	Medium	45 minutes
5	The Invitation	Building Relationships, Organizational Savvy	Foster relationships, bridge generational differences, and transfer learning.	Send selected individuals (such as mentors) a printed invitation to meet and share wisdom.	Low	90 minutes
6	Doozie of a Disappointment	Resilience	Encourage perspective and strength to overcome a disappointment by recalling past disappointing events.	Recall past disappointments. Rate them as they occurred and then with the distance of time and perspective.	High	45 minutes

#	Activity	Competencies	Objective	Description	Level	Time
7	Facebook Feed	Impact on Others, Emotional and Inner Awareness, Accurate Self-Assessment	Provide analysis of how we are always sending messages that others are interpreting.	Discuss the analysis of the messages we send as others are interpreting. Use Facebook as an example.	Low	20 minutes
8	Your TED Talk	Self-Confidence	Build confidence and examine the connection between confidence and influence.	Prepare, videotape, and play back a presentation and receive feedback about confidence.	High	70 minutes
9	Hot Potato	Initiative and Accountability	Provide guidance and choices when dealing with conflicting priorities, especially in team environment.	Simulation of multiple priorities in a team environment to generate discussion of stressors and solutions.	Low	60 minutes
10	Your Theme Song	Creating a Positive Work Climate, Conflict Resolution, Emotional Expression	Raise awareness about the tone that people set in their interactions.	Use music to identify and describe tone and how one comes across to others.	Medium	45 minutes
11	If I Had a Billion Dollars	Understanding Purpose and Values	Help participants clarify and identify what they view as purposeful work.	Structure thinking and discussion around purpose.	Low	30 minutes
12	Finish Line!	Goal Orientation	Build awareness and move forward on goals by analyzing steps used to obtain past goals.	Use worksheet to move forward on a present goal.	Low	45 minutes
13	Selfie Listening	Respectful Listening	Learn listening and empathy skills and the impact they have on others.	Orchestrate listening and nonlistening behaviors, and solicit discussion regarding impact.	Low	30 minutes
14	To Talk or Not to Talk—That Is the Question	Social Bonds, Impact on Others, Feeling Impact on Others, Building Relationships	Sensitize people to the impact of talking too much or not enough.	Role play "talkers" and "nontalkers," and discuss impact.	Medium	45 minutes

FIGURE 4-1 *Continued*

ACTIVITY NUMBER	ACTIVITY NAME	ALL COMPETENCIES EXHIBITED	PURPOSE	SUMMARY	LEVEL OF DISCLOSURE	ESTIMATED TIME
15	Gumball	Emotional Expression, Collaboration	Participants identify their typical M.O. related to stressful tasks.	Ask participants to complete a task with built in stressors.	Low	30 minutes
16	What Do You Assign to the Pictures of Your Life?	Impact on Others, Optimism	Recognize how thinking affects our view and how optimism and pessimism can be influenced by changing our view.	People assign meaning to pictures based on their initial assumptions and then are asked to change their view.	Low	35 minutes
17	Practice Assigning New Thoughts/ Feelings to Something in Your Career	Emotional and Inner Awareness, Optimism, Flexibility, Feeling Impact on Others	Examine our thinking about situations or people and how it affects our behavior.	Analyze current thinking about a person or situation, challenge the thinking, and then predict different behavior.	High	30 minutes
18	Puzzler	Service Orientation, Getting Results through others	Examine service orientation and leadership in a challenging group setting.	Ask participants to build puzzles with incomplete pieces and without being able to communicate.	Low	40 minutes
19	Last Name	Understanding Purpose and Values	Reflection on individual purpose and passion.	Worksheet based reflection to stimulate thinking and discussion around purpose and passion.	Low	25 minutes
20	ROYGBIV	Leading Others	Explore and build skill around influence.	A leader must influence the group to align themselves in a particular order.	Low	40 minutes

#	Activity	Competency	Description	Summary	Level	Time
21	Look Around	Organizational Savvy	Build observational skills in the moment to enhance one's ability to navigate organizational dynamics.	Participants complete worksheets that enhance observation skills during an actual (or orchestrated) meeting.	Medium	40 minutes
22	States	Emotional and Inner Awareness, Emotional Expression, Collaboration	Identify emotional reactions. Use collaboration to perform task.	Alphabetize states as individuals and as a group.	Low	30 minutes
23	Good Enough	Goal Orientation	Provide insight on self-directed goal setting and task achievement.	Worksheet based analysis of one's goal orientation for insight and discussion.	High	30 minutes
24	Reflection Errors—Part 1	Accurate Self-Assessment	Identify reflection errors in thinking.	Interview regarding something that is problematic. Watch for reflection errors.	High	40 minutes
25	Reflection Errors—Part 2	Accurate Self-Assessment	Turn reflection errors into productive problem solving behavior.	Imagine different scenarios for problem situations.	Medium	60 minutes
26	Swing Set	Building Relationships, Getting Results Through Others	Identify conflicting goals, assumptions, and communication that interfere with success of task because of silo thinking.	Group works in department silos and must complete a simulated task.	Low	60 minutes
27	Restaurant Reviews	Feeling Impact on Others, Impact on Others	Identify the reaction and impact that behaviors cause in others.	Role play specific behaviors when performing a group task and analyze the group dynamic.	Low	45 minutes

FIGURE 4-1 *Continued*

ACTIVITY NUMBER	ACTIVITY NAME	ALL COMPETENCIES EXHIBITED	PURPOSE	SUMMARY	LEVEL OF DISCLOSURE	ESTIMATED TIME
28	Using Quotations to Anchor Purpose	Understanding Purpose and Values	Clarify intentions using wisdom of others.	Select and discuss quotations that reflect a life or leadership philosophy.	Medium	60 minutes
29	Academy Award	Emotional and Inner Awareness	Identify false rational beliefs that impact one's behavior.	An assigned actor and challenger role play to demonstrate the impact of irrational thinking on behavior.	Low	40 minutes
30	Judgment Day	Emotional and Inner Awareness, Conflict Resolution	Examines judgments we make that interfere with our actions toward others.	Groups are given scenarios and asked to list assumptions that come to mind.	Low	30 minutes
31	Let's Go!	Collaboration, Conflict Resolution	Gives participants a process to use in resolving conflict by focusing on interests.	Teams must resolve a conflict over where to go on vacation by using a process for conflict resolution.	Low	40 minutes
32	A Wondering Mind or a Plan for the Future?	Understanding Purpose and Values	Help people understand and clarify their purpose.	Use daydreams as a source of data regarding purpose.	High	60 minutes
33	Actions Speak Louder Than Words	Taking Actions Toward Purpose	Encourage action toward purpose and dreams.	Use the worksheet to define actions that could be taken to explore purpose or dreams.	High	50 minutes

34	Shoots and Scores	Resilience	Examine emotion and resilience related to a difficult task.	Group is asked to perform a task that requires members to think differently and identify what is affecting their performances.	Low	40 minutes
35	Blind Vote	Courage	Examine courage and its value to leadership positions and organizations.	Scenarios presented with various resolutions. The group rates and discusses resolutions based on courage.	Medium	40 minutes
36	Are you Flexible? Let's Find Out	Flexibility, Accurate Self-Assessment	Obtain feedback regarding flexibility.	Use 360-interview format to assess flexibility.	High	45 minutes
37	How am I doing?	Leading Others	Gain direct feedback about one's leadership.	Use 360-interview format to gain feedback about one's leadership.	High	45 minutes
38	Authenticity —A Reflection	Authenticity	Build reflection around authenticity for the purpose of improving it.	Reflection worksheet and guided discussion on behaviors that lead to authenticity.	High	60 minutes
39	Better Method	Creating a Positive Work Climate	Frame language that creates positive climate and tone in teamwork interactions.	Choices of language are given to address various situations, and participants select and discuss best language to maintain teamwork.	Low	30 minutes

FIGURE 4-1 *Continued*

ACTIVITY NUMBER	ACTIVITY NAME	ALL COMPETENCIES EXHIBITED	PURPOSE	SUMMARY	LEVEL OF DISCLOSURE	ESTIMATED TIME
40	Flexibility—A New Leader Exercise	Flexibility	Create internal guidelines for leaders for balancing fair and consistent actions with the desire to be flexible.	Reflection worksheet and discussion on leadership flexibility.	High	90 minutes
41	Help Who?	Service Orientation	Explore importance and what service orientation looks like when dealing with peers.	Use scenarios with various options to select the best course of action and discuss reasons why.	Medium	40 minutes
42	Reflection on Courage	Courage	Increase self-awareness related to one's courage.	Reflection worksheet to create thought, dialogue, and goals related to courage.	High	60 minutes
43	Authenticity Explored	Authenticity	Examine actions that are viewed authentically in teamwork and in career advancement.	Capture group thinking and norms around behaviors that are viewed as authentic and inauthentic.	Medium	60 minutes
44	Advertise-ment	Creating a Positive Work Climate	Demonstrate how to create (and destroy) a positive work climate.	Group is asked to create an advertisement. One member either positively or negatively changes the climate of the group.	Low	60 minutes
45	The Rebuttal	Respectful Listening, Conflict Resolution	Illustrates difference between respectful listening and rebuttal listening.	Orchestrated debate on contentious issues while observing listening behavior.	Medium	40 minutes

46	Confidence Builder	Self-Confidence	Addresses criticism and confidence, and the impact criticism can create in some individuals.	Small groups produce a list and the larger group offers criticism. Focused discussion about criticism and confidence.	Medium	40 minutes
47	Flying High	Leading Others, Feeling Impact on Others	Demonstrates influence of the leader using influence tactics.	Group task of building airplanes is either enhanced or thwarted based on leader's behavior.	Low	45 minutes
48	Shoe Switch	Feeling Impact on Others	Encourages empathy when reviewing situations in the workplace.	Work with a partner to review a situation that didn't go well to determine how the other party may have been reacting.	High	40 minutes
49	What Have You Done?	Taking Actions Toward Purpose	Stress value of taking actions toward goals and one's purpose.	Review through a worksheet the actions one has taken to achieve a particular career path.	High	60 minutes
50	Review of Emotional Intelligence Using Quotations	Review of Several Areas of Emotional Intelligence, Emotional and Inner Awareness	Reinforce concepts of emotional intelligence.	Use quotations as part of a review of concepts of emotional intelligence.	Medium	30 minutes

THE ACTIVITIES

EQ 1 ## The Critic

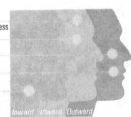

Self-Awareness
and Control

Empathy

Social
Expertness
Personal
Infuence
Mastery of
Purpose and
Vision

Inward Inward Outward

EQ Area and Competency

Social Expertness: Organizational Savvy
Empathy: Feels Impact on Others
Personal Influence: Getting Results Through Others;
    Creating a Positive Work Climate

How to Use This Activity

• To raise awareness about group dynamics and how they affect group members.

• To observe how group members read group dynamics and adjust their positions accordingly.

Use this activity to highlight the dynamics that occur within working groups. In particular, this activity examines the leader and who influences the leader and how other members deal with the influencer. This activity is appropriate for the classroom.

Applicable Content Area

Multiple: Leadership development, New /aspiring leadership development

Audience: Classroom

Estimated Time: 30 minutes

Level of Disclosure/Difficulty: Low

Materials: A slide or PowerPoint of a piece of modern abstract art that is not well known.

Purpose/Why This Is Important

Organizational savvy is defined as the ability to understand how to maneuver within organizations to get things done. Skill and savvy in understanding the organization will play a vital role in one's success. This important skill has four aspects: the ability to read the political climate of the group; to determine who has influence and who does not; to determine how to get a sponsor for an idea; and to understand how to get buy-in for decisions.

Set the Stage

Tell the group members that they are a panel of prestigious art critics and their job is to come up with a group critique of a piece of artwork. Every member of the group is encouraged to state his opinion and rate the artwork based on several criteria listed on the flip chart. However, the chairperson's opinion will weigh most heavily, so other members must convince the chairperson to include their ideas. It is highly desirable to get your point of view included in the review.

The Activity

1. Divide the class into groups of six. Appoint a chairperson for each group.

2. Give the chairperson her instructions. Tell the other members of the group that all must express their opinions on all the factors for the piece of art displayed on the PowerPoint slide. Write the following factors on the flip chart for the groups to use for their discussions. The group is to discuss and form opinions about the following:

   a. Color
   b. Balance
   c. Form
   d. Light
   e. Expression
   f. Emotion

3. Give the group members several minutes (10 to 15) to interact.

4. After 10 minutes, call time.

5. Ask the chairperson to summarize his critique of the artwork based on the criteria.

6. Debrief the activity.

Key Debrief Questions

➤ Whose point of view was included in the chairperson's critique? Whose was not?

➤ What did the team members observe about their group?

➤ How would the team members describe their group? Did everyone in the group have equal power and influence?

➤ How did you assess the power and influence of the members?

➤ What did you think about the distribution of power and influence?

➤ Did any of you feel as though your opinions were heard? Not heard? Why or why not?

➤ What body language did you observe in the group?

➤ Did it appear as though the chairperson was unduly influenced by one member of the group?

➤ What tactics did you observe group members using to exert more influence with the chairperson?

➤ What tactics worked? What tactics didn't work?

Key Learning Points

The facilitator should help the participants arrive at the following conclusions:

➤ Sometimes certain group members have influence over others. The leader pays more attention to that person's opinions or ideas.

➤ We must be able to read this group dynamic. Once we are aware of it, we have several ways to address it. We can challenge it openly in the group; we can challenge it privately with the leader; we can choose to use the influencer as a sponsor for our idea; or we can choose to argue that our idea has more merit.

➤ The critical skill is to be able to see and understand the dynamic and then to create a strategy that best addresses it.

➤ If we are unable to observe the dynamic, we are unable to come up with a strategy to address it.

➤ In a perfect world, all group members would be equal and all leaders would be open minded about everyone else's opinion. However, in reality that is rarely the case.

The Critic Handout

The chairperson should instruct participants to ignore or discount all team members' opinions except for the person seated two seats to their right. If that person says something, they should validate it and include it in their summaries. If anyone else says something, ignore it or discount it. It is not necessary to give a reason for ignoring or discounting something.

Self-Awareness and Control

Empathy
Social Expertness
Personal Infuence
Mastery of Purpose and Vision

Inward   Inward   Outward

EQ 2   Know a Guy

EQ Area and Competency

Social Expertness: Building Relationships

How to Use This Activity

- To show the importance of building relationships in the workplace.

- To provide insight into the necessity of nurturing relationships.

"Know a Guy" can be used as part of emotional intelligence training, as a teamwork exercise, or for customer-service training. It can also be used as part of a communications, diversity, or leadership-development process.

Applicable Content Area

Multiple: Leadership Development, Teamwork, Customer Service, and Communications

Audience: Web-Based, Classroom

Estimated Time: 30 minutes

Level of Disclosure/Difficulty: Low

Materials: "Know a Guy" handout—one per participant

Purpose/Why This Is Important

This activity is designed to provide insight into how social bonds are built and the importance they serve in our everyday lives. Building relationships requires that you become familiar with people's skills and abilities and make each relationship strong and trustworthy. Building relationships in the workplace enables success because it broadens your network and helps get things done.

It can help solve some workplace mysteries, as for example. "Who exactly knows how to fix the copier when it jams?" When individuals build strong, trusting social bonds, they are able to discover that information and leverage those relationships to accomplish goals.

Set the Stage

Give each member of the group a copy of the handout. Introduce the activity by saying, "Think about your social circle and the social circle of people you know. In those circles, many people have specific skills. In this activity, we'll try to think of someone who can help us with the tasks listed on the sheet." If the examples on the sheet do not meet the needs of your audience, you can create your own list for the participants. Ask them to spend a few minutes thinking about the skills on the handout and provide as many people who can help as possible.

The Activity

1. Allow 10 to 15 minutes for the participants to each complete the "Know a Guy" handout.

2. Ask the participants to identify how many skills they could match with a person.

3. Ask participants which skill was hardest to match up with a person. Determine if anyone in the room was able to make that match. Continue with hard skills to identify until you find one that someone was able to make a match.

Key Questions

➤ Was it easy for you to identify people on this list? Would the people you identify be willing to help you? Why would someone be willing to help you? Why wouldn't they?

➤ To whom would you give your contacts? Which contacts? In what situations?

➤ Who at work "knows a guy?" Do you have a relationship with that person? Can you leverage his contacts?

➤ Would you consider this taking advantage of the person? Is it exploitative?

Key Learning Points

The facilitator should help the participants arrive at the following conclusions:

➤ Building relationships that will work for you is critical to accomplishing tasks in the workplace.

➤ Relationships take effort. If you don't build the necessary relationships, you won't ask people to do something for you too often, or you won't be able to use them when you need them.

➤ You need to put effort into relationships so they are not exploitative or one sided. You should always be asking yourself, "What can I do for this person?"

Know a Guy Handout

Think about your social circle and the social circle of the people you know. Try to think of someone you may have access to who can help with the tasks below. "I know a guy/gal who. . . ."

- Could marry two people, legally, this afternoon.

- Could take you skydiving today.

- Would know a restaurant willing to open in the middle of the night and serve you and a dozen friends dinner, and whom to call to make that happen.

- Could introduce you to a U.S. senator.

- Knows the secret to fixing the fax machine when it stops working.

- Makes the perfect pot of coffee, every time.

- Could act as a translator for a client who speaks only Russian.

- Has the phone number for a locksmith memorized or stored in their phone (but no Googling!).

- Has, on her office or on his person, a flashlight and screwdriver.

- Could bake or talk you through baking a loaf of bread without looking at a recipe.

- Owns a working typewriter.

- Could copy files you desperately need off of a 5¼" floppy disk from 1992.

- Can order any office supply you need, no questions asked.

Cups and Ice

Plays Well with Others

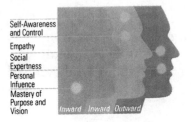

Self-Awareness and Control
Empathy
Social Expertness
Personal Infuence
Mastery of Purpose and Vision

Inward Inward Outward

EQ Area and Competency

Personal Influence: Initiative, Flexibility
Self-Awareness: Emotional and Inner Awareness

How to Use This Activity

- Use this activity to help people see that how we approach mundane tasks can be important because we can demonstrate our commitment and creativity and distinguish ourselves.

- This activity can help people recognize that everyone's career has mundane tasks.

- Use this activity to make the point that everything we do informs people's perceptions of how we perform.

- Cups and Ice can be used at any time, but it is particularly valuable with new hires or with people who feel their careers are stalled.

Applicable Content Area

Multiple: Career Development, Teamwork, Onboarding

Audience: Classroom, Web-Based

Estimated Time: 30 minutes

Level of Disclosure/Difficulty: Low

Materials

The 18th episode of the fifth season of the TV show *Friends*, titled "The One Where Rachel Smokes."
A few minutes of the clip regarding cups and ice discussion.

Purpose/Why This Is Important

Not all tasks are necessarily exciting or glamorous, but how we apply ourselves to those less-than-glamorous tasks builds strong impressions with people. In organizations, these tasks can influence careers and can help decide promotions. Initiative is a key factor in career success. Taking initiative and demonstrating passion for tasks demonstrates to others that we care about doing our best work, regardless of the importance of the task. When we take initiative in the face of the mundane, it demonstrates that we are able to overcome emotions of boredom or frustration that can be associated with routine tasks and commit ourselves to higher goals.

Set the Stage

This activity is best when the group is surprised by the video clip and the content of the message. Therefore, not much is needed to introduce the activity. The best setup would be to say that this next activity will help us look at how we approach our work.

The Activity

1. Ask the participants if they have any tasks or job responsibilities they find mundane or marginal. Ask them to list some of them.

2. Set up the clip using these words: "Phoebe and Monica are organizing a surprise party for Rachel. Monica, who is an organizing freak, takes control of everything, leaving nothing for Phoebe to do. Phoebe points this out to Monica. To appease Phoebe, Monica gives Phoebe marginalized duties: to take care of cups and ice for the party. Watch what happens." Play the clip.

3. Debrief the activity using the questions below.

4. Put people into small groups to brainstorm how they could reframe their attitudes around the tasks they listed in Step 1 and what they could do differently.

Key Debrief Questions

➤ How could Phoebe have reacted to Monica's request?

➤ What happened when Phoebe turned her energy toward cups and ice?

➤ How would you describe Phoebe's performance related to cups and ice?

➤ What was the reaction of other people to Phoebe's attention to cups and ice?

➤ What lessons can we learn from this about our work?

➤ What might we have to change for us to approach our work the way Phoebe approached cups and ice?

➤ What is the potential payoff if we approach our work in a similar manner?

➤ When do you demonstrate initiative toward tasks? When do you demonstrate less initiative? What messages are you sending to others?

Key Learning Points

The facilitator should help the participants arrive at the following conclusions:

➤ Everyone must perform tasks he considers mundane.

➤ Everything you do sends a message to others. Others judge you on your actions.

➤ A negative attitude toward the mundane can demonstrate to others that you are not committed or promotable.

➤ Demonstrating creativity toward the mundane can separate you from your peers.

➤ Your mindset forms your behavior. It also can shape your happiness and satisfaction toward your job.

➤ Your mindset is something you can control.

➤ Initiative is a critical career attribute.

➤ Be aware of the messages you send to others through your behaviors.

EQ 4 Fifteen Minutes

Self-Awareness and Control
Empathy
Social Expertness
Personal Infuence
Mastery of Purpose and Vision

Inward Inward Outward

EQ Area and Competency

Self-Awareness and Control: Emotional and Inner Awareness, Resilience

How to Use This Activity

*   To provide perspective on relative successes and failures.

*   To provides insight into how feelings of success/failure inform our actions.

    This activity can be used as part of EQ training, teamwork, or an on-boarding program. It can also be used as part of a high-potential, leadership-development, or career-development process.

Applicable Content Area

Multiple: Leadership Development, Career Development, Teamwork, Interpersonal Skills

Audience: Classroom, Coaching, Web-Based

Estimated Time: 45 minutes

Level of Disclosure/Difficulty: Medium

Materials: "Fifteen Minutes" handout—one per participant

Purpose/Why This Is Important

Resiliency requires individuals to have the emotional and inner awareness to put things into perspective. This activity is designed to provide insight into how individuals view success and failure and to examine their perspectives on how much "fame" means to them. In "Fifteen Minutes" participants will think about their fame and how they feel when someone else is more popular/more successful/more famous than they are. Yes, someone will always be better at a particular thing, but how we react, accept that information, and move forward is the crux of resiliency.

Set the Stage

Pass out a copy of the handout to each member of the group. Talk about what being famous means and how striving to be the best at something can be a motivator. Some of the best stories of fame come from people who have failed spectacularly, Steven Spielberg, Walt Disney, and Oprah Winfrey to name a few. Ask each person to spend a few minutes thinking about the questions on the handout and then answer them.

The Activity

1. Allow 10 to 15 minutes for each participant to fill out the "Fifteen Minutes" handout.

2. Ask participants to share their responses to the following questions on the handout:

    *   What would you like to be famous for?
    *   How would you feel if someone was better than you?

Key Questions

➤ Why does this matter? Will someone always be better than you, by some definition of "better?"

➤ How do you react when presented with the evidence that someone is better than you? How do you react when presented with a perception that someone is better than you?

➤ Do you dwell on other people's fame? Does this motivate you? Does it distract you?

- How much effort do you put into the skill you'd like to be famous for? How much time/effort do you put into becoming famous? Why is the balance important?

- Do you have any skills you could become famous for in your workplace? Do you promote those skills? Should you? How?

Key Learning Points

The facilitator should help the participants arrive at the following conclusions:

- Chances are someone will be better than you. How you react matters.

- Learning how to react to both fame and failure defines your character. How you choose to act when you are the best or when you fail at something says something about the kind of person you are.

- The ability to focus not just on a skill but on appropriately promoting your own skill can help you.

- Resilience requires that you keep trying and keep picking yourself up, even if things did not turn out very well. It's whether you show up again, ready and willing to work, that matters.

Fifteen Minutes Handout

Name someone who is famous for doing something. What did he or she do? Is it something you could do? Why did this person become famous? How did he or she respond to the fame?

Name someone who is famous for failing at something. At what did he or she fail? Is it something you could do? Why did this person get famous? How did he or she respond to the failure?

What would you like to be famous for?

What could you be famous for in your workplace?

How do you react at your wildest successes?

How do you react when you fail?

How would you feel if someone was better/more famous than you?

EQ 5 | The Invitation

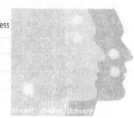

Self-Awareness
and Control

Empathy

Social
Expertness
Personal
Infuence
Mastery of
Purpose and
Vision

EQ Area and Competency

Social Expertness: Building Relationships, Organizational Savvy

How to Use This Activity

*   To help form relationships in the workplace that may otherwise not occur.

*   To bridge generational differences.

*   To transfer organizational learning.

"The Invitation" can be used as part of a formal or informal mentoring program or an on-boarding program. It can also be used as part of a high-potential, leadership-development or career-development process.

Applicable Content Area

Multiple: Leadership Development, Teamwork, Communications, Diversity, Generational Awareness, Conflict Resolution, Mentoring, Career Development

Audience: Classroom, Coaching

Estimated Time: 90 minutes

Level of Disclosure/Difficulty: Low

Materials

Formal invitations obtained at a stationery store
Printing template
Suggested wording or topics
A list of volunteers—Prepare a list of individuals within the organization who would be willing to share experiences or advice with others. You may ask for volunteers, or you may designate individuals based on their job titles or

levels. Either way, the individuals should be willing participants who would represent the organization's values.

Purpose/Why This Is Important

Use this activity to build bridges and social bonds between individuals in the workplace and to transfer organizational learning. A formal invitation to share one's experience honors the individual. In addition, the person who invites someone to share knowledge gains valuable insight into something he deems important. Therefore, both individuals benefit. This activity strengthens bonds between individuals. When someone in the organization can share experiences or knowledge, she transfers organizational learning that may otherwise be lost. The invitation also opens communication pathways between individuals that may never have been forged. By opening communication, a company makes new resources available and transfers tacit knowledge. These relationships can prove fruitful for years to come. They also can provide on-going informal mentoring opportunities between the individuals.

Set the Stage

Ask the group members to think about times when they received formal invitations in the mail. Discuss how they feel whenever someone they care about sends them a formal invitation. Explain that although a formal invitation typically comes for an event such as a wedding or special milestone, it is a powerful way to build bonds and give people a sense of significance in their organizations, particularly when they are invited to share their experience and insight. In essence, a formal invitation acknowledges a person's desire to learn from someone's experiences. A significant way to build bonds with people in an organization is to honor the fact that they have things of value to share. Explain that a critical element of this activity will be for the participant to listen, acknowledge, ask questions, or otherwise indicate interest to the individual who is invited to share his or her knowledge. Ask participants to draw on their personal experiences to think about how they would feel if someone were genuinely interested in their experiences.

The Activity

1. Give each participant a predetermined number of stationery store invitations, envelopes, a printing template, and a list of individuals willing to be interviewed. (Decide if you will assign individuals to each participant, or if you will permit participants to determine whom they wish to invite to share their experiences.)

2. Brainstorm with the group members various topics they could invite people to discuss. Depending on the objectives of your course or coaching, the topics could be related to leadership, career development, organizational savvy, enculturation, diversity, or other topics.

3. Ask participants to develop a list of questions for the topic they would like the individual to address. This list will serve as an interview guide when she is speaking with the person.

4. Set a time frame for sending out the invitation and conducting the interview.

5. Ask participants to come to the next meeting prepared to discuss what they learned.

Key Debrief Questions

➤ What did you learn?

➤ How did you ensure that you were listening and honoring the person you invited?

➤ How would you describe the encounter?

➤ How can you incorporate the experience or knowledge this person shared into your career or life?

➤ How does something like this increase your bonds with others in the organization?

➤ Why is it useful to deepen your bonds with others?

Key Learning Points

The facilitator should help the participants arrive at the following conclusions:

➤ Learning can take many forms: book learning, personal experience, and the experiences of others.

➤ The experiences of others in the same organization provides insight into the culture and unspoken rules of success.

➤ Seeking advice and counsel from others builds strong bonds that you can call on in the future.

➤ If you continue to cultivate these relationships, you can straighten out your learning curve about the organization. You can also produce strong allies and sponsors for your career and help yourself solve important organizational problems.

The Invitation Handout

FIGURE 5-1 An Example of an Invitation Handout

You are invited to share your experience on

Leadership

With: Jan O'Brian, Operations Lead

When: At a time convenient for you in April

Where: A comfortable spot of your choice

Share: Something significant that you learned in your leadership career that you think would benefit others interested in leadership

RSVP: Jan@yourcompany.com x123

EQ 6

Plays Well with Others

Doozie of a Disappointment

Self-Awareness and Control
Empathy
Social Expertness
Personal Infuence
Mastery of Purpose and Vision

Inward   Inward   Outward

EQ Area and Competency

Self-Awareness and Control: Resilience

How to Use This Activity

- To help people overcome disappointing news.

- To demonstrate to people that they have internal power.

- To encourage perspective when looking at life's events.

When individuals are trying to recover from disappointing news, this activity can give them a sense of resilience based on past experience. Since all people at some point during their career will face disappointment, this activity will prepare them to handle it and ensure that it doesn't derail their ultimate success. Therefore, it is appropriate as part of a training session on career development or leadership development. This activity works particularly well when coupled with the "Cups and Ice" Activity for career development because the "Cups and Ice" Activity addresses boring and mundane assignments that can lead to career disappointment.

Applicable Content Area

Multiple: Career Development, Leadership Development

Audience: Coaching, Classroom

Estimated Time: 45 minutes

Level of Disclosure/Difficulty: High

Materials

The "Doozie of a Disappointment" handout
Masking tape

Purpose/Why This Is Important

Managing our reaction to disappointment is an important skill to master. Everyone will face some sort of disappointment in his career and life. However, how people react may separate those who eventually reach their goals from those who do not. When faced with career disappointment in an organization, one's reactions will often be noted and labeled. If person who doesn't get what he wants reacts by pouting, shouting, or otherwise withdrawing his performance, he can incur a costly label that will cling to him. As a result, he may be passed over for the next promotion. However, if people react to disappointing news with resilience, this attribute will likely help them. In addition, they will benefit from the inner strength they muster in times of disappointment. Emotional intelligence requires that we gain perspective on life's disappointments. Of course, all disappointments are not created equal. A bad hair day is not as bad as a day on which one learns of a terminal illness. Perspective building helps us face and measure the next disappointment life may bring. The emotional intelligence competency of resilience will serve us in all aspects of our lives—both personal and professional.

Set the Stage

Begin a discussion on the subject of disappointment. Suggest a mild disappointment, such as the weekend weather forecast. Ask group members to offer a recent disappointment they have had. Ask the group if all disappointing events are equal. Ask if there is anything we can gain from disappointment.

The Activity

1. Ask the participants to think of a few disappointments they have had in their lives. Assure

them that they will not be asked to share the disappointing event with others.

2. Instruct people to complete the "Doozie of a Disappointment" handout.

3. While the participants are completing the handout, use masking tape to create a 1-to-10-point continuum on the floor. Use a piece of tape to mark points 1, 5, and 10.

4. When participants have completed the handout, ask them to gather around the continuum. Demonstrate how to arrange themselves on the continuum based on the severity of the disappointment they experienced, for example, a bad hair day is a 1, a bad hair day on picture day is a 2, someone who has a terminal illness is a 10.

5. For the first disappointment they recorded on the handout, ask people to rate the disappointment based on how they feel now and how they felt when it occurred, both on a scale of 1 to 10, with 10 as the most intense.

6. Ask the participants to rate disappointment number three on the handout. Ask the group if the intensity is the same now as it was when the disappointment occurred.

7. Put people into pairs to discuss how they overcome disappointments.

Key Debrief Questions

➤ How does time change our perspective about disappointments? How can we use this knowledge to help us today?

➤ What happened when we focused our attention on a disappointment?

➤ What are some of the ways that we have overcome disappointment?

➤ What can we apply to our current lives that will help us become more resilient?

➤ What can we learn about examining our role in the disappointing event?

➤ Is this adjustment in our perspective a skill? How can we practice it? How can it assist us today and in the future?

Key Learning Points

The facilitator should help the participants arrive at the following conclusions:

➤ Generally, time lessens the intensity of our disappointments. However, occasionally, there are exceptions. For example, perhaps when you were in high school and didn't apply yourself, you didn't care at the time. However, looking back, you now wish you had worked harder so that you could have gone to school to become an engineer.

➤ The more we focus on the disappointment, the stronger it becomes. Replacing our thoughts about the disappointment with positive aspects of our lives helps us to temper our emotional reactions to the disappointment.

➤ Changing our thinking is an important strategy for improving our emotional reactions to events and can contribute to our resilience. It is a hallmark of emotional intelligence.

➤ It is important to distinguish between healthy and unhealthy rationalization. For example, when examining a disappointment, it would be fruitless to try to change outside circumstances that we can't control. However, it is useful to examine our role in a disappointment to determine if there is something we can do to cause a different outcome the next time around.

➤ Learning from our mistakes makes it more likely we will avoid repeating errors in the future.

Doozie of a Disappointment Handout

1. Think about a disappointing event that happened when you were a child between the ages of 5 and 15. Jot down a couple of notes about the event to help you remember it.

2. Think about a disappointing event that occurred when you were between 15 and 22 years of age. Jot a couple of notes about the event to help you remember it.

3. Think about a disappointing event that occurred in your career. Jot a couple of notes about the event to help you remember it.

   a. What outside influences or circumstances contributed to the disappointment?

   b. How did you contribute to the disappointment?

4. Think about a disappointing event that occurred within the past six months to one year. Jot a couple of notes about the event to help you remember it.

   a. What outside influences or circumstances contributed to the disappointment?

   b. How did you contribute to the disappointment?

EQ 7 Facebook Feed

Self-Awareness and Control

Empathy

Social Expertness

Personal Infuence

Mastery of Purpose and Vision

Inward   Inward   Outward

EQ Area and Competency

Self-Awareness: Impact on Others, Emotional and Inner Awareness, Accurate Self-Assessment

When to Use This Activity

- To use familiar social media norms to resonate with audiences.

- To help develop self-awareness of how messages may be sent unintentionally by people.

- To provide insight into how communications are interpreted.

"Facebook Feed" can be used as part of a formal or informal mentoring program, EQ training, teamwork building, communications training, or an on-boarding program. It can also be used as part of a high-potential, leadership development or career development process.

Applicable Content Area

Multiple: Leadership Development, Teamwork, Communications, Interpersonal Skills, and On-boarding

Audience: Classroom, Web-Based

Estimated Time: 20 minutes

Level of Disclosure/Difficulty: Low

Materials: Negative Nancy's social media page

Purpose/Why This Is Important

This activity is designed to reinforce the concepts of message selection and setting the tone. These are critical emotional intelligence skills, as they require consideration of how the message will im-

pact others and what consequences that impact may have. The activity also provides insight into how individuals may be sending unintentional messages, which are a key aspect of emotional and inner awareness.

Set the Stage

Ask the group the following while displaying or sharing Negative Nancy's page: "Have you ever encountered someone with a social media profile like this? Is this the kind of person you would like on your team at work?" Ask individuals to draw on their personal experiences to think about how messages are perceived by others.

The Activity

1. Duplicate Negative Nancy's social media page and place it in a visible location. (This can be done in a couple of different ways. You can duplicate it on a large piece of poster board so you can reuse it. You can write it on flip chart paper. Or, you could project it on a screen or wall using an LCD projector.) It should be visible to all members of the team.

2. Ask individuals who desperately want to work with Negative Nancy to raise their hand. Count the respondents.

3. Ask individuals who do not want to work with Negative Nancy to raise their hand. Count the respondents.

Key Debrief Questions

➤ Why did you choose to work or not to work with Nancy?

➤ Is Nancy really negative? Based on her messages, does it matter?

- How might people's messages affect us in the workplace?

- How do you send messages in the workplace? Through social media? What others ways do we send messages?

- Are we always aware of the messages we send? How can we increase our awareness of these messages?

- What power do we have over our messages?

- What can you do to change your message?

- Is changing our message "fake"?

Key Learning Points

The facilitator should help the participants arrive at the following conclusions:

- Messages can be deliberate choices or unintended reactions. It is much better to deliberately plan the messages we wish to send to others.

- Messages can be sent via social media, email, and meetings, but also via tone and body language. In fact, many messages we send every day in the workplace are sent by way of our attitude, our nonverbal language, and even the way we dress or carry ourselves.

- Be aware of unintentional messages that may sabotage your intentions.

- Think about how you may be shaping people's opinion about you by the way you respond to an email or your facial expression in a meeting. The more mindful you are, the better your chances of sending the intended message.

Facebook Feed Handout

FIGURE 5-2 Negative Nancy's Social Media Page

Negative Nancy

I don't even know why I bother sometimes, people are so stupid....

Negative Nancy

It is days like today that I just want to quit my entire life, or maybe just get a new job

Negative Nancy

I think my job is giving me an ulcer; maybe I'll call in sick again

Negative Nancy

Why can't I catch a break?

Negative Nancy

Didn't sleep well again last night. Definitely not going to be giving it my all today, not that anyone will notice anyway. . . .

EQ 8 Your TED Talk

Self-Awareness
and Control
Empathy
Social
Expertness
Personal
Infuence
Mastery of
Purpose and
Vision

Inward Inward Outward

EQ Area and Competency

Personal Influence: Self-Confidence

How to Use This Activity

- To help people confidently express themselves.

- To demonstrate the effect that confidence has on others.

- To examine the connection between confidence and influence.

Use this activity in career development, leadership development, or personal development. Although appropriate for both coaching sessions and classroom learning, it is most effective with an audience. The awareness activity illustrates the importance of expressing confidence and the effect that confidence has on others. It benefits someone who believes his influence is weak or her voice often goes unheard. It can also be valuable for people who think they have reached a career plateau or who have suffered a string of rejections from job interviews, possibly related to how they present their ideas or opinions.

Applicable Content Area

Multiple: Career Development, Leadership Development, Communications, Interpersonal Skills

Audience: Classroom

Estimated Time

10 minutes of group discussion to set the stage for the activity.
1 hour per person (1/2 hour for the person to prepare, 5 to 10 minutes to present, 20 minutes for feedback).

Due to length of this activity for each participant, it would be best to keep the group size down to 8 to 10 participants

Level of Disclosure/Difficulty: High

Materials

Video recording and playback equipment
Confidence rating sheet
Confidence preparation sheet

Purpose/Why This Is Important

Influence has many tentacles. One way to improve a person's influence is to increase the confidence with which he expresses ideas. If a person has a great idea or point of view, but doesn't express it with conviction and interest, it may be missed in an organization in which many ideas compete for attention. When ideas are expressed with confidence, people listen. During a person's career, promotions are often based more on confidence than on competence. Although we are not arguing in favor of confidence over competence, we recognize that career opportunities align with the person who is able to convince others of her worth. Therefore, confidence becomes an important element in emotional expression. It can also be effective at demonstrating the line between confidence and arrogance.

Set the Stage

Ask the group if anyone is familiar with TED Talks. TED Talks is a not-for-profit organization devoted to the concept of "ideas worth spreading." One of the services of TED Talks is videotaped presentations of people sharing their ideas with people all over the world. Some of the videos have become very popular and serve to change people's thinking. (If you wish, you can play a TED Talk for the group.)

Explain that in an organization, people have opportunities to present worthwhile ideas. Some do this quite effectively; others do not. The level of confidence the presenter displays can influence whether or not an idea is taken seriously.

Begin a discussion on the subject of confidence. Ask the group:

- To define confidence.

- How they know it when they see it.

- To think about people who display great confidence.

- How confidence affects others.

- To discuss the difference between confidence and arrogance.

- When confidence is important.

- Why it is important in those circumstances.

Then explain that the purpose of this activity is to help people display self-confidence because it is an important emotional expression that helps others become engaged in our ideas and opinions so they become followers and supporters. Be sure to discuss the connection between the perception of confidence and leadership and career advancement.

Ask the group members to think about a time when they were feeling confident and a time when they did not feel confident. What messages or voices were going on inside them at such times? How were they different? Ask how these messages could affect their performance and the perceptions that other people have of them.

The Activity

1. Ask participants to think about an idea or opinion related to work about which they feel strongly. It could be a new system, a new way of processing something, a new product or product improvement, an improvement of some other kind, or anything else that would benefit their company. They should think about it from their supervisor's point of view. Give participants the planning handout and the rating handout to help with their preparation.

2. Instruct people to work independently and come up with a 5- to 8-minute presentation of their idea. If you are in a group training setting, tell participants that they will be asked to present the idea in front of the group. If you are in a private coaching session, tell the participant that he will present the idea to you and can also invite others to join the presentation. Either way, inform participants that their presentation will be videotaped.

3. Videotape the presentation.

4. Ask participants, including the presenter, to use the attached rating handout to evaluate whether the person displayed self-confidence during the presentation.

5. Play the videotape of the presentation.

6. After the videotape playback, give the presenter an opportunity to rate himself again. Ask the presenter the following questions: Did your rating go up or down? Why?

7. Have the participants give the presenter feedback. Be sure that each person giving constructive feedback offers an alternative way to communicate the concept to the presenter. Ask the presenter the following questions: Did you become more or less confident based on the feedback? Why? Did you agree or disagree with the feedback? Why? How did the feedback affect your internal dialogue?

8. Ask each presenter to summarize two or three key learning points she learned that can increase her level of confidence.

Key Debrief Questions

➤ What have you learned about confidence?

➤ Based on the videotape and our discussions and feedback, how would you describe confidence?

➤ How does confidence affect us?

➤ How does our confidence affect others?

➤ How does your internal dialogue affect your confidence?

➤ What internal dialogue do you need to change in order to display more confidence?

- What techniques did you use if your internal dialogue was getting in the way of your confidence?

- What internal dialogue can help boost confidence?

Key Learning Points

The facilitator should help the participants arrive at the following conclusions:

- Confidence is a key factor when influencing others.

- If we feel confident, we have to learn to project it when we speak.

- If we don't feel confident, we have to determine ways to increase our feelings of confidence in order to persuade others.

- If you are well prepared and well versed, your confidence will increase. It also helps your confidence to rehearse your position, to anticipate and prepare for opposition and objections and to provide research and facts.

- If you "manage" or control your negative, self-doubt internal dialogue, your confidence will increase.

- You can improve your influence if you shift your internal dialogue from trying to "prove our idea to be right" to a collaborative discussion of an idea or suggestion that the group believes may have merit.

- To shift your internal dialogue, you must first determine what your internal dialogue is saying, and then replace negative messages with helpful messages. For example, if your internal dialogue is saying: "I don't think anyone will listen to me," shift it to: "I am presenting this idea because I care about this company and I think it might help."

Your TED Talk Handouts

My TED Talk Handout

1. My idea about my organization. . . .

2. Why is it important to my organization?

3. How can my organization benefit?

4. What do I want to convince others they should know about this idea?

5. What doubts do I have about this idea?

TED Talk Rating Sheet

Rater: Please rate the presenter on the level of CONFIDENCE he or she displays, not on the merit of the idea.

1. On a scale of 1 to 10, I would rate this person's overall level of confidence as:

2. Why did you rate the person as you did? Be as specific as possible.

   a. At what moments did the presenter act confidently? Be as specific as possible.

   b. At what moments did the presenter not act confidently? Be as specific as possible.

3. Offer two suggestions that would have improved your rating.

   a.

   b.

EQ 9 Hot Potato

Self-Awareness and Control
Empathy
Social Expertness
Personal Infuence
Mastery of Purpose and Vision

Inward Inward Outward

EQ Area and Competency

Personal Influence: Accountability, Initiative

How to Use This Activity

- To provide insight into the need to focus on goals, not just on tasks.

- To mimic fast-paced work environments with conflicting priorities.

"Hot Potato" can be used as part of EQ training, teamwork building, or an on-boarding program. It can also be used as part of a high-potential, leadership-development, or career-development process.

Applicable Content Area

Multiple: Leadership Development, Teamwork, On-Boarding

Audience: Classroom

Estimated Time: 60 minutes

Level of Disclosure/Difficulty: Low

Materials

Scrap paper of three different colors, cut into two or three pieces each
Markers

Purpose/Why This Is Important

This activity is designed to reinforce the concepts of prioritizing, taking responsibility, and working in a team. It also provides insight into how individuals may be reacting to stressors in the workplace, where it is easy to focus only on your most immediate tasks. As a result, those that require long-term focus can be forgotten. In a team environment, the focus can be on the goals that the team is trying to accomplish and not on the long-term goals of individual team members. This activity reminds participants to balance both. It also emphasizes the social pressures that come from a team environment.

Set the Stage

Ask the group to take several sheets of each color scrap paper. On one color, pink for example, participants should write what responsibilities they owe someone else. For example: "I need to deliver the inventory numbers to Joe every Tuesday." Each individual item they owe someone else should be on a separate piece of paper. Each participant should fill out three to five pieces of paper with his owed responsibilities.

On the next color, blue for example, the participants should write what others owe them in order to complete their jobs. For example: "Joe needs to give me information on his tasks so I can complete the status report." Each individual item they need should be on a separate piece of paper. Each participant should fill out three to five pieces of paper with needed items.

On the third color, green for example, the group members should write the things that they really value in their careers. For example: "I want to keep learning about this software program." Each individual item they really care about should be on a separate piece of paper. All participants should fill out three to five pieces of paper with what they really care about.

The Activity

1. Have participants crinkle each of the 9-to-15 pieces of paper into a ball. Ask them to gather

them and stand in a circle. It should be difficult for them to hold all of the papers.

2. Identify the colors—pass pink papers to the right in the circle, pass blue papers to the left in the circle, and place green papers behind the participant. (The colors listed above refer to the example colors above, but any colors will do).

3. Ensure everyone understands what to do with the various colors.

4. Begin the activity by calling out colors. For example, pink, blue, blue, pink, pink, green, green, blue, pink, blue. Call out the colors quickly, leaving only a second or two for the group to respond to the command. Continue the activity as individuals become frustrated, drop papers, and become confused as to the direction.

5. Instruct the group to pass items to a particular member. For example: "Pass a pink to Joe." "Pass a blue to Anne." Then ask them to pick up green items that are on the floor behind them. Continue to call out colors as you issue more specific commands. Try to ensure that one person is balancing too many papers, while others may be left without a certain color.

Key Debrief Questions

➤ What happened during the activity?

➤ Did anyone become frustrated? Was anyone confused? Did anyone want to give up?

➤ What happened to the green items? Were they forgotten? Stepped on?

➤ Did anyone feel like she couldn't hold all of the papers?

➤ Did anyone drop any balls?

➤ What did it feel like when one person was handed so many extra responsibilities?

➤ Does it ever feel like you have too many responsibilities in the workplace? Too few? What happens then?

➤ Does it ever feel like your priorities are changing too rapidly? What happens to tasks and responsibilities then?

➤ What do others see when we start dropping things or handing things off?

➤ What can a team do when they are experiencing multiple priorities and items are being missed?

Key Learning Points

The facilitator should help the participants arrive at the following conclusions:

➤ Team members have a responsibility to deliver on items promised to others.

➤ It is stressful when priorities change suddenly. Be mindful of this and try to minimize shifts.

➤ When someone is frustrated, he or she may be more likely to react negatively to others.

➤ Managing oneself during those stressful times is important because your team mates may not understand what you are experiencing and your individual goals can be lost.

➤ Individuals need to spend extra energy ensuring that their individual goals are nurtured.

➤ Open dialogue about priorities and communication when problems arise is critical.

EQ 10 Your Theme Song

Self-Awareness
and Control

Empathy

Social
Expertness

Personal
Infuence

Mastery of
Purpose and
Vision

Inward   Inward   Outward

EQ Area and Competency

Personal Influence: Creating a Positive Work
Environment
Social Expertness: Conflict Resolution
Self-Awareness and Control: Emotional Expression

How to Use This Activity

- To help people see the value in "pre-think-ing" the tone they want to set for a particular encounter.

- To examine how tone affects others' percep-tions of us.

- To highlight the role of setting tone in con-flict resolution.

Use this activity in career development, lead-ership development, or personal development. It can be used in both coaching sessions and class-room learning to help people understand that the tone they set can affect the outcome of all encounters, as well as the perceptions that people have of them. In addition, leaders, customer ser-vice personnel, and others who address conflict must understand that setting a tone for meetings and discussions is an essential skill. Rather than being "hijacked" to anger or frustration by a particular situation, these people must bring a measured tone to discussions, especially during conflict, in order to move the discussion to a positive outcome. If not, the conflict can become worse.

Applicable Content Area

Multiple: Customer Service, Leadership Devel-opment, Conflict Resolution, Teamwork, On-boarding

Audience: Web-Based, Classroom, Coaching

Estimated Time: 30 to 45 minutes

Level of Disclosure/Difficulty: Medium

Materials: Music and movie clips of your choice

Purpose/Why This Is Important

In every situation, we "show up" in a particular manner. Everything about us—the way we carry ourselves, the words we choose, the way we look at people—communicates a message and sets a tone for the encounter. If we are aware that setting tone is important and can influence the outcome of our encounters, then we have more power over our situations.

Further, everyone experiences conflict. The emotionally intelligent person understands that he has power to positively influence the outcome if he is able to set the appropriate tone for the discussion. Conflict intensifies if the tone is neg-ative, accusatory, loud, or angry. If, instead, the person sets a tone of mutual respect and encour-ages open communication, the conflict can often be solved. However, often people don't recognize the tone they are setting, or the fact that they have power to set it more positively.

Set the Stage

Ask the participants how the soundtrack of a movie affects their impressions of a scene. (If possible, show a movie clip without the music soundtrack.) Explain that all of us play a "soundtrack" when encountering others. Describe the example of an executive who often uses "war-rior language." He uses phrases such as: "I think he's on my side," "I have a strong hand," "I know we are right," "I think this battle is worth fight-ing," or "I know we can win." This language is a visible expression of his thinking. His theme song might well be the *Ride of the Valkyries* by Wagner, popularly known as the chopper attack song for *Apocalypse Now*. (Play a short clip.) He always appears to be at war. When others describe this person, they say things such as: "He isn't a team player," "He only looks out for himself and his area," or "He only cares about himself." Many people's perceptions are rooted in the tone this leader sets when he interacts with others.

Explain that setting the tone of an encounter enables us to form a perception in the minds of others. That perception can be positive or negative depending on the way we come across. (Play some short music clips, and ask: "How would you expect this person to come across?" Select clips that set a distinct mood such as fast and furious, slow and mellow, sad and somber. You can also select songs with lyrics that demonstrate positive or negative tones.)

The Activity

1. Ask the participants to complete the handout and be prepared to discuss their answers.

2. Ask participants to form pairs to discuss their answers.

3. Debrief with the following questions.

Key Debrief Questions

➤ When you think about the coworkers you enjoy working with, what tone do they set?

➤ When you think about coworkers who are unpleasant to work with, what tone do they set?

➤ Does our tone differ during conflict?

➤ What impact does it have on others?

➤ How can tone influence outcomes?

➤ What is the advantage to having a predetermined tone in mind when encountering others?

Key Learning Points

The facilitator should help the participants arrive at the following conclusions:

➤ The key to effective encounters is to deliberately set the tone.

➤ If you react from anger or frustration, the tone you set may negatively influence how you are perceived. It may also negatively influence your outcomes.

➤ During conflict, it is particularly important to set a positive tone.

➤ Each day you have a choice in how you "sound" to others. If you aren't intentional about your tone, you may be signaling to others a negative attitude that will affect your career or your ability to influence people.

➤ To shift your tone, you must be aware of negative factors that influence you and deliberately switch your tone.

Your Theme Song Handout

1. Think about your average day at work. What song or tempo describes your day?

2. Think about others at work. Can you imagine some music that describes the tone they set?

3. Using music, how would others describe you in the workplace? Are you an upbeat song that inspires high energy, such as the one that makes you want to dance? Or, are you a funeral march? Name some songs that others might use to describe you. What impact does your tone have on others?

4. Think about a conflict you encountered. Using music to describe your tone, what song would describe your encounter? What impact did your tone have on the other party?

5. What is the ideal tone you wish to set each day as you enter the workplace? What song would describe how you wish to "show up?"

EQ 11 If I Had a Billion Dollars

Self-Awareness
and Control
Empathy
Social
Expertness
Personal
Infuence
Mastery of
Purpose and
Vision

Inward Inward Outward

EQ Area and Competency

Mastery of Purpose and Vision: Understanding One's Purpose and Values

How to Use This Activity

- To provide clarity around an individual's dreams.

- To discuss job roles/responsibilities that meet an individual's needs.

"If I Had a Billion Dollars" can be used as part of EQ training or an on-boarding program. It can also be part of a high-potential, leadership development, or career development process.

Applicable Content Area

Multiple: Leadership and Career development

Audience: Classroom, Web-Based, Coaching

Estimated Time: 30 minutes, recommend smaller groups

Level of Disclosure/Difficulty: Low

Materials

Envelope with dollar signs on the outside—one
    per participant
"If I Had a Billion Dollars" Handout—one per
    participant

Purpose/Why This Is Important

This activity clarifies what participants would do in an ideal setting. It also provides insight into how individuals see their current position as compared to their ideal. Talking about an ideal job is easy for participants, and the discussion creates excitement and enthusiasm. By identifying key aspects of an appealing job, individuals can better articulate what they would like in current and future positions. This can help them better understand their core values and what they need to be fulfilled in a career. If, in a worst case scenario, they can find nothing about a current job that is interesting or satisfying, then that information is important for the learner to take into consideration regarding his or her future.

Set the Stage

Pass the envelopes and handouts out to each member of the group. Let the individuals know that you are giving them the opportunity to do anything that they would like to do in life; money is not a problem. The envelope with the billion dollars represents freedom. They can do anything at all with it, but there is one condition. They must do something. They cannot choose to spend all their time in their new mansion without doing anything. Ask them to spend a few minutes thinking about the questions on the worksheet and then provide answers.

The Activity

1. Have each participant fill out the "If I Had a Billion Dollars" handout. Provide 10 to 15 minutes to complete the handout.

2. Ask the participants to share their responses to the following questions on the handout:

   a. What is one fun/frivolous thing that you would do with a billion dollars?

   b. How would you spend your time if you had a billion dollars?

Key Debrief Questions

➤ What in particular appeals to you about the job you selected?

➤ Can the appealing aspect of your billion-dollar job be found in other jobs too?

➤ What would the best moment of your billion-dollar job be every day? What appeals to you about the idea of that moment? How would you feel in that moment?

➤ Do any moments in your current job make you feel that way?

➤ Can any other career paths help you feel that way?

Key Learning Points

The facilitator should help the participants arrive at the following conclusions:

➤ Focusing on what exactly about a job will make someone happy can help open up other options for careers.

➤ Focusing on what exactly about a job will make someone happy can help an individual identify what they enjoy about their current career, helping increase job satisfaction.

➤ Sometimes, just focusing on the positive aspects of any job brings greater satisfaction. Rather than concentrating on what is negative, it is important to realize that each job could have positive aspects.

If I Had a Billion Dollars Handout

1. What is one fun/frivolous thing that you would do with a billion dollars?

2. How would you spend your time if you had a billion dollars?

3. What in particular appeals to you in your "billion-dollar job"?

4. What do you think the best single moment of everyday at your "billion-dollar job" would be? Why?

EQ 12　Finish Line!

Self-Awareness
and Control

Empathy

Social
Expertness

Personal
Infuence

Mastery of
Purpose and
Vision

Inward　Inward　Outward

EQ Area and Competency

Personal Influence: Goal Orientation

How to Use This Activity

- To help people recognize goals they have achieved.

- To demonstrate the power of focusing on small steps to achieve goals.

- To build internal confidence and goal orientation.

Use this activity in coaching sessions or classroom learning for career development, leadership development, or personal development. It will help people recognize that achieving goals helps make them feel empowered. In addition, when people achieve goals, they begin to feel mastery over their lives, as they gain confidence and overcome victim mentality. Even small goals enable people to feel victorious. This activity also can be used to generate enthusiasm and motivation for setting new goals.

Applicable Content Area

Multiple: Leadership Development, Career Development, Teamwork

Audience: Coaching, Classroom, Web-Based

Estimated Time: 30 to 45 minutes

Level of Disclosure/Difficulty: Low

Materials: Finish-Line Handout

Purpose/Why This Is Important

In most cases, goals are achieved through a series of small steps. The sprinter can burst out of the starting blocks with a clear path to the finish line, but the Olympic hurdler must clear 10 obstacles, each nearly a meter high (a little over one yard) depending on the event. The hurdler in the 400-meter event, for example, reaches the first obstacle 45 meters into the race, then encounters another every 35 meters, and then must sprint the remaining 40 to the finish line. Even before clearing the first hurdle, each athlete must take the initiative to begin. Lao Tzu, the Chinese philosopher (604 BC–531 BC), said it best: "A journey of a thousand miles begins with a single step." People with high emotional intelligence recognize the need for self-discipline in setting goals and in taking action toward achieving goals. They are able to take small steps and not let frustrations, distractions, or other obstacles stop them from focusing on the goal.

In addition, people sometimes don't recognize the goals they have already achieved. By recording and acknowledging achieved goals, people build an internal reserve that can be called on when needed. By examining the role that others may have played in keeping us motivated or focused on our goals, we can determine what type of support system we need to achieve them.

Set the Stage

Ask the group to think about goals they have achieved in their lives. Ask if anyone is willing to share a goal she accomplished. Note that all of us have achieved goals, but we often don't spend much time analyzing the steps we had to take, what kind of support we needed, or even how we set that particular goal. Explain that this activity enables us to think about some goals we've achieved and what characteristics helped us. It also will help us identify future goals and the steps we have to take to achieve them.

The Activity

1. Ask participants to complete the handout and be prepared to discuss it.

2. Ask participants to form pairs to discuss their answers.

3. Debrief with the following questions.

Key Debrief Questions

➤ Did you encounter any setbacks on the path to your goal?

➤ Did you ever think about quitting?

➤ How did you persuade yourself to go on? Did anyone help you?

➤ What goal do you have right now?

➤ What are the first steps toward achieving that goal?

➤ Who could help?

➤ How would you feel if you achieved it?

Key Learning Points

The facilitator should help the participants arrive at the following conclusions:

➤ Reaching goals requires taking first steps.

➤ Getting started is often difficult. Talking to others who have achieved a similar goal may help.

➤ If you become discouraged, think about past goals that you've achieved. Allow yourself to draw strength from past achievements.

➤ Seek out people who can assist if you become discouraged.

Finish Line! Handout

Think about a difficult goal you achieved in your life. Write that goal on the destination line to the right in Figure 5-3. For each stop sign, write down steps you had to take for that goal to become a reality. You should also indicate any setbacks you encountered along the way. Think about times when you may have wanted to give up. Name some people who helped you continue. Next, think about a goal you would like to achieve, and write it at the end point of your trip. At each stop, write down small steps you need to take for that goal to become a reality. List people or resources that can help you if you get stuck.

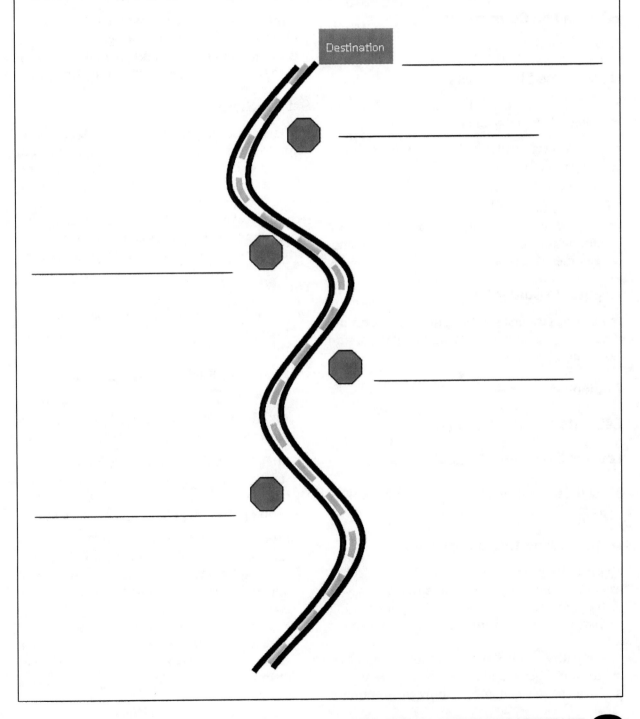

EQ 13

Selfie Listening

Self-Awareness
and Control
Empathy
Social
Expertness
Personal
Infuence
Mastery of
Purpose and
Vision

Inward Toward Outward

EQ Area and Competency

Empathy: Respectful Listening

How to Use This Activity

- To show the importance of careful listening to build empathy and bonds.

- To emphasize known listening skills that can help build bonds.

  "Selfie Listening" can be used as part of emotional intelligence training, teamwork, or diversity training. It can also be used as part of a communications, conflict-resolution, or leadership-development process.

Applicable Content Area

Multiple: Leadership Development, Conflict Resolution, Teamwork, Interpersonal Skills, and Communications

Audience: Classroom

Estimated Time: 30 minutes

Level of Disclosure/Difficulty: Low

Materials: A paragraph for each of two speakers to read.

Purpose/Why This Is Important

This activity provides insight into how respectful listening builds empathy. Empathy requires you to truly comprehend people, so they are willing to share information with you. To do so, you must listen.

Empathy is a key workplace tool that allows others to feel heard and understood. Without empathy, a speaker may present only the minimum information required and could hold back data or problems that would otherwise be shared. Respectful listening is the fundamental and easiest skill to use in building empathy in the workplace.

Set the Stage

Introduce the activity by saying: "Today we're going to listen to two speakers. I'll observe your listening skills in the first round and provide some tips and suggestions that you could do better for the second speaker. If you do well, we'll skip the second speaker and take an early break." You should provide an appropriate incentive for the participants to actively listen to the first speaker.

The Activity

1. Identify two speakers from the group. Ask them to leave the room with the paragraphs they will read.

2. Remind the listeners of the incentive to listen attentively.

3. Ask the first speaker to come in and read. Observe the behavior of the listeners.

4. After the first speaker concludes, ask the speaker to leave the room and inform the second speaker that he will have a turn as soon as you provide suggestions to the listeners.

5. Let the listeners know that you'd like to try to surprise the speaker this time with some typical listening behaviors. Ask everyone to pull out their cell phones and make sure they're on. Ask one person to doodle on a notepad, another to text someone in the room, another to take notes on a phone, another to take a selfie with the speaker, and ask rest to be as disinterested as possible in what the speaker is saying.

6. Ask the second speaker to come into the room. Remind the group of the listening tips they received.

7. Ask the second speaker to read the paragraph. Observe the behaviors of the listener and the speaker.

8. Call the first speaker into the room and ask the following:

   a. Speaker 1, "How did your listeners do?"
   b. Speaker 2, "How were your listeners?"

Key Debrief Questions

➤ Which speaker did a better job? Why?

➤ Was it easy or hard to listen to Speaker 1? What about Speaker 2?

➤ Speaker 2, what did it feel like when you were talking? What did you do? Talk louder? Stop speaking? Did you look forward to talking to the group again?

➤ What did it feel like as a listener? Did you want to listen to Speaker 2?

➤ Was anyone using technology to listen more attentively (specifically, the individual asked to take notes with a cell phone)? Was it still distracting to the speaker? How could you mitigate the distraction?

➤ Did you already know how to listen attentively?

➤ How does this apply in the workplace?

Key Learning Points

The facilitator should help the participants arrive at the following conclusions:

➤ You already have great listening skills. Use them.

➤ If you want to use technology to help you, do so in a way that lets the speaker know you are engaged.

➤ Listening makes a big impact on the person talking.

➤ If we listen to others in the workplace, it shows respect. Respect is the basis of trusting relationships. Listening skills are fundamental to empathy.

EQ 14

To Talk or Not to Talk— That Is the Question

Self-Awareness and Control
Empathy
Social Expertness
Personal Infuence
Mastery of Purpose and Vision

Inward Inward Outward

EQ Area and Competency

Social Expertness: Building Relationships
Self-Awareness: Impact on Others
Empathy: Feeling Impact on Others

How to Use This Activity

- To help people recognize the impact that "too much" talking has on others.

- To help people recognize the impact that "too little" talking has on others.

- To practice one's opposite preference.

- To practice reading nonverbal cues indicating that a person is uncomfortable with the amount of conversation.

Knowing when to speak up, how much to say, and when to listen are essential skills in life. This activity builds awareness of one's preference for talking or being silent, and the impact those preferences have on others. In addition, this activity can help people build their skill in reading nonverbal cues. It helps in career development, leadership development, or personal development. It can be used most effectively in a classroom setting.

Applicable Content Area

Multiple: Leadership Development, Career Development, Communication Skills, Customer Service, Conflict Resolution

Audience: Classroom

Estimated Time: 35 to 45 minutes

Level of Disclosure/Difficulty: Medium

Materials:

2 flipcharts and markers
Masking tape

Purpose/Why This Is Important

Emotional intelligence requires understanding one's impact on others. A key area of impact is the "amount" of conversation one contributes. Is it too much? We've heard the expressions, "He can talk your ear off," or "My ears are bleeding," or "I couldn't get a word in edgewise" to describe people who just don't stop talking. We also know individuals about whom we say, "It's like pulling teeth to get a word out of her," or "He's a man of few words." It's not that being either talkative or quiet is a problem. However, we must be sensitive to the messages our tendencies can send in certain situations and learn to adjust if the impact is negative. For example, if someone has a natural tendency to say little, he may not be adequately communicating and that may adversely affect his career. On the other hand, talking too much can also affect one's career. Developing sensitivity to the appropriate "amount" of conversation can serve one well. Attention to nonverbal cues enables people to adjust the "amount" of conversation that best suits the situation. Of course, it is important to understand that one's impact is also measured by the substance of the conversation, and in most cases, substance is more critical than how many or how few words one speaks. However, the focus of this activity is to help people gauge quantity, rather than substance.

Set the Stage

Ask group members if they know people who talk too much or too little. Share the expressions "He can talk your ear off" or "My ears are bleeding" or "It's like pulling teeth to get a word out of her" or "He's a man of few words." Be sure to tell the group that being talkative or quiet is an individual preference, and there isn't anything wrong with either. However, explain that, at times, it is important for people to understand how their individual tendencies impress others. Say that in some situations and with some individuals their natural preferences will be just fine. At other times, people might find it necessary to adjust. Tell the group that this activity will help them understand and build awareness regarding the impact of the "amount" of conversation one shares. Explain that the substance is also critical, but that we won't be addressing substance at this time.

The Activity

Part 1

1. Prepare two flipcharts. Label one, "Talks Too Much." Label the other, "Talks Too Little."

2. Ask participants to think about people who talk too much and brainstorm a list of words that describe the effects this can have on others. List these items in Column 1 of a flipchart labeled "Talks Too Much." Also, ask participants to brainstorm the disadvantage this can have for the "overtalker." List those in Column 2 on the flipchart labeled "Talks Too Much."

3. Ask participants to think about people who talk too little, and brainstorm a list of words that describe the effect this can have on others. List these items in Column 1 of a flipchart labeled "Talks Too Little. Also, ask them to brainstorm the disadvantages this can have for the "undertalker." Write the group's responses in Column 2 on the flipchart labeled "Talks Too Little."

Part 2

4. Using masking tape to make a 1-to-10 continuum. Place an "x" on the floor at one end and an "x" on the floor at the other end of the continuum. You can also place a hash mark at midpoint.

5. Ask people to place themselves on the continuum based on the following question: "How would you rate your natural preference compared to those of other people? Do you tend to be very talkative (10 on the continuum) or very quiet (1 on the continuum)?

Part 3

6. If participants are widely distributed on the continuum, pair people who are on opposite ends. However, often people will congregate around the middle. If so, just pair people randomly.

7. Instruct the pairs to assign one person as the talker and one as the nontalker. The activity will require the pair to talk for five minutes. Hand out instruction sheets for the nontalker. Do not let the talker see the instructions. As per the instruction sheet, cue the nontalkers three minutes into the activity. Allow the activity to continue another two minutes.

8. Ask the following questions. List the answers on the flipchart.

   a. What nonverbal cues did you receive that indicated that you were talking too long?

   b. What did you experience during the activity? As the talker? As the nontalker?

Part 4

9. Now that they've had an opportunity to practice responding to nonverbal clues, instruct the pairs to converse about anything they choose. They will have ten minutes to converse. Ask the pairs to be mindful and try to share the time equally. However, pairs should not assign five minutes to each person to talk.

Key Debrief Questions

➤ Did any talkers find that they had to hold back on the conversation because they were dominating?

➤ Did any talkers find that they had to step up the conversation because they were not sharing time equally?

➤ Were you more comfortable listening or speaking?

➤ What do you think your natural tendency is?

➤ When do you need to adjust your natural tendency? Why?

➤ How can you read nonverbal cues to help you?

➤ How can talkers help nontalkers share the conversation? How can nontalkers help talkers share the conversation?

➤ During times of high stress, do you tend to talk or not?

Key Learning Points

The facilitator should help the participants arrive at the following conclusions:

➤ Acknowledge that the substance of a conversation will always have an effect on people.

However, sometimes, substance can get lost because someone is talking too much or not talking enough. Therefore, the "amount" of conversation matters.

➤ You must be mindful of your natural tendency. Adjust your natural tendency to the situation and the person.

➤ Talkers may need to learn to be comfortable being silent or drawing out those who are quiet to balance the conversation.

➤ Those who are quiet may need to insert themselves into the conversation.

➤ Learn to look for cues to help you adjust your level of conversation.

To Talk or Not to Talk—That Is the Question Handout

Instructions for "Nontalker": During the first part of the activity, give your partner cues that you are attentive. Ask questions, lean in, nod, and give verbal recognition to comments. However, be sure that your partner is the focus of conversation. When the facilitator announces that you have two minutes left in the activity, give your partner subtle nonverbal signals that he or she is talking too much. Nonverbal signals can be removing eye contact, fidgeting, being distracted by other activities, tapping, or otherwise signaling that you have had enough.

EQ 15 Gumball

Self-Awareness
and Control

Empathy

Social
Expertness

Personal
Infuence

Mastery of
Purpose and
Vision

Inward   Inward   Outward

EQ Area and Competency

Self-Awareness and Control: Emotional Expression
Social Expertness: Collaboration

When to Use This Activity

- To show how easily emotions can take a person away from a task.

- To demonstrate that team tasks often have individual components that still contribute to team success.

"Gumball" can be used as part of emotional intelligence training, teamwork, or diversity training. It can also be used as part of a communications, conflict resolution, or leadership development process.

Applicable Content Area

Multiple: Leadership Development, Teamwork, Conflict Resolution, and Communications

Audience: Classroom

Estimated Time: 30 minutes

Level of Disclosure/Difficulty: Low

Materials

A displayed photo of a complex image, such as a large gumball machine with many different colored balls. Add dividing lines to help segment the image into four quadrants.
Instructions for the "Blue Gumball Team"—One per participant
Instructions for the Distractors—3 to 5 participants

Purpose/Why This Is Important

This activity is designed to provide insight into how everyday distractions and stressors can cause a simple task to become much more complicated. It also helps participants identify their typical emotional reaction when under pressure. By asking participants to do a frustrating task, the participant will gain insight into how they react under pressure. By understanding what their usual emotional reaction to a situation is, an individual can be better prepared to change that reaction in the future.

Although this activity is best accomplished as a team effort, the instructor should not assign teams. This will test if the group members know to reach out, ask for help, and volunteer to help others. Collaborating in the workplace is a crucial skill to accomplishing tasks that are larger than the individual can take on alone.

Set the Stage

Introduce the activity by saying, "Tasks often take intense concentration to accomplish. These are often the ones that require strong individual effort to accomplish. I will provide instructions to each of you that describe the task at hand. Your instructions are for your eyes only, don't share them." Set this up as an individual task, such as counting the blue gumballs, that could be more efficiently accomplished as a team effort, "you count the gumballs in this quadrant; I'll count the ones here, etc."

Note to facilitators: The goal of the activity is not to arrive at a particular number of gumballs, but if you have participants who are particularly data driven, they may not be satisfied arriving at this number. If you suspect your group may be too curious to avoid learning the total number, you may want to have a count of the total number of gumballs.

The Activity

1. Hand out instructions to everyone in the group. Most people will receive the instructions for the Blue Gumball Team; a handful of individuals (3 to 5) will receive the Distractors instructions. Remind the group that the instructions are for their individual task.

2. Display the image of the gumball machine. Tell the group to start.

3. At intervals, prod the group to increase the stress level. For example, "I can't believe you aren't done yet." Or, "I had a group last week that finished in 3 minutes; you are taking a lot longer."

4. Watch for the group to become frustrated with the task, watch for emotional reactions, and call a halt to the task when someone completes the task or when a number of individuals have become frustrated.

Key Debrief Questions

➤ Who became frustrated with the task? Did anyone get angry? Did you want to quit? Did you notice a physical reaction?

➤ What is your normal reaction to stress?

➤ Did you feel supported from others in the room? What happened? Do distractions like this happen at work?

➤ Did you ask for help? Did you realize that others in the room had the same task?

➤ Did anyone pull together a team to solve the puzzle? Did you consider it? Why did/didn't you?

➤ Distractors, did you feel bad? Did you want to help? Why didn't you?

Key Learning Points

The facilitator should help the participants arrive at the following conclusions:

➤ Distractions and other stressors can cause a physical and emotional reaction. These reactions are bigger and more intense the more you care about the task at hand.

➤ Understanding your typical emotional reaction can help you predict your reaction in the future and prepare for that reaction. Reaching out to collaborate on a task can help everyone achieve their goals.

➤ Each person reacts to stress differently. Some may become frustrated, others frozen, and still others angry. Understanding that we each have a different modus operandi when under stress is important.

Gumball Handouts

Instructions for the Blue Gumball Team: Your job is to count all the blue gumballs in the machine that are visible or partially visible. There are quadrants across the gumball image. There may be more than one shade of blue gumball in the machine. It is critical to determine how many gumballs of each shade of blue are in each quadrant and are in the gumball machine as a whole.

Instructions for the Distractors: Your job is to try to ensure that the others in the room do not finish counting the gumballs. Interrupt them with questions, call out random numbers, and talk loudly to other distractors in the room. Do whatever it takes to make sure they don't finish!

EQ 16

What Do You Assign to the Pictures of Your Life?

Plays Well with Others

Self-Awareness and Control
Empathy
Social Expertness
Personal Influence
Mastery of Purpose and Vision

Inward Inward Outward

EQ Area and Competency

Self-Awareness: Impact on Others
Personal Influence: Optimism

How to Use This Activity

- To help people recognize how their thought processes affect their perspectives on events.

- To help people experience how optimism affects mood and behaviors.

- To determine one's pattern of thinking related to optimism and pessimism and to recognize how to influence those existing patterns.

Use this activity either in coaching or in a training class to help people recognize how their thinking affects their moods and behaviors. The attitudes people take toward events in their careers or lives have lasting effects on them. This activity helps people explore how they can change their worldviews by changing their thinking. This activity also explores optimism as a learned skill.

Applicable Content Area

Multiple: Leadership Development, Career Development, Conflict Resolution, Customer Service

Audience: Classroom, Web-Based, Coaching

Estimated Time: 30 to 35 minutes

Level of Disclosure/Difficulty: Easy

Materials

Various pictures of people who depict a situation or emotion that is open to interpretation and do *not* clearly evoke a negative or positive emotion. Thus, inappropriate pictures would include a fu-

neral that clearly evokes the emotion of sadness or of a mother holding her newborn with a warm smile on her face that clearly indicates joy or love. Select pictures in which the situation, thought, and emotion are not evident. For example, a man with his head tilted down and walking away on a wooded path could depict sadness, contemplation, calm, peace, a troubled state, or confusion. The interpretation is open to the viewer. In addition, be very sensitive to cultural issues when selecting pictures. Be sure to avoid negative cultural stereotypes in the pictures.

Purpose/Why This Is Important

The thoughts and emotions we assign to various events and situations in our lives affect our well-being, success, and happiness. Common research findings in the area of optimism show that it correlates with many positive life outcomes, including increased life expectancy, general health, better mental health, increased success in sports and work, greater recovery rates from heart operations, and better strategies for coping with adversity. Emotional intelligence requires that people understand how they assign emotions and thoughts to situations. Once they develop this awareness, they can recognize optimism and pessimism as part of their thinking and the effects optimism and pessimism have on them, the people they lead, and their careers.

Set the Stage

Share the following quote by Epictetus, a Greek philosopher, and ask participants to comment on what it means to them: "People are not disturbed by things, *but* by the *view* they *take* of them." Ask if they know people who view the world as optimists and others who view the world as pessimists.

Ask how these viewpoints can influence how one behaves. Ask if these viewpoints can affect others. Ask whom they prefer as teammates. How about as leaders?

The Activity

1. Show a picture to the group. Ask the participants, "What do you think the person is thinking and /or feeling?" Two different viewpoints should emerge.

   Note to Trainer: Please be mindful of cultural issues that could surface. As a facilitator, you must be aware that the purpose of this activity is to help people neutralize their interpretations rather than assign emotions and stereotypes to situations.

2. Divide the class participants into two equal groups.

3. Give one half of the class instruction sheet A. Give the other half instruction sheet B.

4. Share a few more pictures with the group. Ask them to interpret the pictures based on the instruction sheets they hold.

5. Show the pictures used in Step 4 again. Ask participants, "What do you think the person is thinking and /or feeling?" You should have two different viewpoints depending on which instruction sheet a participant received.

6. Now, ask the groups to switch instruction sheets. Show the pictures from Step 4. Ask group members, "What do you think the person is thinking and /or feeling?" (The participants should be able to change their answers.)

Key Debrief Questions

➤ What determines how we view a situation?

➤ Is it possible to change how we think/feel about a situation?

➤ What could you gain from changing the way you view certain situations?

➤ Can the way we view things make us more frustrated? More satisfied?

➤ How does our viewpoint affect others?

➤ How can it affect our careers?

➤ How can applying optimism and positive thinking affect our lives?

Key Learning Points

The facilitator should help the participants arrive at the following conclusions:

➤ We do not have control over some of the events or situations in our lives, but we can control how we view them.

➤ How we view events and situations can affect our happiness and our success.

➤ We assign a viewpoint to each situation. We choose to make them good or bad. We also assign viewpoints based on our past and our societal/cultural experiences.

➤ It is possible to change our viewpoint about a situation.

What Do You Assign to the Pictures of Your Life? Handouts

Instruction Sheet for Group A: When you view the picture, use the following words or synonyms to shape your response to the question, "What do you think the person is thinking/feeling?"

Stressed	Demoralized	Upset
Overwhelmed	Sad	Worried
Fearful	Angry	Annoyed

Instruction Sheet for Group B: When you view the picture, use the following words or synonyms to shape your response to the question, "What do you think the person is thinking/ feeling?"

Happy	Excited	Content
Confident	Pleased	Inspired
Inquisitive	Playful	Imaginative

EQ 17

Plays Well with Others

Practice Assigning New Thoughts/Feelings to Something in Your Career

Self-Awareness and Control
Empathy
Social Expertness
Personal Influence
Mastery of Purpose and Vision

Inward · Inward · Outward

EQ Area and Competency

Self-Awareness: Emotional and Inner Awareness
Personal Influence: Optimism, Flexibility
Empathy: Feeling Impact on Others

How to Use This Activity

- To increase awareness of thinking patterns around a particular person or situation.

- To help people reshape their thinking around a particular person or situation.

Use this activity either in coaching or in a training class. However, it is better suited to a coaching relationship, in which you would have more time to help the person review the consequences of his current thinking and reshape it. It is a very powerful activity to use when someone is struggling with a particular person or situation, as it helps people clarify their current thinking and establish how that thinking can be counterproductive. It is particularly useful in conflict resolution. You can use this activity in conjunction with "EQ 16, "What Do You Assign to the Pictures of Your Life?"

Applicable Content Area

Multiple: Leadership Development, Career Development, Conflict Resolution, Teamwork, Interpersonal Skills

Audience: Coaching, Classroom

Estimated Time: 20 to 30 minutes

Level of Disclosure/Difficulty: High

Materials: No materials are necessary for this activity.

Purpose/Why This Is Important

The way we think about situations or people affects how we approach them. If we think negatively, we will often act in a manner that aggravates the situation. For example, if we dislike dealing with Joan from accounting, we anticipate an unpleasant encounter whenever she calls. If we dread the visit to our in-laws, our minds find all the flaws in them during our visit just to prove that we were right. This confirmation bias is well known and documented. It can also be very destructive for our relationships, exasperate conflict, and create negative experiences for us when none actually exists. In our careers, we must address people and situations that may not be ideal. However, the more we focus on the faults of these people and problem with the situations, the more our behaviors may be construed as negative—and this can affect our careers. Emotional intelligence requires that we manage these reactions. However, it is even more beneficial to be able to "prevent" the reactions by changing our thinking about them.

Set the Stage

Use an example from your experience or the example of the in-laws stated above to explain confirmation bias. ("If we dread the visit to our in-laws, our minds find all the flaws in them during our visit just to prove that we were right.") Confirmation bias blocks us from seeing the full picture. We see only the portion that affirms our preconceptions. Explain that most situations have two sides and that confirmation bias blocks us from seeing both sides.

The Activity

1. Ask the participants to name a current person or situation that bothers them. If this activity

is conducted in a classroom setting, assure the participants that we will not ask them to share names or details of the situation.

2. Ask the participant to "dwell" on the person or situation and think about all the negative things that come to mind.

3. Give the participant a piece of paper divided into two columns. Instruct the participant to write every negative thing that comes to mind in Column 1.

4. Ask the participants to "change their viewpoints." Stress that most situations or people are not all good or all bad. Focus on the person or situation and, instead of thinking negatively, find positive attributes that also describe the person or situation.

5. Instruct participants to write the positive attributes in Column 2.

6. Ask the participants to predict outcome of future encounters if they focus their attention on Column 1. Ask how it might differ if they focus their attention on Column 2.

Key Debrief Questions

➤ What determines how we approach a situation or person?

➤ Is it possible to change how we think/feel about a person or situation?

➤ What could you gain from changing the way you view a situation or person?

➤ Can the way we view things make us more frustrated? More satisfied?

➤ How does our viewpoint affect others?

➤ How can it affect our career?

➤ How can applying optimism and positive thinking affect our lives?

Key Learning Points

The facilitator should help the participants arrive at the following conclusions:

➤ We do not have control over some of the people or situations in our lives, but we can control how we view them.

➤ How we view people and situations can affect our happiness and our success.

➤ We assign a viewpoint to situations and people. We choose to make them good or bad.

➤ It is possible to change our viewpoints about a given situation.

Note to Trainer/Coach: Most of the time a person can change her viewpoint and learn to approach a person or situation in a more positive manner. As a training tool, this method is sound. In addition, as a coach, you will help the person gain positive outcomes by using this method. However, a small number of problem people may also take advantage of others, so the participant may actually suffer instead of gain by using this method. Be aware that most of time, this method is useful, but with a very small number of people, it may not be the best approach.

EQ 18 Puzzler

Self-Awareness
and Control

Empathy

Social
Expertness

Personal
Infuence

Mastery of
Purpose and
Vision

Inward Inward Outward

EQ Area and Competency

Personal Influence: Getting Results Through Others
Empathy: Service Orientation

How to Use This Activity

- To provide an opportunity to lead an effort to work with others.

- To provide insight into self-motivation versus service orientation.

"Puzzler" can be used as part of emotional intelligence training, teamwork, or an onboarding program. It can also be used as part of a high-potential, leadership-development, or career-development process.

Applicable Content Area

Multiple: Leadership and Career Development, Teamwork

Audience: Classroom

Estimated Time: 40 minutes

Level of Disclosure/Difficulty: Low

Materials

One puzzle bag for each participant. Puzzles should have a minimum of 24 pieces. Pieces should be mixed among bags so that at least one bag has all the pieces to complete the puzzle, but the other bags are all missing a few pieces while having duplicates of others. Ensure that each set of puzzle bags has the required puzzle pieces to complete all the puzzles. One set of puzzle bags for each five to seven participants.

Purpose/Why This Is Important

This activity is designed to provide insight into how the participants view individual tasks and their willingness to take initiative and become leaders for their groups. The activity is set up as a silent, individual task, but participants will realize they need pieces from other individuals to complete their puzzles. How they go about receiving those pieces will provide insights into their willingness to help others and their ability to influence others to help them,. They may start putting "extra" pieces into the center of the table, encouraging others to do the same. Or, they may just grab pieces from others in a single-minded pursuit to complete their own puzzles. Others may try to dole out their extra pieces to someone they believe needs the pieces, thus demonstrating their willingness to help others. This exercise shows how the participants use their influence skills, limited in this case by being unable to talk, to get the items they need to complete the task at hand. For an individual in an organization, it is often necessary to obtain the assistance of others on a large job or project, so providing an insight into the natural influence methods can be important. This exercise also demonstrates one's service orientation, which is a key component of empathy and can be used by the participant to build relationships in the organization.

Set the Stage

Ask groups of five to seven participants to sit together around a table. Introduce the activity by talking about the importance of independent work and promise accolades for those who accomplish the task. You can, of course, promise additional incentives for completing the task. Then, reinforce that the primary rule is to not speak to anyone else during the activity and that the objective is to complete the puzzle.

Note to facilitators: The "do-not-speak" rule provides a barrier to the participants in trying to help one another. As a facilitator, do not enforce this rule too strongly, since the challenge of the exercise is to see who will break the rules in order to help everyone complete the task.

The Activity

1. Pass the puzzle bags out to each participant. For groups larger than seven people, have different sets of puzzle bags for each five to seven participants.

2. Ask the participants to begin completing their puzzles after reminding them not to speak.

3. Allow the participants 10 to 15 minutes to complete the puzzle. Allow more time if the participants are struggling with the puzzle. Keep a note of which individual participants and groups of participants completed the puzzle first.

Key Debrief Questions

➤ Who was first to complete the puzzle? Which group completed the puzzle first?

➤ Did you know that there was an incentive for the group to complete the puzzle?

➤ How did you solve the puzzle? Who took pieces from another person to complete the puzzle? How did the individual whose piece was stolen feel?

➤ Did anyone give extra pieces to another person at the table? How did that make the person who received the piece feel?

➤ Did anyone come up with any other approaches to sharing pieces? How did those work?

➤ Do people in organizations steal puzzle pieces? Do they ever offer them without being asked? With whom do you prefer to work?

➤ How did it feel when someone in your group completed the activity before you?

Key Learning Points

The facilitator should help the participants arrive at the following conclusions:

➤ Individuals want to work with and for people who want to help others.

➤ Individuals who need to get results through others need to ensure that they are approaching the situation from a service orientation point of view. Otherwise, they may be viewed poorly in the organization, and their ability to influence others will be compromised.

➤ Influence often increases when one has positive relationships and a willingness to help others.

➤ Competition can create stress that may cause people to act differently.

EQ 19 Last Name

Self-Awareness and Control
Empathy
Social Expertness
Personal Infuence
Mastery of Purpose and Vision

Inward Inward-Outward

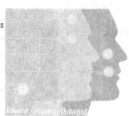

EQ Area and Competency

Mastery of Purpose and Vision: Understanding One's Purpose and Values

How to Use This Activity

- To reflect on the individual's passionate interests.

- To provide insight into how the individual communicates his or her purpose.

"Last Name" can be used as part of emotional intelligence training, coaching, or an on-boarding program. It can also be used as part of a high-potential, leadership-development, or career-development process.

Applicable Content Area

Multiple: Leadership Development and Career Development

Audience: Classroom, Coaching, Web-Based

Estimated Time: 25 minutes

Level of Disclosure/Difficulty: Low

Materials: "Last Name" handout—one per participant

Purpose/Why This Is Important

This activity provides insight into the individual's passionate interests. As an activity in reflection, the participant will be able to think about what his ideal last name would be if it symbolized his passion. It's important for an individual to reflect on what she is truly passionate about and to think about how she now communicates that passion.

When we are passionately excited and interested about something, we are able to inspire others to join our cause and support our endeavors.

Set the Stage

Pass out the handout to each member of the group. Remind them that there is a long history of people whose names describe a job or career pursued by an ancestor, including the Smiths, Bakers, and Thatchers of the world. Imagine if you could be known by one thing that you do: What would your name be? Ask the participants to spend a few minutes thinking about the questions on the handout and providing answers to them.

The Activity

1. Give participants 10 to 15 minutes to fill out the "Last Name" handout.

2. Ask the participants to share their responses to the following questions on the handout:

   - What would your last name be?
   - How will you tell others about your new last name?

Key Debrief Questions

➤ How many people picked a last name that was related to their jobs, careers, or education?

➤ How many people picked a last name that was related to a hobby or interest?

➤ Do you think it is important to work at something you are passionate about? When does it matter?

➤ Did anyone have trouble identifying a passion?

➤ How can you bring the level of enthusiasm for your passion to others? How do you communicate it now? Would you like to communicate it more? How would others help you?

Key Learning Points

The facilitator should help the participants arrive at the following conclusions:

➤ There may be ways to incorporate something you are passionate about into your career.

➤ Communicating passion is infectious; others will help you succeed.

➤ If you never communicate what you are passionate about, others may never know and may never assist you.

➤ It is possible that you may have several things you are passionate about or none at all. It is important to recognize and define your passions.

Last Name Handout

1. What is something that you love talking about to others?

2. What is something you want to spend your spare time reading about, learning more about, or practicing more?

3. What is something that you are passionately interested in doing? Career or hobby—it doesn't matter.

4. What should your new last name be?

5. How will you tell others about your new last name?

6. How do you think they'll react?

7. Who do you think would volunteer to help you? Why would they do so?

8. Who do you think wouldn't support your name change? What could you do to convince them?

EQ 20 ROYGBIV

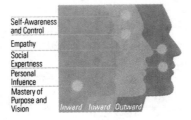

Self-Awareness
and Control
Empathy
Social
Expertness
Personal
Infuence
Mastery of
Purpose and
Vision

Inward Inward Outward

Plays Well
with
Others

EQ Area and Competency

Personal Influence: Leading Others

How to Use This Activity

- To explore the nature of influence.

- To help people determine how to influence others.

- To show that to influence someone you must understand that individual's thinking about an event or situation.

Use this activity in leadership-development training. It is a group activity and is not effective for one-on-one coaching. This activity illustrates the concept of influence. It allows the group to explore the different approaches to influence. The activity addresses the concept of vision and how a strong inspiring vision can motivate or inspire people to put aside their individual agendas for the good of the team. Use it to illustrate the importance of understanding various points of view during conflict resolution. ROYGBIV can be very effective when used with EQ 31, "Let's Go!," as ROYGBIV addresses the critical skills of influence and "Let's Go!" explores ways to have impactful influence during conflict.

Applicable Content Area

Multiple: Leadership Development, Conflict Resolution, Interpersonal Skills

Audience: Classroom

Estimated Time: 40 minutes

Level of Disclosure/Difficulty: Easy

Materials:

For each group of 11 people, you will need the following:

- 2 red handouts

- 2 red ribbons or sticky dots that people can wear

- 3 yellow handouts

- 3 yellow ribbons or sticky dots that people can wear

- 3 blue handouts

- 3 blue ribbons or sticky dots that people can wear

- 2 violet handouts

- 2 violet ribbons or sticky dots that people can wear

- 1 leader handout

- Coach handouts

- 2 hats

- 1 bottle of water

Purpose/Why This Is Important

Personal influence, our ability to influence others, is the essence of leadership. Inspiring others through example, words, and deeds requires a firm foundation in all areas of emotional intelligence. Leaders must be able to engage (social expertness) and understand the perspective of others (empathy.) In addition, the ability to connect the task or situation to a larger or compelling vision is useful. A person with a high degree of personal influence will look for creative ways to get others to buy into her concepts and ideas. She will understand what it takes to move an idea or suggestion forward and will mobilize others to her point of view. Personal influence is also the ability to pursue issues that are important or debilitating to relationships, goals, missions, or visions. If a person realizes that something or someone prevents achieving a goal that he believes in, he will determine how to overcome those obstacles rather than crumble in defeat.

Set the Stage

Tell the group that the following activity is about influence. DO NOT use the name of the activity—ROYGBIV. Explain that influence is an important skill for everyone, whether in leadership or not. However, for leaders, influence is essential. Tell the group that they will be assigned to teams. Each team will have a leader and a task to complete.

The Activity

1. Divide the group into groups of 11. (If you have individuals remaining, make them "coaches" to the leader and provide coach handouts.)

2. Assign 10 individuals a color card and color designating item (stickers or ribbons). (See handouts.) Assign one individual a leader card. (See handouts.) Ensure each team has 2 reds, 3 yellows, 3 blues, and 2 violets.

3. Tell the participants that they are working on a team, and let them know who their leader is. ASK THE LEADER TO LEAVE THE ROOM. It is important that the leader is not aware of the instructions on the handouts. Tell the participants that each handout contains important information and give the participants a couple of minutes to read.

4. Tell the participants that the activity is about influence. Coach the participants to role play according to the instructions on the handout. However, tell them to respond to the leader if they think the leader has in some way convinced, motivated, or inspired them to act in the best interest of the team. The leader's role

is to inspire them to act and give up their own positions. Participants can be as cooperative or uncooperative as they choose. Tell the coaches their role is to make suggestions to the leader to help her succeed.

5. Bring the leader back into the room. Begin the activity. Allow approximately 15 minutes for the leader to complete the task.

Key Debrief Questions

➤ How did the leader gain information about the individuals?

➤ How did the leader use the information he gathered?

➤ What methods did the leader use to convince, motivate, or inspire?

➤ What methods were effective?

➤ What methods were ineffective?

➤ Did the same methods work with each person?

➤ Did "leadership vision" have any impact on the followers' actions?

➤ What can we learn about leadership and influence from this activity?

➤ What can we learn about followership from this activity?

Key Learning Points

The facilitator should help the participants arrive at the following conclusions:

➤ As a leader, you must know the individuals on your team. It is important to talk with them to understand their perspectives. Each person's perspective is different and in order to influence them, you must know how each one is thinking about and interpreting a situation.

➤ Forcing people to do what you want doesn't usually work.

➤ Sometimes a compelling vision will motivate people.

➤ The same methods don't work for all individuals. The leader must adjust the approach to fit the situation and the individual.

➤ Sometimes followers are easy to motivate. Sometimes they are not. When followers are not, the leader must change the approach. If the leader is to be successful with a difficult follower, she must understand how the follower thinks in order to influence him.

ROYGBIV Handouts

VIOLET: You are a VIOLET. VIOLETS don't like BLUES because BLUES act like they know everything. VIOLETS want to avoid BLUES at all costs. VIOLETS enjoy working with REDS or YELLOWS. They will volunteer to work with REDS or YELLOWS, but they will do what they can to stay away from BLUES.

BLUE: You are a BLUE. BLUES are allergic to YELLOWS and VIOLETS. When you are near a YELLOW or VIOLET, you have a severe allergy attack. Your allergy attack can be prevented if the YELLOW or VIOLET wears a hat. You prefer not to talk about your allergies. You don't feel comfortable asking YELLOWS or VIOLETS to wear hats, so the best thing to do is to avoid YELLOWS or VIOLETS so you don't have an allergy attack.

YELLOW: You are a YELLOW. YELLOWS are fiercely independent. They don't want to work with anyone. They find REDS or BLUES particularly annoying because REDS have headaches and BLUES have allergies. As a YELLOW, you are a hard worker and your philosophy is to work independently, get the job done and go home.

RED: You are a RED. REDS get severe headaches if they are near YELLOWS. Your headache can be prevented if the YELLOW holds a bottle of water. You prefer not to talk about your headaches. You don't feel comfortable asking YELLOWS to hold a water bottle, so the best thing to do is to avoid YELLOWS so you don't have a headache.

LEADER: You are the leader. Your job is to get your team to cooperate to form a rainbow. A rainbow consists of the following colors in this order: RED, ORANGE, YELLOW, GREEN, BLUE, INDIGO, and VIOLET. Your job is to get your team members to stand in a line in order of the rainbow colors. You have team members who are RED, YELLOW, BLUE and VIOLET. To make the color orange, you will need to get a YELLOW and RED to join arms. To make the color green, you will need to get a YELLOW and a BLUE to join arms. To make the color indigo, you will need to get a BLUE and a VIOLET to join arms.

COACH: You are the COACH. Your job is to help the leader determine the best approach to get people to cooperate. All communication to the team should come directly from the leader, but you can make suggestions to the leader based on what you know about the team members.

EQ 21 # Look Around

Self-Awareness
and Control

Empathy

Social
Expertness

Personal
Infuence

Mastery of
Purpose and
Vision

Inward   Inward   Outward

EQ Area and Competency

Social Expertness: Organizational Savvy

How to Use This Activity

- To build observational skills that help build awareness in the moment.

- To provide insight into group dynamics and the ability to navigate organizational situations.

"Look Around" can be used as part of a coaching or phased-training program. It is designed to be used after training and coaching on using observational skills to build awareness and to re-inforce training and coaching on navigating organizational dynamics.

Applicable Content Area

Multiple: Leadership Development, Teamwork, Conflict Resolution, Interpersonal Skills

Audience: Coaching, Classroom, Web-Based

Estimated Time: 40 minutes

Level of Disclosure/Difficulty: Medium

Materials

"Look Around" handout—one per participant
Flip chart and markers for the in-class option

Purpose/Why This Is Important

This activity provides insight into people's ability to read the situational dynamics of a meeting. Often in meetings, many verbal and nonverbal clues provide information on who is engaged and who is not. By learning how to read signals in a meeting, individuals can determine the best method for approaching the group. They can also gather information on the social dynamics of the group involved. By learning which parties like and respect each other most, individuals learn about the structure of the organization's informal network.

The activity also challenges individuals to look for power in the organization. Sometimes true power lies in sources that are not obvious, and learning those sources can greatly increase the ability to accomplish things in the organization.

Set the Stage

Pass out the handouts to each participant. Explain that observations you gain from observing group dynamics are valuable. Ask the participants to take the "Look Around" handout with them to complete during a meeting. Ask them to be prepared to talk about their observations following the meeting. There are two ways to conduct the activity, depending on your type of training or coaching situation. If you have ongoing training or coaching, in which you can debrief the participants after a real meeting, then the first option would provide the participant the opportunity to practice these skills in the real world.

Alternatively, if you will not be in another session with your participants, set up a meeting in your classroom. First, ask your participants to list a controversial organizational topic on the flip chart and divide the flip chart sheet in half. On one side, write "Pro" and on the other side write "Con." Select a real business topic that your company is considering, such as whether or not to use offshore labor, consolidate locations, or invest more in research and development; where and how to expand business opportunities; and whether or not to sell portions of the business. (As the facilitator, you will have to prepare in advance to determine the topic or topics to select. If you are an outside facilitator, be sure to discuss appropriate topics with your internal resources.) Alternatively, if you are using this activity at for an event with many organizations, such as a professional conference, you may want to select a topic for discussion that would be relevant to the audience, such as a debate around a type of professional certification or hosting an event in a particular city.

The Activity

Option 1: Classroom, Coaching, or Web-Based Training Appropriate

1. Ask all participants to attend a meeting in which they do not have to be an active participant. Rather, they should be able to observe and listen.

2. Participants should complete the "Look Around" handout at their meetings. Emphasize that they should make their observations during the meeting and not in reflection after the meeting.

3. Ask the participants to bring their "Look Around" handouts with them to your next session.

4. Debrief their observations at the next session.

Option 2: Classroom Training Only

1. Ask group members to select a side based on their true opinions related to the topic.

2. Ask the group to debate the issue and defend their pro or con position.

3. Once the discussion becomes heated, stop it and ask people to complete the "Look Around" handout based on observations made during the discussion.

4. Debrief their observations.

Key Debrief Questions

➤ Did you notice any nonverbal behaviors? What were they? Did they change when the tone of the discussion changed? How?

➤ Did you notice who received the most respect from others in the room? How could you tell?

➤ Can you identify who in the room has the most expertise on the issue at hand? How can you tell he has such expertise? Can you determine if the individual's expertise is backed by knowledge or bravado?

➤ When someone spoke, could you tell who agreed and disagreed? How could you tell?

➤ Did you get the sense that some people liked each other more than others? Disliked each other? How could you tell?

➤ Was anyone able to silence the room with a particular point?

➤ Who had the greatest influence in reaching a final decision? How could you tell?

➤ If you had to speak to this group, how would you change your tone or body language? Whose reaction would you watch while speaking?

Key Learning Points

The facilitator should help the participants arrive at the following conclusions:

➤ Often group dynamics play out in meetings. By learning to read the verbal and nonverbal clues, you gain insights into the power dynamics at work in the group. These insights can prove powerful as you try to understand and navigate group and organizational dynamics.

➤ Pay attention to those who have the real power in meetings; they're not always the ones who say the most. Look for those sources and work to understand them.

Look Around Handout

1. What are you noticing about the individuals in the room? Be specific. Make note of who is talking, who is not, and what people do when they speak. What is their body language? What is their tone of voice? List everyone in the room and note what behaviors, spoken and unspoken, you observe for each individual.

2. Did the tone of the discussion change at any point? If so, did anyone change verbal or nonverbal behaviors? List all the changes you noticed.

States

| Self-Awareness and Control |
| Empathy |
| Social Expertness |
| Personal Infuence |
| Mastery of Purpose and Vision |

Inward Inward Outward

EQ Area and Competency

Self-Awareness and Control: Emotional and Inner Awareness, Emotional Expression
Social Expertness: Collaboration

How to Use This Activity

• To help individuals explore self-control.

• To help people determine how collaboration can change a team dynamic.

• To explore differences between team performance and individual performance.

Use this activity in leadership-development training, teamwork, and personal development. It is a group activity and is not effective for one-on-one coaching. This activity helps participants recognize that some tasks can be frustrating, seem purposeless, and cause people to become hijacked. It is important to learn to separate those reactions from the task. This activity also illustrates that when people collaborate, tasks become easier and frustration decreases.

Applicable Content Area

Multiple: Leadership Development, Teamwork

Audience: Classroom

Estimated Time: 30 minutes

Level of Disclosure/Difficulty: Low

Materials

Flip chart
Markers

Purpose/Why This Is Important

Workplace tasks can be frustrating. Sometimes people don't understand the meaning or logic behind tasks. (It's the leader's job to help them understand why a task is important.) Further, some tasks are menial. How we react to menial tasks, especially frustrating ones, is an activity in self-control. Do we give up, get annoyed, forge ahead, compete, or react some other way? Any of those emotions may indicate we have been hijacked. It's easy to become hijacked in the workplace, so learning when that is likely to happen and how to manage our reactions is the fundamental first step in emotional intelligence—self-awareness and self-control. However, if we can take our learning and development even further and discover how to change our perception about a given task, it benefits our emotional well-being even more. In this activity, the group will experience the frustration of doing a menial task as individuals. Then, they will be asked to experience the same tasks as a group. The instructor will compare the emotional reactions to the two experiences.

Set the Stage

Tell participants that they will be assigned a task. You will be timing their performance. The first person to complete the tasks successfully wins.

The Activity

1. Ask the group members to recite all 50 states in alphabetical order out loud. (Facilitator: alternative tasks include counting backward from 200 by 3s or saying the alphabet backward). (Facilitator: The challenge of the task is both listing the states in alphabetical order

and doing so while hearing everyone else in the room. This makes it much more likely they will become confused about which state comes next). As the facilitator, you should use a timer and encourage the group to keep trying, but provide feedback stating that they could be doing a much more efficient job. For example, tell them they are not completing the task as quickly as other groups you've instructed. (Facilitator: In this case, you are trying to encourage some additional frustration with the task.)

2. After a few minutes, ask the following:

   a. What emotions did you experience during the activity? Write your answers on the flip chart. You may need to ask: "Did anyone feel frustrated? Challenged? Annoyed? Distracted? Defeated?" Explain that those feelings are characteristic of being hijacked. Some can hurt performance.

   b. What caused you to feel that way? Did the facilitator's comparing to other groups help or hurt?

   c. Did anyone drop out or quit?

   d. Did anyone think of another way to complete this task?

3. Instruct the group to collaborate to solve the task. Instruct them to list the states in alphabetical order in unison and make it an enjoyable experience. (The easiest way to do this is to have someone write the list of states and then have the entire group recite the states as someone points to each state. The group should be able to come up with this solution. You may need to assist.)

4. After the group has successfully completed the task, ask the following:

   a. What emotions did you experience? Capture the response on the flip chart. Compare it to the previous stated emotions.

   b. Ask those who may have dropped out the first time if they were more willing to participate this time.

Key Debrief Questions

➤ How do our emotions affect our willingness to perform a task?

➤ How do emotions affect our performance of a task?

➤ How can collaborating on a task change the reaction to the task? Especially menial tasks? Or less desirable tasks?

➤ Does every job have less desirable tasks?

➤ How does changing our mindset about a less desirable task benefit us?

➤ What methods could a leader use to convince or motivate people to do menial or undesirable tasks?

➤ What can we learn about collaboration from this activity?

Key Learning Points

The facilitator should help the participants arrive at the following conclusions:

➤ Workplace tasks vary greatly. Some are meaningful, some may be menial or difficult, and some may seem irrational, but how we react to the less desirable tasks can affect both performance and attitude.

➤ The leader can help people understand the purpose of tasks that may seem meaningless.

➤ Collaboration can make a difficult task easier. It can also make tasks go faster. People may feel less frustrated when collaborating.

➤ Changing our mindset about tasks is critical. We can choose our emotional reactions to a given task. Why get bothered about a task that still has to be done?

➤ Apply creative thinking to tasks to determine if there is a way to streamline them, break them down into easier parts or have others involved in some way.

➤ Approach tasks with a collaborative mindset.

EQ 23 Good Enough

Self-Awareness
and Control
Empathy
Social
Expertness
Personal
Infuence
Mastery of
Purpose and
Vision

Inward, Inward, Outward

EQ Area and Competency

Personal Influence: Goal Orientation

How to Use This Activity

- To provide insight into goal setting and management.

- To help break down goals into achievable chunks.

- To understand when we merely need to complete a task and when we should strive for something more, such as perfection or following a certain process to achieve success.

"Good Enough" can be part of a leadership, teamwork, or on-boarding program. It is an effective tool for coaching and in self-development or team-based training, as well as a very effective career development activity that can help individuals learn how to set appropriate and realistic goals for their careers.

Applicable Content Area

Multiple: Leadership and Career Development, Teamwork

Audience: Classroom, Coaching, Web-Based

Estimated Time: 30 minutes

Level of Disclosure/Difficulty: High

Materials: "Good Enough" handout—one per participant

Purpose/Why This Is Important

This activity provides insight into an individual's ability to set and accomplish. Goal setting is a critical emotional intelligence competency that shows if an individual is self-motivated and directed. It can also affect how he, as a leader, sets goals for others. Sometimes, individuals can also become trapped in an effort to achieve unrealizable goals. An individual must be able to determine how to set goals that can be accomplished and continue to strive for more, but not to let the magnitude of the goal interfere with her ability to accomplish what needs to be done.

This activity asks participants to look at the goals they have met and those they have not accomplished. Participants will be asked to think about how setting too high a goal may be interfering with what they want to accomplish and how breaking them into manageable tasks can help them realize their goals.

Participants who may have a perfectionist voice in their heads may also struggle with accomplishing goals because of their desire to have the item completed perfectly instead of simply accepting its completion. This activity will also challenge those assumptions and show how the perfectionist voice can interfere with realizing a participant's individual goals.

Set the Stage

Pass out the handouts to each participant. Explain that there is value and immense satisfaction in accomplishing a goal and always striving to be better. Sometimes, however, the language of a goal can be limiting, and it is important to think of how to best accomplish what needs to be done, and then strive to do more.

The Activity

1. Ask participants to complete the "Good Enough" handout. Emphasize that they

should focus on goals that would benefit either their organization or themselves.

2. Provide time to complete the "Good Enough" handout.

3. Ask participants to identify both goals they've successfully met and those they've failed to achieve.

Key Debrief Questions

➤ What are some goals at which you've succeeded? What aspect of those goals made it possible for you to succeed?

➤ What are some goals that you could not achieve? What aspects of those goals made it impossible for you to succeed?

➤ Were any goals too big to accomplish?

➤ Did your own feelings of "it has to be right" or "it has to be perfect" interfere with meeting the goal? Does that push to be perfect help you accomplish what you want to accomplish, or does it interfere?

➤ How can you overcome those obstacles? Can you redefine any goals to make them simpler? Is this "one size fits all?"

➤ What can you do individually to help overcome your internal challenges to accomplishing goals?

Key Learning Points

The facilitator should help the participants arrive at the following conclusions:

➤ At times the size and magnitude of a goal or a person's perfectionist tendencies can overwhelm a person's ability to achieve goals. It is important for an individual to develop strategies to overcome internal challenges to meeting goals.

➤ Setting goals in small manageable chunks can help break down a tendency to be overwhelmed or paralysis brought on by perfectionism and still allow for results.

➤ Sometimes, good enough is good enough. It's important to develop a strong sense of when something is worth extra effort and when it is good enough.

➤ Sometimes gaining another person's perspective can help you push through a block that you may have related to achieving a goal.

Good Enough Handout

1. What are some goals you've set for yourself that you've accomplished?

2. Can you think of any goals you've set for which you know that you could have done more/achieved more with more effort?

3. Why did you choose to expend the effort or not?

4. Are any of those goals important enough to keep working on?

5. What are some goals you've set for yourself that you haven't accomplished?

6. Why were you not able to complete the goal?

7. Could you have completed part of the goal and had an impact?

EQ 24

Reflection Errors— Part 1

Self-Awareness and Control

Empathy

Social Expertness

Personal Infuence

Mastery of Purpose and Vision

Inward Inward Outward

EQ Area and Competency

Self-Awareness and Control: Accurate Self-Assessment

How to Use This Activity

- To help individuals determine the reflection errors they make.

- To help people accurately assess themselves.

Use this activity in leadership-development training, teamwork, and personal development in a coaching or classroom setting. This activity helps participants recognize the common reflection errors—rationalizing, justifying, explaining, getting angry all over again, focusing only on intentions instead of the results of one's behavior, blaming, psychoanalyzing, or beating oneself up—as they assess their own performances.

Applicable Content Area

Multiple: Leadership Development, Teamwork, Conflict Resolution, Interpersonal Skills

Audience: Classroom, Coaching

Estimated Time: Minimum of 40 minutes (depends on the option and number of participants)

Level of Disclosure/Difficulty: High

Materials: Handouts

Purpose/Why This Is Important

Wisdom is not about putting in time in this thing called life. It is about the profound knowledge that can come from life experience. Reflection is the most powerful tool we have to develop our emotional intelligence and turn our life experiences into wisdom. The manner in which we reflect on our behavior after a situation will either help us to improve our behavior in a future situation or reinforce behavior that did not produce the desired result. Everyone makes reflection errors. These errors enable people to justify their current behavior. The common reflection errors, as described in *The EQ Difference* by Adele B. Lynn, are rationalizing, justifying, explaining, getting angry all over again, focusing only on intentions—not the results of one's behavior, blaming, psychoanalyzing, or beating oneself up. As long as we are using these errors when we think about our behavior, we will not change our behavior. Instead, we will find reasons to continue. Learning how to reflect free of errors will help us develop our emotional intelligence because we will have a more accurate way of understanding the impact of our behaviors.

Set the Stage

Ask the group if the members have heard the expression, "There's a huge difference between 30 years of experience and one year of experience repeated 30 times." Ask the group to comment on the meaning of that quotation. Also, ask what happens on Tuesday morning after the big football game. Pro football teams spend hours looking at videotapes of the game. Why? What do they hope to accomplish? Tell the group that we can use these same methods to get better for our next "big game." However, it is important that we know what we're looking for when reviewing our situations. State that everyone reflects on situations. However, when we reflect, we often make reflection errors that discourage us from changing our behavior in the future.

The Activity

Note to Trainer: There are three options listed for this activity. Select the option that best suits your time and learning agenda. The debrief questions are the same for all options.

Option 1: 30 minutes (very high disclosure for the volunteer)

1. Give each participant a handout.

2. In a minilecture, describe the reflection errors listed on the handout.

3. Ask for a volunteer to be interviewed. (This is high disclosure activity for the volunteer because he will be exposed in front of the entire group. If you don't think the participants are ready for this type of disclosure, then the instructor should not ask for a volunteer. Instead, the instructor can be the interviewee and should answer the questions. When the instructor answers the questions, be sure to use reflection errors.)

4. Ask a person in the room to ask the questions stated on the handout.

5. Instruct the participants to complete the handout by checking off and briefly describing the reflection errors that they hear during the interview.

6. Debrief the activity. (The debrief questions are the same regardless of the option.)

Option 2: 40 minutes

This option is still high disclosure for the participants, however, it provides the least amount of exposure for participants. It is the lowest disclosure of all options.

1. Put participants into pairs of two.

2. Give each participant a handout.

3. In a minilecture, describe the reflection errors listed on the handout.

4. Ask one person in each pair to volunteer to go first.

5. The other person will ask the questions and listen for and record reflection errors on the handout.

6. After about 10 to 15 minutes, ask the partners to switch. Whoever was the interviewee becomes the interviewer, and vice versa.

7. Debrief the activity.

Option 3: 30 minutes per person plus a 15- to 30-minute debrief for the entire group

This option works very well for one-on-one coaching. It gives the participants the best overall learning experience. It is high disclosure for all participants. Most participants do not enjoy being videotaped, but that experience is quite useful for this learning point. It is the most time consuming option.

1. Arrange to interview and videotape each participant separately before the class.

2. Give handouts to each participant. Each participant should have a handout for each member of the class.

3. In a minilecture, describe the reflection errors listed on the handout.

4. Play each tape. Have class members give feedback on reflection errors they heard during the taped interview.

5. Debrief the activity.

Key Debrief Questions

➤ How do reflection errors prevent us from being our best?

➤ How do reflection errors cement our behaviors?

➤ How can accurate self-assessment help us live our intentions?

➤ What can we gain if we are more aware of our behavior and its impact?

➤ What methods could we use to help us become more aware of our reflection errors?

Note to Trainer: Participants may need additional information about how to become aware of our reflection errors. Trainers should refer participants to the handout at the end of the activity.

Key Learning Points

The facilitator should help the participants arrive at the following conclusions:

➤ Reflection errors prevent us from being our best because they prevent us from changing our behavior.

➤ Reflection errors are common. We hear them everywhere, so it's easy to believe that they are not errors.

➤ Accurate self-assessment allows us to examine our lives to determine if we are living our intentions.

➤ By becoming more aware of the impact our behavior has on others, we can create desirable outcomes in others.

➤ Reflection is the best tool we have to change our behavior.

Reflection Errors Handout—Part 1

Avoid these common reflection errors that can occur as we recall a situation. They are the things we tell ourselves about a particular incident or situation. Making these reflection errors can rob us of our development because we find reasons NOT to try to change our behavior.

- Rationalizing: "I had no choice...."
- Justifying: "Considering the situation, I was right to...."
- Focus on Intentions: "I didn't mean to insult...."
- Explaining: "Well, the reason I did this was...."
- Blaming: "If Joe hadn't____, then I wouldn't have had to....."
- Psychoanalyzing: "He's just upset because he didn't get promoted...."
- Beating Yourself Up: "'I'll never be a good leader...."
- Getting Angry All Over Again: "I'm so mad...."

Interview Question: Tell me about a time when a project or job you were doing didn't go well. What happened? Describe it to me in detail.

Listen to the interview. Place a mark in the box if you hear any of the reflection errors. Jot down a couple of words to capture what you heard.

RATIONALIZING	JUSTIFYING	FOCUSING ON INTENTIONS	EXPLAINING	BLAMING	PSYCHOANALYZING	BEATING YOURSELF UP	GETTING ANGRY ALL OVER AGAIN

How to Improve Reflection

We can use several methods to assist us in our reflections.

1. Reflect with the assistance of a mentor who can help us identify our reflection errors.

2. Journal our reflections and then check our journal entries for reflection errors.

3. Ask key questions such as:

   Q. How well did my interactions with others go today?

   Q. How did others receive my actions?

   Q. What did I do well today?

   Q. What did I do that could be improved?

   Q. What did I do that I should stop doing?

   Q. What positive effect did I have on others today?

   Q. What negative effect did I have on others today?

   Q. What can I be proud of today?

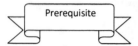

EQ 25 Reflection Errors— Part 2

Self-Awareness and Control
Empathy
Social Expertness
Personal Infuence
Mastery of Purpose and Vision

Inward · Inward · Outward

Prerequisite

EQ Area and Competency

Self-Awareness: Accurate Self-Assessment

How to Use This Activity

- To help individuals transform negative behaviors into more positive behavior.

- To help people imagine behavior that will produce positive results with others.

Use this activity in leadership-development training, teamwork, and personal development. This activity can be done in a coaching or classroom setting. After recognizing common reflection errors in EQ 24—rationalizing, justifying, explaining, getting angry all over again, focusing only on intentions instead of the result of one's behavior, blaming, psychoanalyzing or beating oneself up—this activity replaces the errors with productive thought patterns that lead to behavior change. EQ 24 is a prerequisite to this activity.

Applicable Content Area

Multiple: Leadership Development, Teamwork, Interpersonal Skills and Conflict Resolution

Audience: Classroom, Coaching

Estimated Time: 60 minutes

Level of Disclosure/Difficulty: Medium

Materials: Completed Handouts from EQ 24

Purpose/Why This Is Important

As people become aware of the reflection errors in their thinking (*see* EQ 24), they become more open to exploring new ways of thinking and behaving. Reflection errors cement our behaviors.

By freeing our thinking from describing previous behavior as "right," we can begin to think about other ways to behave that will result in different and, we hope, improved outcomes. Emotional intelligence requires us to think about ways to behave that deliver outcomes consistent with our intentions, goals, or values. If we eliminate reflection errors and think instead about alternative behaviors, we prepare ourselves to act differently in similar situations. We learn from our past behavior and create scenarios in our minds that we can access in the future. This lifelong learning enables us to mature into the people we wish to become.

Set the Stage

Direct the group to think again about what sports teams do after a game, match, or meet. Teams spend hours looking at videotape. Why? Remind the participants that in the last activity we learned about the mistakes we made in our reflections. However, a great coach does more than just point out errors. Instead, he coaches his players on what they could have done to be more effective and get the outcome the team desires. Explain that you can use the same technique. Recognize your errors, and then coach yourself to determine how you could have behaved in that "play" to win the big game. The goal in reflection is always the same. It is to discover new ways to behave that would have delivered a more positive outcome— an outcome that is linked to our goals, intentions, and values.

The Activity

1. Ask participants to recall the situation discussed in EQ 24.

2. Put participants in groups of three.

3. Ask participants to imagine at least one different scenario of how they could have behaved that would have delivered a more positive result.

4. Each participant should volunteer ideas or scenarios. The participants in the triad should comment and offer additional ideas or scenarios.

5. Instruct each participant to select a favorite scenario.

6. Ask participants to mentally rehearse the favorite scenario. Let them imagine themselves in the situation, but imagining a different ending.

7. Debrief the activity.

Key Debrief Questions

➤ How do reflection errors prevent us from being our best?

➤ How do reflection errors cement our behaviors?

➤ How can accurate self-assessment help us live our intentions?

➤ What can we gain if we are more aware of our behavior and its impact?

➤ What methods could we use to come up with different ideas or scenarios to behave differently?

Key Learning Points

The facilitator should help the participants arrive at the following conclusions:

➤ Accurate self-assessment allows us to examine our lives to determine whether or not we are living our intentions.

➤ By becoming more aware of the impact our behavior has on others, we can create desirable outcomes in others.

➤ Reflection is the best tool we have to change our behavior.

➤ Reflect with a friend, colleague, or mentor who is able to help us brainstorm behaviors that would result in a more positive outcome.

➤ Ask key questions during our reflection that are future oriented, such as:

• What could I have done differently?
• What outcome did I want?
• How could I have achieved the outcome I wanted?
• Whom could I have modeled in this situation? What would she have done?
• What will I try next time I am faced with a similar scenario?
• What do I want to change about my behavior? What do I want to change it to become?

EQ 26 Swing Set

Self-Awareness and Control
Empathy
Social Expertness
Personal Infuence
Mastery of Purpose and Vision

Inward Inward Outward

EQ Area and Competency

Social Expertness: Building Relationships
Personal Influence: Getting Results Through Others

How to Use This Activity

- To understand how conflicting goals in an organization can hinder communications.

- To understand how ineffective communications can cause poor results.

"Swing Set" can be used as part of leadership, teamwork, or communications training. It is also an effective tool for remote-work training or team-based training.

Applicable Content Area

Multiple: Leadership Development, Teamwork, Remote Work, Communications, Interpersonal Skills

Audience: Classroom

Estimated Time: 60 minutes

Level of Disclosure/Difficulty: Low

Materials

Instructions for each of the four teams.
Paper
Markers in a variety of colors, but green and blue must be included.
Timer

Purpose/Why This Is Important

This activity shows how team members work to achieve results through others. Organizations want individuals who are able to influence others and maintain quality relationships in all of their interactions. However, often in organizations, communications between departments are far from perfect. Each department has its own view as to what is important for the success of the organization. These views create assumptions and can influence the communications from group to group, can harm relationships in the organization, and can detract from the organization's goals. Navigating an organization successfully requires the ability to understand how each line of business works together toward the overall goal of the organization and to break down organizational silos in order to be successful.

This activity simulates individual departments with conflicting goals, all of which are trying to meet the overall organization's goal. Discussion around how to communicate with other departments with conflicting goals and how to build and maintain those relationships will allow participants to discuss the ramifications of "silo-ing" that may occur in their own organizations.

Set the Stage

Divide the group into four department teams at a design and manufacturing plant. The four departments are Engineering, Design, Marketing, and Sales. Explain that the organization has the opportunity to design a product for a large customer and, if the organization wins the work, it will be a wonderful opportunity that should result in large bonuses for everyone involved.

Pass out instructions to each team and ask the members to read them when told to but not to discuss them with any other team. The organization must present to the potential customer soon, so the activity will be timed.

The Activity

1. Begin the activity by asking the Engineering Department to read its instructions. After the members have read the instructions, ask the team to create a plan and set the timer for 10 minutes. At this time, the Design Department should read its instructions.

2. When the timer goes off, ask the Engineering Department to share its plan with the Design Department. Then set a timer for ten minutes and ask the Design Department to create a design for the Marketing Department. At this time, the Marketing Department should read its instructions.

3. When the timer goes off, ask the Design Department to share its design with the Marketing Department. Then set a timer for ten minutes and ask the Marketing Department to create a pitch for the Sales Department.

4. Once the timer goes off, ask the Marketing Department to hand the Sales Department its plan, and ask the Sales Department to read its instructions.

5. Ask the Sales Department if the organization made the sale.

6. Debrief the activity.

Key Debrief Questions

➤ Were you surprised at what the Sales Department said? Sales, what were you looking for? Was that information included at any point? When was it dropped? Why was it dropped?

➤ What was the failure? How could it have been prevented?

➤ Did everyone want to achieve the overall goal of the organization? What prevented that from happening? How did each department's goals support or detract from the overall goal of the organization?

➤ How did the communications to each team hurt the overall goal? How could they have been crafted differently?

➤ How did not talking to each team hinder the overall goal? Does this actually happen in organizations?

➤ Does your organization have departments with seemingly conflicting goals? Are the goals really conflicting?

➤ How can those seemingly conflicting goals be resolved? Should they always be?

➤ How can you ensure that your goals are nurtured in the organization? How can building relationships across departments help?

Key Learning Points

The facilitator should help the participants arrive at the following conclusions:

➤ Seemingly conflicting goals of departments or individuals can hinder the organization's progress.

➤ Building relationships across the organization can break down "silo-ed" thinking and help maintain a focus on overall goals.

➤ Communications are not always clear and crisp and often do not focus on the overall goals. Rather, they assume knowledge of the larger goals.

➤ Assumptions are a huge factor in creating "silo-ed" thinking.

➤ When communicating goals, the leader can create greater success by calling people together to discuss the overall goal and how each area's goal impacts the others.

Swing Set Handouts

Engineering Department

The overall goal of the Engineering Department is to concentrate on the parts and the key aspect of the design, based on the list of specifications determined by the client and which were received in the message below.

Dear Engineering Team,
We need a swing set designed for a new client. This is a bit of a rush, so please draw up your plans immediately and send them to Design so we can begin manufacturing as soon as possible. The requirements from the client are:

- U.S.-made steel frame supporting two or more swings.

- Each swing supports one child.

- Also include one slide.

- Each slide can handle one child.

- Length of slide should be 6 feet.

- Swing set should be 12 feet long.

- The swing set should be able to handle three children at any time.

- Swing chains should ensure that children's fingers cannot be caught.

- Weight capacity per swing/slide: 100 lbs.

- Maximum weight capacity: 430 lbs.

- Minimal assembly required.

Instructions: Sketch a drawing of the swing set to show design, including relevant information for the Manufacturing Department. When the timer buzzes, walk over to the Design team and show them your drawing. You'll want to keep your copy of the sketch to provide the engineering specifications to manufacturing, but the design team will also need to see your specs so it can determine colors and packaging requirements.

Design Department

The goal of the Design Department is to focus on the colors and the ability to ship the final product to the customers (broken down into flat boxes and designed to be assembled with everyday household tools). The designers receive the message below from their upper management team.

Dear Design Team,
We have an exciting opportunity to work with a new client on a swing set project. If we receive this contract, our company's products will be showcased throughout the state. It is important that we focus on using our corporate colors to identify the product as ours, so green and blue should be featured. We'll also want to make sure that shipping costs are minimized, so we have to think about how we can pack the product as efficiently as possible and make it easy for our end customers to assemble once they receive it.

Instructions: Sketch a clean copy of the swing set featuring key elements of the design. The Marketing Department will need to see your sketch to determine the most important features for its presentation. You'll need to keep your sketch, though, to provide to the Shipping Department so it knows how many items can fit on each truck.

Marketing Department

The goal of the Marketing Department is to focus on the features that will appeal to the end customer. The department received the following information from its management team.

Dear Marketing Team,
Once you've seen a copy of the new swing set design, develop a list of the key features for the Sales Department. Spend time thinking about what the customer really wants from the swing set and how we can meet those needs. Create a list of top advantages for the Sales team to present to the customer.

Instructions: Based on the design team's sketch, create a list of the top advantages and selling points that the sales team can present to the customer. The Design team will need to keep its sketch to begin ordering supplies, but don't hesitate to give your list to the Sales team.

Sales Department

The goal of the Sales Department is to close a contract with the State's school system, which wants to purchase new swing sets for all elementary schools but must comply with a requirement that the materials used are made in this country. If that information is not in the marketing plan, the organization will lose the contract. The Sales team receives the following message from its management team.

Dear Sales Team,
Your customer has provided a very specific list of requirements with which your teams must comply. The customer's number one concern is that the product is made from a majority of U.S. products. If this fact is not in the Marketing team's presentation, we will not get the work. However, it was included on Engineering's list of requirements, so you should be sure it will be mentioned in the presentation.

Instructions: View the Marketing team's presentation and determine if you've made the sale.

EQ 27 # Restaurant Reviews

Self-Awareness
and Control

Empathy

Social
Expertness
Personal
Infuence
Mastery of
Purpose and
Vision

Inward Inward Outward

EQ Area and Competency

Self-Awareness and Control: Impact on Others
Empathy: Feeling the Impact on Others

How to Use This Activity

• To demonstrate how our actions can affect a group's tone.

• To understand and anticipate how our actions will be interpreted by a group.

"Restaurant Reviews" can be used as part of leadership, teamwork, or communications training. It is also effective for customer service training.

Applicable Content Area

Multiple: Leadership Development, Teamwork, Customer Service, Interpersonal Skills, Communications

Audience: Classroom

Estimated Time: 45 minutes

Level of Disclosure/Difficulty: Low

Materials

Timer
1 set of behavior cards for each team

Purpose? Why This Is Important

This activity examines how individuals manage their reactions to the behavior of teammates and how individuals anticipate the reactions they will have in a group. Organizations want individuals who are able to understand and anticipate how their behaviors will be interpreted in a group and who are able to manage their reactions to poor behaviors. We also need to be aware of the impact positive behaviors will have on our group interactions.

This activity allows participants to react to behaviors and discuss anticipated reactions to certain behaviors. It will also look at how groups adapt to good and bad behaviors and the impacts on performance that those behaviors might have. Groups can often be hurt by the poor behavior of a few, as those attitudes can work against the goals of the overall group. Alternatively, groups can also strongly benefit from the positive actions of a few members; however, negative actions do tend to overshadow positive interactions.

Set the Stage

Split the group into teams of eight people depending on the number of participants. Ask each participant to count off 1, 2, 3, 4, etc., and remember his or her number. Then, have the teams create a list of the closest places to eat and rank them by quality. Explain that preparing a list will allow them to practice their teamwork skills and that they will be asked to share their list.

The Activity

1. Provide a stack of behavior cards to each team. The behaviors should not be visible to the teams.

2. Explain that every time the timer goes off, the next person will take a behavior card and act on that behavior. Person 1 begins, then person 2 goes, and so on. When the timer goes off again, the previous person no longer needs to continue to act on his or her behavior card. Take eight timed cycles to complete the activity.

3. Ask the teams to begin discussing places to eat. Set a timer for one minute.

4. Once the timer goes off, ask person 1 to draw a card, and act on it. Set a timer for one minute.

5. Once the timer goes off, ask person 2 to draw a card, and act on it. Tell person 1 he no longer needs to act on the behavior. Set a timer for one minute.

6. Once the timer goes off, ask person 3 to draw a card, and act on it. Tell person 2 she no longer needs to act on the behavior. Set a timer for one minute.

7. Once the timer goes off, ask person 4 to draw a card, and act on it. Tell person 3 he no longer needs to act on the behavior. Set a timer for one minute.

8. Once the timer goes off, ask person 5 or 1 (depending on group size) to draw a card and act on it. Tell person 4 she no longer needs to act on the behavior. Set a timer for one minute.

9. Once the timer goes off, ask person 6 or 2 (depending on group size) to draw a card and act on it. Tell person 5 or 1 (depending on group size) he no longer needs to act on the behavior. Set a timer for one minute.

10. Once the timer goes off, ask person 7 or 3 (depending on group size) to draw a card and act on it. Tell person 6 or 2 (depending on group size) she no longer needs to act on the behavior. Set a timer for one minute.

11. Once the timer goes off, ask person 8 or 4 (depending on group size) to draw a card and act on it. Tell person 7 or 3 (depending on group size) he no longer needs to act on the behavior. Set a timer for 1 minute.

12. Once the timer goes off, tell person 8 or 4 she no longer needs to act on the behavior. Ask groups to quickly finish their lists.

13. Debrief the activity.

Key Debrief Questions

➤ Were you able to complete the list? What helped you? Hindered you?

➤ When there was a behavior change, how did you react?

➤ As the person who had to change your behavior, how did you feel? Did you anticipate how the group might react? Did you correctly anticipate their reactions?

➤ How did you react to "good" behaviors versus "bad" ones? Was the group more or less productive?

➤ What were you thinking or feeling during the activity? Did that change with different behaviors?

Key Learning Points

The facilitator should help the participants arrive at the following conclusions:

➤ Building the skill to anticipate how a group will react can help you craft your message.

➤ Groups can easily become derailed by poor behaviors of a small number of people. It takes effort to maintain work on the task at hand.

➤ It is harder for a positive behavior to affect the behaviors of a group. Pay attention to positive behaviors and work to encourage them.

Restaurant Reviews Handouts

Behavior Cards

Interrupt each time someone speaks.

Tell the next person to talk that her idea is stupid.

Put your feet up on the table or check your cellphone and act bored.

Tell everyone in the group that you don't care, this is stupid, and try to get others to quit.

Get up and leave the room (come back in less than 30 seconds, but don't tell others where you are going or when you'll be back).

Offer to take a turn (or start, if necessary) writing the list of restaurants for the group. Maintain the list.

Give positive feedback to the group—"That list is really great."

Tell the next person who talks that he has a good idea.

EQ 28 Using Quotations to Anchor Purpose

EQ Area and Competency

Mastery of Purpose and Vision: Understanding Ones' Purpose and Values

How to Use This Activity

- To help people clarify their intentions.

- To help people develop an appreciation of the wisdom of others and apply that wisdom to their own lives.

Use this activity in leadership-development training, teamwork, and personal development. This activity can be done in a coaching or in classroom setting. Quotations can serve as a compass to help people clarify their intentions. By selecting certain quotations to live by, participants can clarify guiding philosophies that can serve to anchor their intentions. Because of the open nature of the activity, participants can draw from a variety of sources, so it can be as contemporary as the participants wish to make it.

Applicable Content Area

Multiple: Leadership Development, Teamwork, Interpersonal Skills, Conflict Resolution

Audience: Classroom, Coaching, Web-Based

Estimated Time: 60 minutes

Level of Disclosure/Difficulty: Medium

Materials:

Internet access during class or as a prerequisite to class so participants can access sites such as http://www.bartleby.com/ or http://www.online-literature.com.

Or

Bartlett's Familiar Quotations by John R. Bartlett

Purpose/Why This Is Important

Mastery of purpose requires that you know who you are and what you want to do with your life. It is about being guided by a strong personal philosophy that sets your life's direction. It serves as your inner script, fixing on the plot and giving you constant stage directions for living that purpose. Your purpose comes through in each line you speak, each action you take, each decision you make, and each secondary character and subplot that enters the pages of your life. When you're 80 years old and reading your life book, each chapter speaks to your purpose. What it says will either be unintentional or directed. Mastery of purpose requires it to be directed. Using quotations as a way to anchor your direction in life, can help you remember the individual you strive to be each day.

Set the Stage

Most of us have a favorite quotation that hits some chord within us. Quotations show up on our cube walls, our Facebook pages, our refrigerator doors, and even our vehicle bumpers. Ask if anyone has a quotation hanging on a wall or elsewhere. Share a favorite quotation with the class, and explain why it is important to you. (One of my personal favorites to sum up emotional intelligence is from the Greek philosopher, Epictetus: "Man is not disturbed by things, but the view he takes of them.") Tell the class that quotations can come from many sources, including music lyrics, television shows, literature, and so on.

The Activity

As prework to the class or you can provide time during class for participants:

1. Ask participants to research and identify no more than five quotations that address fundamental concepts that describe their life/leadership philosophies.

During class:

2. Put participants into groups of four.

3. Ask participants to share within their group the quotations they selected, state what it means to them, and explain how they hope to apply it to their own lives.

4. Debrief the activity.

Key Debrief Questions

➤ How does having a life or leadership philosophy help us?

➤ How can a quotation help us stay on track?

➤ What are some other methods to help us stay centered on our leadership philosophy?

➤ When you are acting in a manner consistent with your philosophy, how does that feel?

➤ When you are acting in a manner that is inconsistent with your philosophy, how does that feel?

Key Learning Points

The facilitator should help the participants arrive at the following conclusions:

➤ People who have a strong, well-thought-out philosophy tend to act according to that intention.

➤ By asking ourselves what is important to us and having clearly answered those questions, we make it easier to remain anchored during times of stress or crisis.

➤ When we act in a manner consistent with our philosophy and intention, we feel confident in our actions. We also feel in harmony.

➤ When we act in a manner inconsistent with our philosophy and intention, we feel dissonance.

Note to Trainer: Many creative concepts can flow from this activity that will help to reinforce the person's philosophy. For example, participants can have a favorite quotation framed and hung in their offices. They can have their pictures taken with the quotation. They can write the quotation in sand and, when the tide washes it away, talk about how that affects their lives. They can have the quotation printed on their business cards. Let the participants use their imaginations to help use the quotation to anchor their thinking.

EQ 29 # Academy Award

Self-Awareness
and Control

Empathy

Social
Expertness

Personal
Influence

Mastery of
Purpose and
Vision

Inward   Inward   Outward

EQ Area and Competency

Self-Awareness: Emotional Inner Awareness

How to Use This Activity

- To provide insights on what drives the participant's behaviors.

- To help identify false rational beliefs and the impact they have on our behavior.

"Academy Award" can be used as part of emotional intelligence training and coaching. It is also effective for leadership or teamwork training.

Applicable Content Area

Multiple: Leadership Development, Teamwork, Interpersonal Skills

Audience: Classroom, Coaching

Estimated Time: 40 minutes

Level of Disclosure/Difficulty: Low

Materials

One copy of The Dirty Dozen list for each participant.
A copy of Instructions for the Actor for one person in each pair.
A copy of Instructions for the Challenger for one person in each pair.
A copy of the Actor Role Card and the Challenger Role Card for each pair.

Purpose/Why This Is Important

This activity describes the false rational beliefs, The Dirty Dozen, that often drive our behavior. Although we mistakenly believe they are rational

thoughts, we may not necessarily act in the best manner. By describing The Dirty Dozen and looking at which of those beliefs the participants most often subscribe to, participants will gain insights into the false rational beliefs that drive their behavior. When we have the emotional inner awareness to understand what drives behavior, we can change it. The more aware of inner thinking individuals become, the less likely they are to be victimized by false thinking and the better able they will be to live their intentions. This activity holds a magnifying glass to The Dirty Dozen and allows the participants to see the impact of their false rational beliefs.

Set the Stage

Pair off the participants. If you use this activity for one-on-one coaching, the coach will be a participant. Explain that the purpose of this activity is to identify how difficult it can be to overcome flawed rational thoughts and how easy it is to defend a flawed rational thought. We will exaggerate The Dirty Dozen to show the internal monologues that influence our thoughts.

The Activity

1. Provide a copy of The Dirty Dozen list to each participant and provide time for everyone to read it. Ask the paired teams to count off by 12. Team #1 will take on Dirty Dozen thought #1. Team #2 will take Dirty Dozen thought #2, and so on. If you do not have 12 pairs in the group, randomly assign Dirty Dozen thoughts. For one-on-one coaching, choose a Dirty Dozen thought that will best assist the person being coached.

2. Ask one person in the pair to be the actor and one person to be the challenger. Give the

actor and the challenger the appropriate instruction sheets and the details of their role, listed on the role cards, and provide time for the individuals to read the sheets. For example, for Team #1, provide one member a copy of Actor 1, Needing Approval Role Card, and the other member of the team will be given a copy of the Challenger 1 Role Card. If you do not have an even number of participants in the group, have extra participants help the challengers. So if you have a group of 25, there will be one extra participant after creating twelve groups of 2. Therefore, assign three people to Team #1 and have one individual act as actor 1 and two individuals act as challengers.

3. Ask the teams to begin the activity as described on the instruction sheet. Watch the teams for signs of frustration, exaggeration of behaviors, and heated debates.

4. After some teams become more animated in their discussions, ask the participants to debrief.

5. Debrief the activity.

Key Debrief Questions

➤ Challengers, were you able to convince your actors? If yes, how? If no, why not?

➤ Actors, were you able to maintain The Dirty Dozen thought process? If so, how? If not, why not?

➤ Challengers, was it easy to interact with the actors? Why was or wasn't it?

➤ Do any of The Dirty Dozen thoughts sound familiar to you?

➤ When you have The Dirty Dozen thoughts, what type of thoughts are in your head? How are those thoughts flawed? Do they interfere with what you hope to accomplish? How can you overcome the thoughts?

Key Learning Points

The facilitator should help the participants arrive at the following conclusions:

➤ Identifying our own Dirty Dozen flawed rational thoughts can help us avoid thought traps that may interfere with our ability to live our intentions.

➤ By working to become aware of what drives our behavior, we can set ourselves up to make positive changes in our lives.

Academy Awards Handouts

The Dirty Dozen

No matter how good we become at observation, if our rational thinking is flawed, our interpretations will be flawed as well. Erroneous beliefs and prejudices in our thinking will thus hinder us from living our intentions. These are called "rational hijackings" because they render our rational brain useless. The Dirty Dozen are examples of flawed thinking.

1. Needing Approval: "Everyone I work with must approve of me at all times."

2. Making Mistakes: "I must prove thoroughly competent, adequate, and achieving at all times."

3. Changing Others: "I have an obligation to change others who act unfairly or obnoxiously."

4. Catastrophize: "When I am very frustrated, treated unfairly, or rejected, I have to view things as awful, terrible, horrible, and catastrophic."

5. Others Cause Misery: "My emotional misery comes from external pressures that I have little ability to change."

6. Worry, Fret, and Fear: "If something seems dangerous or fearsome, I must preoccupy myself with it and make myself anxious about it."

7. Avoidance: "It's easier to avoid facing difficulties and self-responsibilities than to do something about it."

8. The Past: "My past remains all important and because something once strongly influenced my life, it has to keep determining my feelings and behavior."

9. Unrealistic Expectations: "People and things should turn out better than they do, and I must fix them."

10. Competition: "My worth can be measured by competitive situations."

11. Source of Problems: "The people and conditions in my life are the source of my problems."

12. Negativity: "Certain occurrences or events are negative by nature."

Role Cards

Actor 1, Needing Approval: "Everyone I work with must approve of me at all times."
Challenger 1: Try to convince your partner to go ahead with an idea that is contrary to what others in the group like.

Actor 2, Making Mistakes: "I must prove thoroughly competent, adequate, and achieving at all times."
Challenger 2: Try to convince your partner that he does not have to be competent at a certain thing. Let him know it is okay to not be perfect.

Actor 3, Changing Others: "I have an obligation to change others who act unfairly or obnoxiously."
Challenger 3: Point out someone who acts obnoxiously and commiserate on how you are unable to change people and that some things are just unfair.

Actor 4, Catastrophize: "When I am very frustrated, treated unfairly, or rejected, I have to view things as awful, terrible, horrible, and catastrophic."
Challenger 4: Point out that at times unfair things happen, but they're just life, they happen sometimes, and it is not the end of the world.

Academy Awards Handouts (*Continued*)

Actor 5, Others Cause Misery: "My emotional misery comes from external pressures that I have little ability to change."

Challenger 5: Try to convince your partner that happiness/unhappiness comes entirely from within each person.

Actor 6, Worry, Fret, and Fear: "If something seems dangerous or fearsome, I must preoccupy myself with it and make myself anxious about it."

Challenger 6: Try to convince your partner that there is no sense in worrying about something.

Actor 7, Avoidance: "It's easier to avoid facing difficulties and self-responsibilities than to do something about it."

Challenger 7: Try to convince your partner to confront something that she may find difficult and do something about it.

Actor 8, The Past: "My past remains all important, and because something once strongly influenced my life, it has to keep determining my feelings and behavior today."

Challenger 8: Try to convince your partner that things that happened previously do not need to influence his life, and that he is making a choice to continue to focus on that thing.

Actor 9, Unrealistic Expectations: "People and things should turn out better than they do, and I must fix them."

Challenger 9: Point out that your partner has no power over how most other people or things turn out and no obligation to fix anything or correct other's mistakes.

Actor 10, Competition: "My worth can be measured by competitive situations."

Challenger 10: Try to convince your partner that she does not have to be the best at things, or even better than most.

Actor 11, Source of Problems: "The people and conditions in my life are the source of my problems."

Challenger 11: Try to convince your partner that some things are within your control and that there are some problems that he could fix just by changing his outlook.

Actor 12, Negativity: "Certain occurrences or events are negative by nature."

Challenger 12: Try to convince your partner that some events are only events and do not have positive or negative connotations assigned to them.

Instructions for the Actor: The challenger is going to try to convince you to do something. Use the actor card assigned to you to convince the challenger that you shouldn't participate in the activity the challenger is proposing. Be firm in your voice and don't give in. (Do not share these instructions with the challenger.)

Instructions for the Challenger: Try to convince the actor to do what is listed on your role card. The roles are vague so that you can fill out the details of the activity yourself. If the actor doesn't want to go along with your plan, do your very best to convince him and work to overcome any obstacles that may prevent him from participating. (Do not share these instructions with the Actor.)

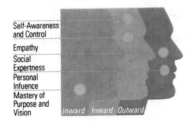

Self-Awareness and Control
Empathy
Social Expertness
Personal Influence
Mastery of Purpose and Vision

Inward   Inward   Outward

EQ 30 # Judgment Day

(With a Special Scenario for Remote Teams or Colocated Teams)

EQ Area and Competency

Self-Awareness: Emotional and Inner Awareness
Social Expertness: Conflict Resolution

How to Use This Activity

- To determine the assumptions we make regarding others.

- To assess how the assumptions we make interfere with our actions toward others.

- To determine the extent to which we reserve judgment when little information is known.

Use this activity to highlight emotional intelligence issues related to working remotely. It addresses issues of leadership and teamwork for remote teams, but it can also be used with an intact office team. This activity is appropriate for the classroom. It can serve as a strong reminder to all teams to refrain from jumping to conclusions or making assumptions. It can help people see the effect of people's assumptions on their actions and may also enlighten individuals who are blind to some of their assumptions.

Applicable Content Area

Multiple: Working Remotely, Leadership Development, Teamwork, Conflict Resolution. Interpersonal Skills

Audience: Web-Based, Classroom

Estimated Time: 30 minutes

Level of Disclosure/Difficulty: Low

Materials: Scenario handouts for participants

Purpose/Why This Is Important

Although we like to think that we are open minded, we often make decisions or take actions with very little data to support them. In *Blink: The Power of Thinking Without Thinking*, Malcolm Gladwell discusses how we think about thinking and how we seem to choices in an instant—in the blink of an eye—that actually aren't as simple as they seem. Learning more about the powerful assumptions we make with very little information helps us to recognize that we may be making judgments that are not in the best interests of our teams or our performances.

Set the Stage

It is best to go directly to the activity, rather than to set the stage about open mindedness and judgment.

The Activity

1. Give one of the roles to each participant. If you have 15 participants, give five participants the role of Employee 1, five participants the Leader role, and five participants role of Employee 2.

2. Ask participants to list what they assume about the situation. Tell them to let their imagination run wild and list all assumptions that come to mind.

3. Have someone read each role and have the participants state their assumptions for the role.

4. Debrief the activity.

Key Debrief Questions

➤ Can quick judgments ever be useful? Under what circumstances?

➤ Under what circumstances should we seek more information?

➤ When we make a judgment about a situation or teammate, how does it affect our behavior?

➤ Do these assumptions and judgments occur only when working in remote teams, or can they occur when working together in the same office?

➤ If we tend to think and judge a person or situation positively or negatively, will we act differently?

➤ What are some methods to use to stop yourself from forming judgments that may not be fair or accurate?

➤ How can working remotely affect the assumptions we make about our remote teammates?

➤ What can you do to gain more information about why teammates or others have not delivered something they promised?

➤ Do you like to be judged?

➤ On what criteria do you want to be judged?

Key Learning Points

The facilitator should help the participants arrive at the following conclusions:

➤ If you sense physical harm, it's probably best to follow your judgment.

➤ For most other nonemergency or nonthreatening situations, working to hold back quick judgments to seek data is probably the best move.

➤ When working with coworkers, quick negative assumptions often lead to negative encounters. Managing these assumptions is best for maintaining positive teamwork.

➤ Often, our assumptions about coworkers who are working remotely can be negative.

➤ The most powerful tool you have to gain more information is to talk with your coworkers and seek to understand their perspectives.

➤ When coworkers don't meet our expectations, asking them about the situation is important in determining the facts.

➤ As a teammate, you have many options to help manage others' assumptions about you. The most important one is to deliver on expectations. Another is to communicate when something is going to be delayed. Explain when it can be expected and why it was delayed. In addition, offering stopgap measures when possible would be appreciated.

Note to Trainer: Working remotely creates huge challenges related to emotional intelligence. The absence of nonverbal cues and tacit knowledge about work practices requires people to be even more emotionally intelligent in their interactions with their remote peers, direct reports, or supervisors. When we don't see people, we often make negative assumptions about their involvement in work-related activities. This activity points out the negative assumptions that can interfere with our working relationships when we work remotely. However, it can also be used to highlight the role that assumptions play when working with one another and how emotionally intelligent team members and leaders must work to overcome the challenges of negative assumptions.

Judgment Day Handout—Working Remotely Scenario

Employee 1: You work on a remote team. Your boss is in another location. You have seen your boss in person three times in the past three years. The two of you communicate almost exclusively by email, and only very rarely by telephone. You are extremely busy on a small portion of a large-scale project—dubbed Project A—that has widespread implications for your organization. You heard through one of your colleagues (Employee 2) that the project was in trouble. You also heard that the budget for your project was being cut. You know that Employee 2 recently met with the boss via conference call. He has met with the boss on several occasions. Your boss sent you an email today wanting a clear update on your activity on the project for the past three months. You send him updates weekly in a report format. Generally you do not hear anything back regarding the updates. Two weeks ago, he responded to your weekly update with an email in which he said he wanted more information on a particular item in the report. You sent him more information and haven't heard back from him. Your work requires you to get information from Employee 2 on a regular basis. Although Employee 2 answers you, his answers are often delayed. Sometimes you have to note in your weekly reports that you are behind on some aspect of the project due to these delays. You know that Employee 2 is working on a cross-functional local team and you wonder why you haven't been asked to take on similar responsibilities.

Leader: You are the leader of a remote team. You have responsibility for team members in seven states. You have a limited travel budget to visit your team members or to pull your team members together. You believe most members of your team are very competent, and your philosophy is to stay out of their way. Your boss has tapped you to design an organizational change that will require drastic changes on an important project that your remote team is working on. The change is extremely confidential, and you are not permitted to discuss it with your team. You believe that Employee 1 may be a good resource to lead a new initiative in the changed organization. Employee 1 always gives you weekly updates that are thorough and informative. Employee 2 gives you updates that are very limited. You have asked him for more information, but you get only limited response to your needs. On several occasions you have reached out to talk to Employee 2 and he never seems available when you call. You are concerned that Employee 2 won't have the skill set required in the new structure. One skill set will be a special certification on XYZ. You wanted to signal to Employee 2 that there may be a problem, so you hinted that the project may not continue as it has in the past, due to budget constraints.

Employee 2: You have been working on a very large remote project—dubbed Project A. Your boss is in another location. You have only seen him three times in three years. You send him weekly updates on your work progress. Lately, your boss has been asking for more information on just about everything. There is a three-hour time difference between you and your boss, who has a habit of calling when you are not available. When you try to call him back, more often than not, the boss is in a meeting. This past year has been particularly challenging. You have been pulled in a lot of different directions at the local level. Your local office has physically moved its location. You were responsible for the cross-functional team that led every detail of the physical move. In addition, you are now working on another cross-functional team at the local level that has you in meetings all day. You've also been working on a special certification. By the end of the month, you'll be certified on XYZ. The training has been intense. It's required hours of preparation and study. However, you're happy that you've been working on it and that it's almost completed. Although you've mentioned the cross-functional teams to your boss, you don't include the details of them in your weekly reports because the boss just wants to know about the activities focused on Project A. You recognize that sometimes Employee 1 needs information from you, but he isn't always able to get it as timely as possible because you've been juggling so many extra duties. You have noticed that Employee 1 has much more detail in his reports. You expect to be able to deliver to that same level once you are finished with your certification.

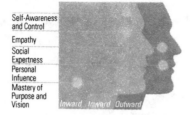

Let's Go!

EQ 31

Plays Well with Others

Self-Awareness and Control

Empathy

Social Expertness

Personal Infuence

Mastery of Purpose and Vision

Inward Inward Outward

EQ Area and Competency

Social Expertness: Collaboration, Conflict Resolution

How to Use This Activity

- To provide insights on how to build collaboration.

- To help identify ways to work around conflict positions.

"Let's Go!" can be used as part of emotional-intelligence, conflict-resolution, leadership, and teamwork training. "Let's Go!" is an effective exercise to be used with ROYGBIV, as ROYGBIV addresses the critical skills of influence and Let's Go! explores ways to have impactful influence during conflict.

Applicable Content Area

Multiple: Leadership Development, Teamwork, Conflict Resolution, Interpersonal Skills

Audience: Classroom, Web-Based

Estimated Time: 40 minutes

Level of Disclosure/Difficulty: Low

Materials

A copy of Team A Instructions for each participant in Team A

A copy of Team B Instructions for each participant in Team B

Purpose/Why This Is Important

This activity is designed to create a conflict within teams and provide different methods for working through that conflict. The teams will use the different methods to answer a simple question, "Where should we go on vacation?" The different methods of answering the question provide insights into how we can resolve conflict in an emotionally intelligent way. This is important because good working relationships and teamwork are critical in the workplace, and with groups of people, conflict is inevitable. Since conflict will happen, individuals need a way to resolve the conflict without damaging the relationships in the workplace. Otherwise, serious impacts can affect future performance and group productivity. This activity challenges participants to consider the importance of thinking about interests, not positions, which allows the discussion to center on what is truly important.

Set the Stage

Divide the group into two teams. Each group has the same goal: to decide where to go on vacation. Everyone in the group must agree to go to the same location.

The Activity

1. Give Team A its instructions. Give Team B its instructions.. Ask them to take a few minutes to read the instructions and to discuss vacation plans.

2. Allow each group time to determine where to go on vacation.

3. If one team settles on a location and the other doesn't, provide a few more minutes for the second team, but you can wrap up the discussion at any time.

4. Debrief the activity.

Key Debrief Questions

➤ Team A: Were you able to decide where to go on vacation? Does everyone on Team A agree with the choice?

➤ Team B: Were you able to decide where to go on vacation? Does everyone on Team B agree with the choice?

➤ If you don't agree, how did the discussion go?

➤ Team A: Were you able to come to consensus? How?

➤ Team B: What happened? Why was it difficult?

➤ What were the differences in the approaches?

➤ Why was it easier for Team A to agree?

➤ How does focusing on interests make conflicts easier to resolve? How does focusing on positions make conflicts more difficult to resolve?

➤ What conflicts in your workplace could benefit from a different approach?

Key Learning Points

The facilitator should help the participants arrive at the following conclusions:

➤ By focusing on interests, teams can often resolve conflict in a manner that preserves the relationship.

➤ Starting with positions can hinder a group's ability to resolve a conflict and can, instead, lead people to defend their positions, which causes defensiveness and gets the group stuck.

➤ In organizations, learning to approach situations with interests in mind, rather than positions, allows people to step back and open their minds about what is best for everyone.

➤ Less competition and less need to "win" someone over to one's position occurs when we focus on interests. The objective is to create a solution where both parties are able to get their interests met.

Let's Go! Handouts

Team A Instructions

When thinking about planning a vacation spot, be open minded and do not immediately jump to a place you'd like to go. Instead, use the following process:

Step 1: Focus on identifying your interests in a vacation. Be specific about the interest without immediately naming a location.

For example: I am interested in being near water. I am interested in golf. I am interested in hiking. I am interested in good food.

Step 2: Clarify the interests of everyone in the group.

For example: Let me understand: You'd like to be near any body of water. Is there a particular watersport you're interested in, or is it just being near the water?

Step 3: Confirm the understanding of the interests.

For example: So the interests of everyone in the group are being near a body of water, playing golf, hiking, and so on.

Step 4: Start suggesting locations. At this point you can be specific about the places and explain how each of the interests could be met by the locations.

Step 5: Try to resolve any concerns so that everyone's interest is met.

Step 6: Set the location for your vacation.

Team B Instructions

Each person on the team should conceive of a specific vacation spot. Then, you should convince your team to go to a specific vacation spot that you love. Try to convince the members how special the specific city, town, or spot is, including the specific activities, restaurants, museums, etc., that make the place special.

EQ 32

A Wondering Mind or a Plan for the Future?

Self-Awareness and Control

Empathy

Social Expertness

Personal Infuence

Mastery of Purpose and Vision

Inward   Inward   Outward

EQ Area and Competency

Mastery of Purpose and Vision: Understanding Purpose and Values

How to Use This Activity

- To help people clarify their purposes.

- To help people use their daydreams constructively to gain insight about their futures.

Use this activity in leadership-development training and personal development. This activity can be done in a coaching or in classroom setting. Everyone daydreams. We daydream about happy times in the past; we daydream about ways to reconstruct unpleasant pasts; we daydream about the future. It is those daydreams about the future that can help us write our autobiography. This activity can tap into people's unrealized passions, interests, and purposes that can provide important motivation for living their lives in purposeful and meaningful ways. It is best to assign this activity over a period of time. The activity is designed to elicit thought patterns over the course of a few weeks. So, the handout could be assigned as prework between leadership, personal-development sessions, and coaching sessions.

Applicable Content Area

Multiple: Leadership Development, Career Development

Audience: Classroom, Coaching, Web-Based

Estimated Time

Prework—Journaling two to four weeks prior to session

Session: 45 to 60 minutes

Level of Disclosure/Difficulty: High

Materials: "A Wondering Mind" Handout

Purpose/Why This Is Important

Many people live purposeful lives. Others wonder through life aimlessly. Purpose gives people a reason to wake up in the morning. People who demonstrate purpose are dedicated to a cause, a mission, a reason for being. They are guided by a strong compass that sets their lives' directions. People who live purposeful lives have visions of their lives. They "see" themselves living and working in certain ways toward specific purposes. They set goals to achieve these purposes. For example, if your purpose is to bring health and joy to the lives of animals, you can do this in many ways. You can open an animal shelter; you can volunteer to foster animals; you can become a veterinarian. Each goal would require a different set of actions and skills. Opening an animal shelter may require intense fund-raising and organizational skills, whereas becoming a veterinarian would require serious commitment to the study of science. But either path may enable you to live your purpose of bringing health and joy to the lives of animals. The first question for each of us to answer is that of purpose. Then, we must assess our skills and abilities to determine the right path to live our purposes. Purposeful living gives our lives meaning. At the end of our lives, we can look back with satisfaction that we lived and accomplished something that we valued.

Set the Stage

Daydreams take on many forms. Typically, they fall into a few categories: thinking about our past experiences, imagining an event that might take place in the future, trying to understand what other people are thinking, and assisting us in making moral decisions. Using our daydreams, especially those that focus on imagining ourselves in the future, can be a rich source of information that can help us tap into our interests. People who live purposeful and meaningful lives do so from their interests. They also state that they can't imagine themselves doing anything else. So, if we can be mindful of our daydreams, they can help us write our future autobiography. What do you want your future to be? Ask your daydreams; they may have the answer.

The Activity

As prework

1. Ask participants to complete the prework handout before the session. Be sure to remind people to focus on daydreams about their futures. In addition, inform them that they will be asked to share the information in the next scheduled class or coaching session. Help people to distinguish between the two parts of the handout. Part 1 asks participants to catch themselves daydreaming about the future without prompting. Part 2 asks participants to purposefully generate daydreams about their future. It is often more difficult to catch ourselves daydreaming about the future, so you'll have to encourage people to pay attention.

During class

2. Ask participants to reflect on Part 1 of the handout on free-form future-focused daydreams. For each future-focused daydream, the participants should be instructed to evaluate the item based on the following characteristics:

   a. Natural Ability—Using a 1-to-10 scale, ask participants to evaluate their natural abilities regarding this characteristic or quality. For example, if you have a future-focused daydream to be a world-class ballerina, but have absolutely no natural ability to dance, you would rate yourself a "1."

   b. Existing Skill—Using a 1-to-10 scale, ask participants to evaluate their existing skill regarding this characteristic or quality.

   c. Interest Level—Mark this column with an H for High, M for Medium, or L for Low to indicate your interest level.

   d. Realistic—Is this future-focused daydream at all possible? Mark this column with a Yes or No. (The instructor can note that although it is important to be realistic, this isn't intended to kill a dream. Before marking "no," coach participants to ask if there is something that can make it more realistic?)

   e. Explore—Is this future-focused daydream something you wish to explore? Mark this column with a Yes or No.

3. Ask participants to pair with another person in the group. They should share their future-focused daydreams and how they rated the items in each column. For the items that ranked highest, ask people to share with their partners why the item was ranked high. What was the appeal? What do they think the item would give them that their current situation doesn't give them? Encourage people to dig deep and try to uncover what is appealing about the dream. For example, someone might say she wants to be the head of her own company. When asked why, she might say it's because she wants freedom over her schedule or perhaps the power to make her own decisions. It is essential that the discussion uncover "why" these ideas have appeal.

4. Ask participants to repeat Steps 1 to 3 of this activity for Part 2 of the handout on structured daydreams.

5. Debrief the activity.

Key Debrief Questions

➤ How difficult was it for you to catch yourself daydreaming?

➤ What differences do you see between your structured daydreams and your free-form daydreams? What similarities exist?

➤ When you dig deep to uncover why these ideas have appeal, did you discover any similarities?

➤ What is the value of evaluating our daydreams against our natural ability, skills, and interests?

- What insight can you gain from your daydreams?

- How do you turn daydreams into reality?

- When do you want to turn daydreams into reality?

- Is it always worthwhile to pursue your dreams?

Key Learning Points

The facilitator should help the participants arrive at the following conclusions:

- Daydreams can be an important source of information about our interests and purposes.

- Daydreams can also lead us to understand what could be added to our current lives to make them more fulfilling or meaningful.

- Pursuing a daydream doesn't necessarily mean we give up our current lives. It could be more about adding to our current lives to deepen their purposes.

- What we think about defines what we pursue. If we don't think about something, then the chances of its occurring are much less than something we think about often.

- Thoughts alone, however, do not make things happen. They inform us about what may be important, but without action, dreams do not come true.

- Aligning our interests, skills, and natural abilities is a winning tactic that often leads to satisfaction.

- People who pursue their purposes will often say that when they are working at something it feels natural. It feels like they are aligned and in flow. However, people who pursue their purposes don't necessarily have an easier life or time, especially if they are doing something with an uncertain financial return or something that may seem impractical to friends, family, or others.

- When people must act in a manner inconsistent with their interests, skills and abilities, they often feel dissonance. Although they can learn to be good at something, it may never feel it is what they were born to do. Many people may experience this. In fact, when talking with peers or friends, it may seem like the norm.

Note to Trainer: If you are working with a group for leadership development, you could use Part 2 of the handout as a specific structured daydream activity to engage people's thoughts about how to become more effective as a leader. Instead of asking people to imagine themselves doing something different, ask them to imagine themselves leading in a better, new, or bigger way. They would structure the daydream by completing the following: "I can picture myself being even more effective as a leader if I . . . ."

A Wondering Mind. . . Daydream Your Future Autobiography Handout

Part 1—Freeform Daydreaming

Record at least one of your future-focused daydreams per day for two weeks. In addition, record the reason this idea appeals to you. Future-focused daydreams place us in the future doing or interacting in a certain way. For the sake of this exercise, just record or focus on daydreams related to work or career aspirations. Leave the columns to the right blank. Bring your worksheet to class.

FREE-FORM FUTURE FOCUSED DAYDREAMS	NATURAL ABILITY 1–10	EXISTING SKILLS 1–10	INTEREST H M L	REALISTIC Y N		EXPLORE Y N	
Day 1—Daydream notes Why does this appeal to you?							
Day 2—Daydream notes Why does this appeal to you?							
Day 3—Daydream notes Why does this appeal to you?							
Day 4—Daydream notes Why does this appeal to you?							
Day 5—Daydream notes Why does this appeal to you?							
Day 6—Daydream notes Why does this appeal to you?							
Day 7—Daydream notes Why does this appeal to you?							

FREE-FORM FUTURE FOCUSED DAYDREAMS	NATURAL ABILITY 1—10	EXISTING SKILLS 1—10	INTEREST H M L	REALISTIC Y	N	EXPLORE Y	N
Day 8—Daydream notes Why does this appeal to you?							
Day 9—Daydream notes Why does this appeal to you?							
Day 10—Daydream notes Why does this appeal to you?							
Day 11—Daydream notes Why does this appeal to you?							
Day 12—Daydream notes Why does this appeal to you?							
Day 13—Daydream notes Why does this appeal to you?							
Day 14—Daydream notes Why does this appeal to you?							

Part 2—Structured daydreaming

If you've ever heard yourself saying, "I can picture myself doing that," you may be tapping into some important information about your future. This mental visualizing of ourselves in the future is an important step in defining our purpose. To help tap into important information about the future, try structured daydreaming. It is intentional daydreaming for the purpose of determining our interest and purpose. Each day for two weeks, allow yourself to daydream about a particular path that interests you. You can get inspiration from an article you read, a person you meet, a picture you see, a movie or book, or any other source. The idea is to take something that draws you in and allow yourself to explore the idea. Every day for two weeks, the goal is to hear yourself saying, "I can picture myself doing that," to at least one idea. Write it down.

If you are already engaged in work that you believe fulfills your purpose, then use this exercise to refine it. Instead of imagining yourself doing something different, it is imagining yourself doing what you are already doing in a better, new, or bigger way. You would say to yourself, "I can picture myself doing that and being even more effective at my purpose."

STRUCTURED FUTURE FOCUSED DAYDREAMS	NATURAL ABILITY 1–10	EXISTING SKILLS 1–10	INTEREST H M L	REALISTIC Y　　N		EXPLORE Y　　N	
Day 1—Daydream notes Why does this appeal to you?							
Day 2—Daydream notes Why does this appeal to you?							
Day 3—Daydream notes Why does this appeal to you?							
Day 4—Daydream notes Why does this appeal to you?							
Day 5—Daydream notes Why does this appeal to you?							
Day 6—Daydream notes Why does this appeal to you?							

STRUCTURED FUTURE FOCUSED DAYDREAMS	NATURAL ABILITY 1–10	EXISTING SKILLS 1–10	INTEREST H M L	REALISTIC Y	N	EXPLORE Y	N
Day 7—Daydream notes Why does this appeal to you?							
Day 8—Daydream notes Why does this appeal to you?							
Day 9—Daydream notes Why does this appeal to you?							
Day 10—Daydream notes Why does this appeal to you?							
Day 11—Daydream notes Why does this appeal to you?							
Day 12—Daydream notes Why does this appeal to you?							
Day 13—Daydream notes Why does this appeal to you?							
Day 14—Daydream notes Why does this appeal to you?							

EQ 33 Actions Speak Louder Than Words

Self-Awareness and Control
Empathy
Social Expertness
Personal Infuence
Mastery of Purpose and Vision
Inward Inward Outward

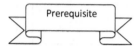

Prerequisite

EQ Area and Competency

Mastery of Purpose and Vision: Taking Action Toward Purpose

How to Use This Activity

- To help people take actions toward their purposes.

- To encourage people unsure of their purposes to take steps to explore the question.

Use this activity in career-development, leadership-development, and personal-development training programs. This activity can be done in a coaching or in a classroom setting. It is particularly helpful for people who are exploring options related to their career or life paths. EQ 32, "A Wondering Mind or a Plan for the Future?" is a prerequisite. The completed handouts for EQ 32, "A Wondering Mind or a Plan for the Future?" will be required for this activity. If you are using this in leadership development and have asked leaders in EQ 32 to use structured daydreaming for the following scenario, "I can picture myself being even more effective as a leader, if I. . . ," then use the completed responses to that scenario.

Applicable Content Area

Multiple: Career Development, Leadership Development

Audience: Classroom, Coaching, Web-Based

Estimated Time: 50 minutes

Level of Disclosure/Difficulty: High

Materials: Completed handouts from EQ 32, "A Wondering Mind or a Plan for the Future?"

Purpose/Why This Is Important

Daydreams, or any other types of dreams, without action are nothing more than wishful thinking. Action toward goals designed specially to move oneself closer to the dream or purpose differentiates a person who lives a life of purpose from someone who just dreams of a purposeful life. Someone can be very productive and goal oriented, but those goals could have nothing to do with getting closer to one's purpose. One can pursue and achieve many accomplishments, but the accomplishments may seem empty and meaningless because they aren't anchored in one's true purpose. In the example stated in EQ 32, we spoke of someone who may have a purpose to bring heath and joy to the lives of animals, and we said this purpose could manifest itself in many different paths, such as opening an animal shelter, volunteering to foster animals, or becoming a veterinarian. Each path would require reaching for many goals or milestones on the quest toward purpose. And each goal requires an action: some small step to begin the journey toward the goal and, therefore, a life of purpose. So, no matter how productive and goal oriented a person may be, unless his or her actions are deliberately tied to his or her purpose, a life of meaning and purpose will be elusive.

Set the Stage

The instructor should ask the group to name some individuals throughout history whom they believe lived a purposeful life. Generally names such as Gandhi, Martin Luther King, Mother Teresa, or Beethoven may surface. However, it can also be someone in life that they know and admire, such as a family member, coach, mentor, pastor, teacher, or other person. Ask the group to think about small actions those individuals may have taken to put them onto their paths. Allow the group to talk about actions these individuals have taken. Point out that purpose and interests alone will not produce a purposeful life. Explain that without action, these individuals may be nothing more than dreamers.

The Activity

1. Ask participants to refer to their completed handout from EQ 32, "A Wondering Mind or a Plan for the Future?"

2. Ask participants to reflect on all items that were marked "Yes" under the column headed "Explore." Ask participants to rank the items marked "Yes" from highest to lowest. The items should also have a "Yes" in the "Realistic" column. Then, ask participants to determine the item that has the most appeal.

3. Ask participants to write actions they could take to begin exploring these items. These could be simple actions, such as talking with someone who is currently doing this.

4. Instruct the participants to form groups of four. Ask each person to share his action steps with the group. Group members should be encouraged to brainstorm other ideas or actions that the participants could include. Instruct the group to allow 10 minutes for each participant. Be sure to remind participants when 10 minutes is approaching and ask them to switch.

5. Debrief the activity.

Key Debrief Questions

➤ How difficult was it for you to determine some actions to take that would put you on a path to living your purpose?

➤ Do you think that all actions will lead to the right path?

➤ Do you think you may change your mind about your purpose?

➤ What happens if you discover that you are not on the right path?

➤ What can you do to foolproof your plans?

➤ Is it worthwhile to explore your dreams?

Key Learning Points

The facilitator should help the participants arrive at the following conclusions:

➤ Daydreams can be useful to point us in the right direction of our passions and purposes. However, we must act on our dreams in order to realize them.

➤ Small actions could be all we need to begin to pursue our dreams.

➤ The actions can produce great results, no results, or mixed results.

➤ The success or failure of an action doesn't necessarily determine whether or not the dream is worth pursuing. It only gives you data.

➤ You will probably have many unsuccessful attempts and will likely want to quit. Pay attention. Is it still worth pursuing? Only you can answer that question.

➤ There is no such thing as a foolproof plan. You will more than likely meet many obstacles, many of which seem insurmountable.

➤ After exploration, if you decide not to pursue your interests, so be it. At least, you made a decision to end it, rather than to continue throughout life wondering, "what if."

EQ 34 # Shoots and Scores

Self-Awareness
and Control

Empathy

Social
Expertness
Personal
Infuence
Mastery of
Purpose and
Vision   *Inward Inward Outward*

EQ Area and Competency

Self-Awareness and Control: Resilience

How to Use This Activity

- To examine the energy and effort that is required to accomplish goals of various sizes and to control the emotional reaction to failing at goals.

- To examine ways to shift a goal's paradigm to help accomplish the goal.

Shoots and Scores can be used as part of emotional-intelligence training and leadership and career-development sessions. It is also effective for use in new-hire sessions.

Applicable Content Area

Multiple: Leadership and Career Development

Audience: Classroom

Estimated Time: 40 minutes

Level of Disclosure/Difficulty: Low

Materials

Ping pong balls
Hula hoop—larger than the exercise ball
Exercise ball—hidden from the group until needed
   in the activity

Purpose/Why This Is Important

This exercise challenges participants to manage their emotional reactions to a difficult task and discover new ways to accomplish the task. Resilience is a key emotional intelligence competency, as it is integral to managing disappointment or failure. Organizations want to encourage resilience in their leaders, because it is a characteristic that leads us to keep trying, even in the face of obstacles. Resilience allows an individual to avoid becoming overly discouraged with a task and to continue working to solve a problem. Some of the most creative solutions come from a resilient thinker.

This activity will provide an opportunity for participants to examine how they react to a challenging situation and determine how their resilience can help them overcome frustrations and rethink a problem to find creative solutions.

Set the Stage

The instructor should explain that as we move forward in our careers, a task that we might find simple can become more complicated, but it is important to keep practicing the task to make sure that we can master our skills.

The Activity

1. Ask someone in the group to help you demonstrate the activity. Have the volunteer hold the hula hoop toward you, stand 6 to 8 feet away from that person, and toss the ping pong ball through the hula hoop. In order to ensure that your participants know where to stand, you can even place two pieces of tape on the floor to mark the spot.

2. Ask each participant to practice tossing the ping pong ball through the hula hoop. Ask everyone to keep repeating the toss until successful. The person who tosses can hold the hula hoop for the next person to allow everyone an opportunity to throw.

3. After everyone tosses a ping pong ball, remind participants of how tasks become more difficult as they become more complex. Bring out the exercise ball and ask the participants to toss the exercise ball through the hula hoop. Ask them to keep repeating the toss until they are successful.

4. Watch for signs of frustration, for individuals wanting to give up, and for those in the group who are trying to problem solve to find different ways of accomplishing the goal and for those who are complaining that the rules/parameters have changed.

5. Debrief the activity.

Note to Trainer: By setting up the paradigm when we toss the ping pong balls from one place, we are getting the participants stuck on that as the rules of the activity. As the instructor, you should not state that they can move from this place, but also allow it if some participants experiment. For example, a participant may choose to walk the balls to the hula hoop and easily push them through.

Key Debrief Questions

➤ Was the ping pong task easy?

➤ Were you able to throw the exercise ball through the hula hoop? Was it as easy?

➤ If you weren't able to succeed with the exercise ball immediately, what did you do to continue to work on the task?

➤ Did you try something different? Did anyone think to walk the exercise ball up to the hula hoop and push it through? Did any hula hoop holders try to move to help catch the ball?

➤ Have you been faced with the increasing complexity of tasks in your position? How does that make you feel? How do you manage the emotion?

➤ How did the instructor set you up to fail? Do any current tasks you are working on have limiting paradigms? Are they necessary to complete the task? How could you shift them?

Key Learning Points

The facilitator should help the participants arrive at the following conclusions:

➤ Managing the emotions around difficult tasks is a key factor in successfully completing a task.

➤ Looking at what paradigms may exist and determining if there are other ways to solve the task are key aspects of resiliency.

➤ Even though things change, a leader's role is to remained focused on solving the problems.

➤ We have to be careful that our frustration doesn't impact our creativity. We must look for creative ways to solve problems and not give up.

EQ 35 Blind Vote

Self-Awareness and Control
Empathy
Social Expertness
Personal Infuence
Mastery of Purpose and Vision

Inward   Inward   Outward

EQ Area and Competency

Self-Awareness and Control: Courage

How to Use This Activity

- To examine the courage it requires to take action on an issue.

- To push participants to rank appropriate actions and then discuss the courage required.

Blind Vote can be used as part of emotional-intelligence training and leadership development sessions. This activity can also be useful in conflict-resolution and teamwork sessions.

Applicable Content Area

Multiple: Leadership Development, Conflict Resolution, Teamwork

Audience: Classroom, Web-Based

Estimated Time: 40 minutes

Level of Disclosure/Difficulty: Medium

Materials

A copy of the scenario and possible resolutions for each person

Three clear jars 1, 2, and 3 or three posters with Resolution 1, Resolution 2, Resolution 3 written on them

Poker chips or stickers of three different colors

A displayed value indicator for the poker chips or stickers

Purpose/Why This Is Important

This activity considers the emotional intelligence competency of courage. Courage is key in an or-ganization because while individuals can often tell right from wrong in egregious cases and would act, it takes courage to speak the truth, challenge popular opinions, or confront a coworker who are taking shortcuts or otherwise shortchanging others. In leaders, courage helps you manage your people, as confronting issues is a necessary part of the job, but one that is very difficult for leaders to take on. Instead, some leaders will avoid confronting issues or individuals, allowing problems to fester and morale to deteriorate. By having courage, a leader can create better working environments for everyone.

This activity will provide an opportunity for participants to examine their natural responses to a situation that requires courage. Some participants will learn that their natural responses are courageous ones and others will learn that they may need more courage. The activity will also look at situations in which more than one answer may be appropriate, and the discussion will focus on how to navigate those situations.

Set the Stage

The instructor should explain that we will be faced with situations that can be difficult to address. We will look, through a blind voting process, at how most people would address a certain situation and look at times when there may be more than one possible resolution and how each of those resolutions could be appropriate.

The Activity

1. Explain the participants will receive a scenario that has three possible resolutions and that everyone will rank the resolution they would be most likely, next most likely, and least likely to complete. Display the colors for each selection. For example, if you are using red,

white, and blue poker chips, red may be least likely, white may be the next most likely choice, and blue would be what the participant would be most likely to do. Stickers would follow a similar scheme.

2. Pass out poker chips or stickers, the scenario, and possible resolutions to each person. Ask each person to read the scenarios and resolutions.

3. After all have read the scenario, ask them to face the opposite wall and come to the front one at a time to vote for their most likely, next most likely, and least likely response to the scenario according to the displayed rank. Have everyone vote.

4. After the vote, do a count of how many votes of each category were placed for each of the possible resolutions.

5. Debrief the activity.

Key Debrief Questions

➤ Were you surprised at the results? Did the majority of the votes match how you voted?

➤ Did anyone have a hard time selecting a course of action?

➤ Did you think that more than one course of action may have been appropriate?

➤ Which of the possible resolutions would have required the most courage to address? Did anyone feel lacking in that courage? What was holding you back? How could you address the situation?

➤ Was there anything wrong with any of the possible resolutions?

➤ Was your natural response a courageous one? Why or why not?

➤ Does courage to confront things help or hurt workplace morale? How?

➤ Do some situations have more than one right answer? Tell us about them.

➤ Can you describe a situation when you were courageous? Can you describe a situation where you should have been more courageous?

Key Learning Points

The facilitator should help the participants arrive at the following conclusions:

➤ It can take courage to address a situation that you know isn't correct, but courage can help improve the organization.

➤ Taking a stand defines who you are. Give thought to this and then do so in a respectful, yet clear direction.

➤ Some situations have more than one right answer. It is okay to go for the option you feel most comfortable with if it is right.

➤ In ethical or legal issues, it is important to consult with others. Careers can be broken if inappropriate action is taken when faced with an ethical or legal issue.

Note to Trainer: You can create other scenarios that may be appropriate for the organization in which you are training.

Blind Vote Handout

Scenario: You work in a restaurant kitchen. You are fairly certain that your coworker Jane has been taking shortcuts at work. These aren't super serious, but you are certain that Jane has been leaving food out of the refrigerator longer than is allowed by the county health inspector. You don't believe that this is a malicious action on Jane's part. Instead she just gets busy preparing food for customers and doesn't immediately put the ingredients back where they belong.

Possible Resolution 1: You are fairly certain that your boss has noticed Jane's behavior, so you'll continue doing your job and not say anything about Jane leaving things out. It isn't your job to correct Jane's behavior—it's your boss's, and you don't want Jane to be angry at you since that won't help anyone get the work done.

Possible Resolution 2: You know that Jane has good intentions, so you decide to approach her gently. You decide to let her know the restaurant could get in trouble with the health inspector for leaving food items out. Explain that you know it's only because she gets so busy filling orders for customers. Still, it is important in the future to make sure things are put away so that you both don't get in trouble.

Possible Resolution 3: You are fairly certain your boss has noticed Jane's behavior, but you're not 100 percent sure, so you approach your boss to let him know that you've noticed Jane leaving food items out. You explain that you're sure it's only because she gets distracted because she cares so much about filling the orders for the customers.

EQ 36

Are you Flexible? Let's Find Out

Plays Well with Others

EQ Area and Competency

Personal Influence: Flexibility
Self-Awareness and Control: Accurate Self-Assessment

How to Use This Activity

- To get feedback about how participants are perceived around the emotional intelligence competency of flexibility.

- To gain insight into what others perceive as flexibility in the organization or structure in which they operate.

Use this activity in leadership-development, career-development and personal-development training. This activity can be done in a coaching or in a classroom setting. The activity gives people important feedback regarding their flexibility. Because the activity asks for feedback from others, it also can be used to build relationships with others and provide open, honest dialogue that can improve performance. Prior to the activity, it is important to coach participants on how to receive the feedback they will be soliciting. Also, because prework is required, be sure to give enough time for participants to complete the interviews before the class or coaching session.

Applicable Content Area

Multiple: Leadership Development and Career Development

Audience: Coaching, Classroom

Estimated Time

Prework—Interview others two to four weeks prior to session
Session—45 minutes

Level of Disclosure/Difficulty: High

Materials: Handouts—One per interviewee

Purpose/Why This Is Important

Change is routine in most workplaces. Rapid change is the norm in many. Our ability to meet the world where it is today and will be tomorrow largely depends on our ability to be flexible or adapt—flexible in our thinking, flexible in our decision-making, flexible in our behavior, and flexibility in our relationships. How we address changes that come our way is often an important factor in our success, as well as in our personal lives. Do we try to meet others' needs, or are we driven solely by our own demands? Do we try to rearrange our schedule to accommodate others, or must we maintain the timetable conceived in our minds? Adapting to new technology, new markets, global influences, mergers and acquisitions, new systems, new bosses, new building space, and even virtual space all exercise our flexibility muscle. And one thing for certain is that the rate of change will continue and accelerate.

Set the Stage

Discuss with the group why flexibility is an important attribute. Talk about how changing technology, changing markets, changing bosses, and even changing organizations all require flexibility. Ask the group members to identify changes they have experienced and ask how those changes may have required them to be flexible. Further, ask the group if flexibility is always desired. Explain that it isn't always useful to be flexible. For example, paying taxes isn't an option. We don't want to exercise flexibility in interpreting certain laws. Make the point that the position and requirements of the job will dictate the level of flexibility required. Describe and assign the prework. Explain that each person will be asked to interview five to seven people to obtain feedback about their flexibility. Tell people they will be using the handouts to obtain information about themselves regarding how flexible they appear to others. When assigning the prework, explain that getting feedback from others is a true gift. Explain that sometimes we have blind spots regarding our strengths and areas for development and that getting feedback from others can provide important insights about our behavior. Explain that during the interviews they must be very careful to listen and not react or defend themselves. This is not a conversation; it is an interview. They should simply ask the questions, ask for clarification as needed and record the answers. Tell them that this is a great opportunity to practice listening skills.

The Activity

Prework

1. Ask participants to interview five to seven people using the handouts provided. Instruct them to interview a few peers, a few direct reports, their bosses, and, if they wish, a family member.

During class

2. Ask participants to reflect on their feedback with a partner. Write the following questions on a flip chart for discussion in their pairs:

   a. Do others see you as flexible?
   b. Did others' perception of your flexibility match your own?
   c. Are you more flexible with some groups than with others? For example, are you more flexible with peers than with your direct reports?
   d. What conclusions can you draw?
   e. What would you like to adjust or change about your flexibility?

3. Bring the full group together. In the full group ask each person to describe something he or she learned by talking with others about their flexibility. Be sure to include all group members so that all have an opportunity to share what they learned.

4. Instruct the group members to thank the individuals who provided feedback. It may also be appropriate for them to share with the individuals some lessons learned about their flexibility.

5. Debrief the activity.

Key Debrief Questions

➤ Was it difficult to ask for feedback?

➤ When conducting the interviews, were you tempted to defend yourself?

➤ Did you find the information from the interviews useful?

➤ What should you do if you don't agree with the information?

➤ Given your role, when are you appropriately flexible? Appropriately inflexible?

➤ How can being flexible help us in our relationships?

➤ How can being flexible help us in our careers?

Key Learning Points

The facilitator should help the participants arrive at the following conclusions:

➤ Getting feedback is sometimes difficult when that feedback doesn't meet our vision of ourselves. However, when that happens, it is important to gain insight into how others interpret our actions.

➤ If we receive feedback that our actions do not align with our intentions, that is a perfect opportunity to exercise some new behaviors. This is the essence of emotional intelligence: aligning our behaviors with our intentions.

➤ All feedback is not necessarily something that you must act upon. Looking for trends in the feedback is a strong indicator that the data are perceived by many, not a solitary person. When many people perceive us in a particular way, there is probably something in our behavior that causes that perception.

➤ With all solicited feedback, be gracious and then decide if it is something you want to act on.

➤ Flexibility is quite useful in many situations. However, not all situations lend themselves to flexibility. You must use your judgment to determine when to be flexible and when not to be flexible. You can use mentors, confidants, and others familiar with your role to help you determine your actions.

Are You Flexible—Interview Handout

Interviewee Name

Explain to the interviewee that you would like some feedback from his or her perspective about your flexibility. Explain that it is important to be flexible with coworkers and others. Tell people that you would value their candid responses. Ask the following questions for each interviewee. Record the answers below.

1. As you think about our working relationship (or personal relationship if interviewing a family member), can you describe a time when you considered my actions to be flexible?

2. Can you please describe a time when you considered my actions to be inflexible?

3. In our working relationship (or personal relationship), how often do you think I try to flex to your needs, concerns or demands?

1	2	3	4	5	6	7
Almost Never	Never	Sometimes	Average	Often	Almost Always	Always

4. Under what circumstances do you consider me to be most flexible? Least flexible?

5. What suggestions do you have for me to be more effective in this area?

6. On a scale of 1 to 10, with 10 being the highest, how would you assess my flexibility?

1	2	3	4	5	6	7	8	9	10
Low									High

EQ 37 How Am I Doing?

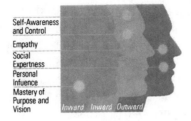

Plays Well with Others

EQ Area and Competency

Personal Influence: Leading Others

How to Use This Activity

- To gain insights on the strengths and weaknesses of the participants' leadership style from others' points of view.

- To encourage people to examine their current thinking and definition of leadership.

Use this activity in leadership-development and new and aspiring leadership-development programs. It is ideal for high-potential candidates who are in the pipeline for future leadership positions. This activity can be conducted in a coaching or in a classroom setting. Because the activity asks for feedback, it also can be used to build relationships with others and provide open, honest dialogue that can improve performance. Prior to the activity, it is important to coach participants how to receive the feedback they will be soliciting. Also, because prework is required, be sure to allow enough time for participants to complete the interviews before the class or coaching session.

Note to Trainer: This activity is structured in the same way as EQ 36, "Are you Flexible? Let's Find out." They can be used in conjunction effectively by conducting the interviews for both activities simultaneously.

Applicable Content Area

Multiple: Leadership Development, and New/ Aspiring (high-potential) Leaders

Audience: Classroom, Coaching

Estimated Time

Prework—Interview others prior to session
Session—45 minutes

Level of Disclosure/Difficulty: High

Materials: "How Am I Doing?" handout

Purpose/Why This Is Important

A leader's ability to lead can, in the simplest sense, be defined as instilling in others the willingness to follow them and accomplish goals. Leading others is a key skill to develop because there is only so much you can do by yourself. You can do so much more by inspiring others to work with you toward common goals.

This activity asks individuals to look to their communities and reach out to others with whom they interact to gain feedback on what they do well as a leader and what they could do better. Some participants will receive feedback that surprises them, either because they thought they were more skilled than they actually are or because they have more skills than they realized. Those leaders who have more skills than they realized have unrealized strengths that they can leverage in order to accomplish even more. Others may have unrealistic views of their skills and may need to take a hard look at where they need to develop further.

Set the Stage

Talk to the group about the amount of time we spend learning new skills to develop leadership ability, but how we do not often simply ask those around us for feedback on how we're doing as leaders. Ask the group to think about good pieces of advice they've received and applied, and how that advice can be life changing. It is also important, when we talk about leading others, to check in occasionally with those that we are supposed to be leading. Describe and assign the prework. Explain that each person will be asked to interview five to seven people to obtain feedback about their leadership skills. Tell participants they will be using the handout to obtain information about themselves regarding their own strengths and weaknesses as leaders. When assigning the prework, explain that feedback from others is a true gift. Explain that sometimes we have blind spots regarding our strengths and areas for development and getting feedback from others can provide important insights about our behavior. Explain that during the interviews, they must be very careful to listen and not react or defend themselves. This is not a conversation; it is an interview. They should simply ask the question, ask for clarification as needed and record the answers. Tell them that it's also a great opportunity to practice listening skills.

The Activity

Prework

1. Ask participants to interview five to seven people using the handouts provided. Instruct them to interview a few peers, a few direct reports, their bosses, and if they wish, a family member.

During class

2. Ask participants to reflect on their feedback with a partner. Write the following questions on a flip chart for discussion in their pairs:

   a. Do others see you as a good leader?
   b. Did others' opinion of your leadership skills match your own?
   c. Are you a better leader with some groups than with others? For example, are you better able to lead with direct reports than with your peers?
   d. What conclusions can you draw?
   e. What would you like to adjust or change?

3. Bring the full group together. Ask all participants in that group to describe something they

learned by talking with others about their skills at leading others. Be sure to include all group members, so they have an opportunity to share what they learned.

4. Instruct the group members to thank the individuals who provided feedback. Also, it may be appropriate for them to share with the individuals some lessons learned about their ability to lead others.

5. Debrief the activity.

Key Debrief Questions

➤ Was it difficult to ask for feedback?

➤ When conducting the interviews, were you tempted to defend yourself?

➤ Did you find the information from the interviews useful?

➤ What should you do if you don't agree with the information?

➤ What are your key skills when leading others? How can you better use those skills?

➤ What are your key weaknesses when leading others? How can you mitigate those weaknesses?

➤ How can leading others help us in our careers? To achieve our goals?

Key Learning Points

The facilitator should help the participants arrive at the following conclusions:

➤ Getting feedback is sometimes difficult when that feedback doesn't meet our vision of ourselves. However, when that happens, it is very important to gain insight into how others interpret our actions.

➤ If we receive feedback that our actions do not align with our intentions, that is a perfect opportunity to exercise some new behaviors. This is the essence of emotional intelligence: aligning our behaviors with our intentions.

➤ All feedback is not necessarily something that you must act on. Looking for trends in the feedback is a strong indicator that the data are perceived by many, not a solitary person. When many people perceive us in a particular way, there is probably something in our behavior causes that perception.

➤ With all solicited feedback, be gracious about it and then decide if it is something that you want to act on.

➤ Leading others is a key competency to further your ability to accomplish your purpose. It is especially critical to request feedback from those you are intended to lead to ensure your leadership style helps you effectively lead those around you.

How Am I Doing? Interview Handout

Interviewee Name

Explain to the interviewee that you would like some feedback from his or her perspective about your ability to lead others. Explain that it is important to be able to lead others, not just with those who directly report to us, but to coworkers and others as well. Tell people that you would value their candid responses. Ask the following questions for each interviewee. Record the answers below.

1. As you think about our working relationships (or personal relationship if interviewing a family member), can you describe a time when you thought I did a good job leading others?

2. Can you please describe a time when you thought I did poorly at leading others?

3. What are my greatest strengths when it comes to leading others?

4. What are my greatest weaknesses when it comes to leading others?

5. What suggestions do you have for me to be more effective in this area?

6. On a scale of one to ten with ten being the highest, how would you assess my ability to lead others?

1	2	3	4	5	6	7	8	9	10
Low									High

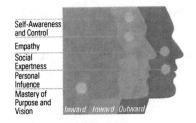

Self-Awareness
and Control

Empathy

Social
Expertness

Personal
Infuence

Mastery of
Purpose and
Vision

Inward   Inward   Outward

EQ 38 Authenticity— A Reflection

EQ Area and Competency

Mastery of Purpose and Vision: Authenticity

How to Use This Activity

- To help people take stock of their actions to determine their authenticity.

- To encourage people to examine their actions on a regular basis so they can create authenticity in their relationships.

Use this activity in career-development, leadership-development, and personal-development training programs. This activity can be done in a coaching or in a classroom setting. Authenticity is an important quality for everyone. In fact, it is a distinguishing factor that defines trusting relationships at all levels, including those in our personal lives. It is particularly helpful for leaders because authenticity is a critical quality for leaders. If a leader is perceived as having high authenticity, his followers find him believable and trustworthy. New leaders must examine their actions on a regular basis to be sure that organizational pressures and politics are not creating situations that can jeopardize their authenticity, so this activity is particularly useful for new or aspiring leaders.

Applicable Content Area

Multiple: Career Development, Leadership Development, New /Aspiring Leaders, Teamwork

Audience: Coaching, Classroom

Estimated Time: 60 minutes

Level of Disclosure/Difficulty: High

Materials: Handout

Purpose/Why This Is Important

When interacting with others in the workplace, authenticity is a highly desired trait. People want to interact with people whose values, motives, and actions are aligned and transparent. They don't want to be concerned with dual agendas and politics. Of course, no organization is free of these things, but the more a leader can transcend them, the better. When we are interacting with someone who is authentic, we feel a natural trust. We feel safe to express the truth about a situation. Leaders, of course, must lead from facts, and if they create authentic relationships, people are more apt to speak the truth. Authenticity in leadership is best described as showing oneself honestly to followers. The authentic leader doesn't hide for fear of looking weak. Also, he acts out of mission and focuses on results rather than on pursuing goals for his own power or ego. Besides leaders, all peers and colleagues in the workplace can benefit from displaying high authenticity.

Set the Stage

The instructor should ask the group to talk about authentic leaders who come to mind. What qualities or characteristics do they embody? State that all of us must take stock of our authenticity. Explain that authenticity creates value for people because they become approachable and credible with others. Explain that people form impressions about someone's authenticity around three items:

- A person's value system and whether or not the person's actions align with their values.

- The person's trustworthiness.

- The person's commitment to the mission or task at hand.

Explain that the following activity will allow people to reflect on their authenticity by giving participants quiet reflection time to address questions on the handout. Tell participants that they will not be asked to share the private details of their answers, but they will be asked to comment on what they have learned by answering the questions.

The Activity

1. Give each participant a worksheet. Ask participants to complete the handout. You can encourage people to go to a private space if the area is conducive to such. Tell people to return in 30 minutes with a completed handout.

2. Ask participants to form groups of four to reflect on authenticity, including the roles of values, trust, and commitment. Each group is to produce some key learning or truths that members believe are important in each of these areas. Write the three areas (Values, Trust, Commitment) on a flip chart to make them visible to the group and instruct the groups to write at least three key learnings for each area.

   a. Values—List truths that the group believes are important to one's values.
   b. Trust—List truths that the group believes are important to trust.
   c. Commitment—List truths that the group believes are important to commitment.

3. Ask a spokesperson from each group to tell the full group of participants its key learnings. Point out similarities as well as differences between the groups.

4. Debrief the activity.

Key Debrief Questions

➤ How can authenticity help you as a leader?

➤ When someone is authentic, how do you feel when dealing with that person?

➤ Is it always possible to be authentic?

➤ Under what conditions is authenticity most difficult?

➤ What happens when you continually compromise your authenticity?

➤ Does acting with authenticity have consequences?

Key Learning Points

The facilitator should help the participants arrive at the following conclusions:

➤ As a leader, authenticity will increase your influence.

➤ Authenticity also increases the amount of truth that people are willing to disclose. Authenticity can discourage "yes" people.

➤ When interacting with someone who is authentic, people generally feel a high level of trust. Trust is a critical foundation for influence.

➤ It is most difficult to be authentic when there is organizational pressure to think or act in a way that runs counter to your beliefs. Depending on how strong the pressure and consequences are, it can become challenging to say what you really believe.

➤ If a person's values or goals are out of sync with the organization's, he or she may not be able to act authentically without consequences. Consequences could be extreme, including losing one's job. Therefore, when examining one's life for the purpose of living authentically, a person may find that they would be better to leave an organization if not in sync.

➤ There is skill involved in HOW to speak the truth. Addressing conflict honestly and authentically requires skill.

Note to the Trainer: If you are working with an intact team, the key learnings that the small groups produce can be captured and circulated as an output from the session. These key learnings can form a moral and behavioral compass for the group.

Authenticity—A Reflection Handout

Values

1. Describe a situation in which you found yourself in a values conflict. What did you do?

2. Describe a situation at work in which you thought you had to compromise your beliefs or values.

3. Think about a time when a situation at work was an affront to your values. What did you do?

4. Describe a time when you were able to persuade people to agree with your values. How did you do that?

Trust

1. Think about someone you trust. Why do you trust that person?

2. How do you gain people's trust? What actions did you take?

3. Think about a situation in which you lost someone's trust. What do you think you could have done differently?

Commitment

1. When did you honor a difficult commitment?

2. When did you not honor a commitment? Why? How did you feel?

3. Was there ever a time when you didn't carry your weight regarding an assignment or a commitment?

EQ 39 Better Method

Self-Awareness and Control
Empathy
Social Expertness
Personal Infuence
Mastery of Purpose and Vision

Inward   Inward   Outward

EQ Area and Competency

Personal Influence: Creating a Positive Work Climate

How to Use This Activity

- To look at ways to adapt our language to avoid creating a negative work environment.

- To provide phrases that can diffuse tensions and help groups remain positive.

"Better Method" can be used as part of emotional-intelligence training and leadership development sessions. This activity can also be useful in conflict resolution and teamwork sessions.

Applicable Content Area

Multiple: Leadership Development, Conflict Resolution, Teamwork, Interpersonal Skills, Communications

Audience: Classroom, Coaching, Web-Based

Estimated Time: 30 minutes

Level of Disclosure/Difficulty: Low

Materials: Handout

Purpose/Why This Is Important

Creating and maintaining a positive work environment enables employees to solve large problems, effectively work together, and become high-performing and high-functioning teams. A positive work environment is a key reason why people choose to go above and beyond in their roles. It also helps create a positive impression of the organization as a whole. With a positive work environment, turnover decreases, and it's easier to recruit other strong performers to the organization. However, a positive work environment can often be undermined with just a few words. This activity examines common upsets of a positive work environment, most often seen during conflict, and provides alternatives for how to address the conflict in a positive manner and deescalate negative conflict scenarios.

Set the Stage

The instructor should explain that maintaining a positive work environment has many benefits for the organization and individuals in it. Everyone is responsible for helping to maintain a positive environment. This is most difficult to do when we are faced with conflict because we are likely to react emotionally and react without considering our words. The handout will present alternatives to addressing an issue and ask you to select the best method for preserving a positive work environment.

The Activity

1. Pass out the Phrases handout and ask the participants to choose the best method for preserving a positive work environment.

2. Provide time for the participants to complete the handout.

3. After everyone has finished, ask everyone to share how they voted for each scenario.

4. Debrief the activity.

Key Debrief Questions

➤ Was it easy to identify the items that help maintain a positive work environment?

➤ Do you hear or say any of the negative work environment phrases in your own workplace?

➤ How can changing your language help?

➤ Which positive phrases do you think you could use in your workplace?

➤ What does having a phrase like this help you do?

➤ What would interfere with your using phrases like this? How can you mitigate the interferences?

Key Learning Points

The facilitator should help the participants arrive at the following conclusions:

➤ It is easy to recognize the phrases that create a positive work environment, but it can be challenging to always use them in a heated moment.

➤ By using positive phrases as an instinctive, first response, you can buy yourself time to calm the initial emotional response to a conflict.

Better Method Handout

Circle the option you think would be best for maintaining a positive work environment.

When you aren't sure that your coworker is doing a task correctly...	
Option 1: "I want to work with you to come up with something that is acceptable for our client."	*Option 2:* "You're doing this wrong."

When your coworker isn't addressing a situation correctly...	
Option 1: "You're wrong."	*Option 2:* "Let's talk about it so we can both understand what we need in this situation."

When you don't agree with your colleague's positon...	
Option 1: "Please help me to fully understand your position."	*Option 2:* "Yes, but...."

When you believe your colleague is presenting incorrect information...	
Option 1: "What would you think if we involved the xyz expert on this?"	*Option 2:* "You don't have your facts right."

When your expectations weren't clearly understood...	
Option 1: "No, YOU don't understand how important this is."	*Option 2:* "Let me explain as clearly as I can what I need from this. Please ask me to clarify if I'm not making myself understood...."

When someone really disagrees with your position...	
Option 1: "I appreciate you letting me know this information. This new information helps me understand the situation more clearly."	*Option 2:* "Why would you think that!?!"

When there is clearly a problem that needs to be solved...	
Option 1: "Well if we just do it my way, we can stop talking about it."	*Option 2:* "I believe if we put our heads together we can come up with an acceptable solution to both of us. Tell me what comes to mind to you to resolve this situation."

When you don't think a colleague will meet a deadline...	
Option 1: "You're always late."	*Option 2:* "I'm concerned about the deadline on the xxx project. You said you would review my report by noon yesterday, and to my knowledge it hasn't been done yet. Can you help me?"

When another party is clearly angry...	
Option 1: "I know that this is a difficult issue. I would like to hear your perspective. Please help me by remaining calm."	*Option 2:* "How could you be so disrespectful!?!"

When you don't have a good relationship with a colleague...	
Option 1: "You just want to disagree with me because that's what you always do."	*Option 2:* "I know that we have a disagreement right now, but I want to work hard to have a positive outcome."

When someone brings up an issue with your idea...	
Option 1: "Please tell me more, I want to understand your position."	*Option 2:* "Well, that's not likely to happen anyway, it's silly to talk about...."

When you have an issue about another's idea...	
Option 1: "Ok, if we do that, I'm concerned that ___ might result. How might we mitigate my concern if we choose your option?"	*Option 2:* "We can't do that! That's not going to work."

EQ 40 Flexibility—A New Leader Exercise

Self-Awareness and Control
Empathy
Social Expertness
Personal Infuence
Mastery of Purpose and Vision

Inward   Inward   Outward

EQ Area and Competency

Personal Influence: Flexibility

How to Use This Activity

- To help new leaders maneuver the complicated decision making regarding leading, consistency, and flexibility.

- To encourage people to examine their current thinking and definitions of flexibility.

Use this activity in leadership-development, and new and aspiring leadership-development programs. It is ideal for high-potential candidates who are in the pipeline for future leadership positions. This activity can be done in a coaching or in a classroom setting. One of the classic issues that leaders must face is balancing the fine line between being flexible and being consistent and fair. This activity will encourage new leaders to grapple with these issues and create some internal guidelines to help the decision-making process.

Applicable Content Area

Multiple: Leadership Development, and New/ Aspiring (high-potential) Leaders

Audience: Coaching, Classroom

Estimated Time: 90 minutes (60 minutes if handout is assigned as prework)

Level of Disclosure/Difficulty: High

Materials: Handout

Purpose/Why This Is Important

Leaders are sometimes between a rock and hard place. How can they be both flexible and fair at the same time? Under what circumstances is flexibility related to favoritism? What's the difference between micromanaging and adhering to set procedures? How can a new leader know what approach is best? When interacting with direct reports in the workplace, a flexible leader is valued. No one wants to work with someone who is regarded as completely inflexible. However, new leaders often struggle with the issues of how much flexibility is too much and how much is not enough.

Set the Stage

The instructor should ask group members to think about their leaders who have demonstrated great flexibility, as well as those who demonstrated little to none. What feelings did working for a flexible leader create in followers? What feelings did working for an inflexible leader create in followers? You can capture these on the flip chart for visibility. State that all of us must take stock of our flexibility with our direct reports. New or aspiring leaders will especially need to think about how they will determine the appropriate level of flexibility they demonstrate with their staff.

The Activity

1. Give each participant a handout. Allow participants about 30 minutes to complete the handout. (This could be assigned as prework.)

2. Ask participants to form groups of four to reflect on flexibility. Based on the discoveries on the handout, each member of the group should raise questions or issues for which they would like comments from the full group.

3. Each group is to produce some key guidelines members believe are important to assist leaders in making decisions about how flexible

they can be in the workplace. Ask each group to list these guidelines on a flip chart and assign a spokesperson.

4. Ask a spokesperson from each group to tell the full-group participants their key learnings. Point out similarities as well as differences between the groups.

5. Debrief the activity.

Key Debrief Questions

➤ What is the benefit of being viewed as flexible as a leader?

➤ What is the drawback?

➤ How can you be flexible and fair?

➤ How can having some guidelines help you?

➤ What's the difference between a guideline and a hard-and-fast rule?

➤ When can you appropriately allow people to complete a task in his or her own way?

➤ When must you insist that a task be completed according to procedure?

Key Learning Points

The facilitator should help the participants arrive at the following conclusions:

➤ For you as a leader, flexibility is a desired asset and will increase your influence. However, if your flexibility benefits some at the exclusion of others, then you will be viewed as being unfair.

➤ Generally, having guidelines will help you maintain a sense of fairness.

➤ Certain rules or procedures should never be broken. Safety procedures, conduct issues, and other rules are important to adhere to all the time.

➤ When possible, look at and evaluate the outcome of a person's work rather than the process he or she uses (unless the process has safety or other issues that could affect the quality of output.) Otherwise, you can be viewed as inflexible and micromanaging.

➤ Getting input from others can be very valuable when deciding on an action.

➤ Assessing the impact of your decision on others is also a critical step.

Note to the Trainer: If you are working with an intact team or teams within the same organization, the guidelines that the small groups produce can be captured and circulated for future reference.

Flexibility—A New Leader Exercise Handout

1. Think about a time as a leader when you found it necessary to bend the rules.

   - What did you do?

   - Why did you do it?

   - What criteria did you use to decide?

2. Think about a time as a leader when you were tempted to bend the rules, but decided not to.

   - What did you do?

   - Why did you do it?

   - What criteria did you use to decide?

3. Think about a time as a leader when you were asked to bend the rules, but definitely knew it was the wrong move.

   - What did you do?

   - Why did you do it?

   - What criteria did you use to decide?

4. Think about a time when you were flexible and accommodated someone on your staff.

   - What did you do?

   - Why did you do it?

   - What criteria did you use to decide?

   - How do you think others viewed your actions?

5. Think about a time when you were flexible and later regretted it.

   - What did you do?

   - Why did you do it?

   - What criteria did you use?

   - What went wrong?

   - What would you do differently?

EQ 41 Help Who?

Self-Awareness
and Control
Empathy
Social
Expertness
Personal
Infuence
Mastery of
Purpose and
Vision

Inward Inward Outward

EQ Area and Competency

Empathy: Service Orientation

How to Use This Activity

- To look at a participant's natural inclination to assist for the best of the organization.

- To provide insight into a participant's willingness to help a less well-liked individual.

    "Help Who?" can be used as part of emotional-intelligence training. This activity can also be useful in customer service and teamwork sessions.

Applicable Content Area

Multiple: Customer Service, Teamwork

Audience: Classroom, Web-Based

Estimated Time: 40 minutes

Level of Disclosure/Difficulty: Medium

Materials

"Help Who?" scenario for each participant
Reaction 1, Reaction 2, and Reaction 3 for each participant

Purpose/Why This Is Important

The emotional intelligence characteristic of empathy brings about a desire to be of service toward others. This desire to help extends to coworkers, peers, and others in the organization and creates a positive climate for everyone in the workplace. Our desire to help others is magnified when the individual is someone we genuinely like and care about. On the other hand, it is more challenging to help someone we do not like. It is important, though, to continue to serve everyone in the organization and to place the needs of the whole environment ahead of a personal feeling. The ability to see the needs of others and react to them is a key factor for organizations because it leads to a customer- and team-minded workforce. This is especially true since service orientation can be contagious and can create groups of people who are happy to better serve the goals of the organization.

Set the Stage

The instructor should explain that we need to make decisions every day in the workplace. The scenario and reactions from the coworkers are all possible situations. You should choose which coworker you are more likely to behave like after reading the scenario and reactions.

The Activity

1. Pass out the scenario and the reactions of the coworkers.

2. Provide time for the participants to read all of the information.

3. After everyone has finished, ask participants who agreed with the actions of Reaction 1 to go to the right side of the room, participants who agreed with the actions of Reaction 2 to go to the left side of the room, and participants who agreed with the actions of Reaction 3 to go to the front of the room.

4. Debrief the activity.

Key Debrief Questions

➤ What was it about the response that you thought was right? Ask all sides of the room.

➤ What was the coworker's intention? Ask all sides of the room.

➤ Did that intention influence their behavior? How? Ask all sides of the room.

➤ Will that intention have an impact? On whom? Ask all sides of the room.

➤ What is the cost of not assisting? What is the cost to the company? To your customer? To you personally?

➤ Why would you allow yourself to not assist? What was the motivation? How can you change the motivation?

Key Learning Points

The facilitator should help the participants arrive at the following conclusions:

➤ It is easy to provide help and assistance when you genuinely like someone; it is harder when you do not.

➤ There are costs associated with not helping, and those costs could have consequences throughout the organization and on your own career.

Help Who? Handout

Scenario: You work in a shipping facility with two other coworkers. Orders that must be packed and shipped are assigned as they come in on a rotating basis. For example, Order 1 will be assigned to you, Order 2 will be assigned to Sue, and Order 3 will be assigned to Joe. Then when Order 4 comes in, it will be assigned to you again, and so on. You have filled several large orders today and know that you can finish everything else assigned to you by the end of the day. You had to rush quite a bit this morning in order to meet a noon shipping deadline for a very large order, and now you are pleased that you have met your goals and that your customers will receive what they need.

   With only an hour left in the shift, Joe is assigned a very large order that must be filled by that evening's shipping deadline. It will take a tremendous amount of effort for Joe to fill the order and it would be very hard for one person to do that amount of work on his or her own. What do you do?

Reaction 1: You know that you should probably help Joe, but Joe has been a bully to you and Sue lately. Joe has been making rude comments and has been telling crude jokes that make both of you uncomfortable, so you are not looking forward to spending extra time in his presence. You know that he cannot easily make the evening shipping deadline and the customer will have its shipment delayed.

   You also know that unless you concentrate for the rest of your shift on filling the orders that are left in your queue, you won't be able to complete all of them. Joe took several breaks earlier and a very long lunch, and you know he is behind on his queue. He also didn't help you when you were scrambling earlier to fill the order for the noon shipment, so you complete the work assigned to you and leave work at the end of your shift.

Reaction 2: Joe has been a difficult coworker to deal with lately. He's a bully to you and Sue, and he's been making rude comments and telling crude jokes that make both of you uncomfortable. You are not looking forward to spending any extra time with Joe, but you know that if he doesn't get help, he'll miss this evening's shipping deadline and the customer will have to wait for his order. You find it frustrating that earlier today when you were scrambling to fill your order for the noon deadline, Joe took a long lunch and didn't help you out.

   You also know that unless you concentrate for the rest of your shift on filling the orders left in your queue, you won't be able to complete all of them this evening, but since they do not need to go out until tomorrow at noon, you probably could spare the time to help Joe fill the order as long as you scramble tomorrow morning. You know the customer that placed this order and you know they really do need the order quickly, so you decide to help Joe fill the order with the time remaining on your shift. By doing so, the order makes it onto the evening shipment.

Reaction 3: Joe has been a difficult coworker to deal with lately. He's a bully to you and Sue, and he's been making rude comments and telling crude jokes that make both of you uncomfortable. You are not looking forward to spending any extra time with Joe, but you know that if he doesn't get help, he'll miss this evening's shipping deadline and the customer will have to wait for his order. You find it frustrating that earlier today when you were scrambling to fill your order for the noon deadline, Joe took a long lunch and didn't help you out.

   You also know that unless you concentrate for the rest of your shift on filling the orders left in your queue, you won't be able to complete all of them this evening, but since they do not need to go out until tomorrow at noon, you could spare the time to help Joe fill the order. You approach Joe and offer to help him with his order this afternoon as long as he helps you with your orders in the morning. Joe agrees, so you decide to help Joe fill the order with the time remaining on your shift. By doing so, the order makes it onto the evening shipment. You leave work hoping that Joe will keep his word and help you fill your remaining orders in the morning.

Self-Awareness
and Control
Empathy
Social
Expertness
Personal
Infuence
Mastery of
Purpose and
Vision

EQ 42 Reflection on Courage

EQ Area and Competency

Self-Awareness and Control: Courage

How to Use This Activity

- To help people take stock of their actions to determine their level of courage.

- To encourage people to examine their actions on a regular basis so they take courageous actions to address issues.

Use this activity in leadership-development and personal-development training programs. This activity can be done in a coaching or in a classroom setting. It is particularly helpful for leaders and managers because courage is a critical quality for leaders. If a leader does not have courage, having challenging conversations around goal setting and performance issues can be avoided, causing significant problems in the future. New leaders must examine their actions on a regular basis to be sure that they are acting with courage, so this activity is particularly useful for new or aspiring leaders.

Applicable Content Area

Multiple: Leadership Development, Conflict Resolution

Audience: Classroom, Coaching

Estimated Time: 60 minutes

Level of Disclosure/Difficulty: High

Materials: "Reflection on Courage" handout

Purpose/Why This Is Important

Courage is a critical emotional intelligence competency for everyone in the organization, but especially for leaders and managers. Courage enables people to challenge the status quo, to have challenging conversations, and to speak up when they believe in something and offer a countering opinion. If individuals lack courage, teams and organizations may suffer from a lack of innovative ideas that push boundaries, and they may suffer from group-think and broken processes that aren't being challenged.

Courage and assertiveness allow a leader or manager to have the difficult conversations around performance improvements with employees. Without those conversations, performance problems can go unaddressed and lead to big problems for both the employee and the organization. Appropriately confronting an issue with peers or leaders also requires courage, but without addressing issues with peers and leaders, the organization as a whole will suffer. Leaving issues unaddressed can cause tension between groups and a loss of focus on the overall goals of the organization.

Set the Stage

The instructor should ask the group to talk about courageous individuals who come to mind. What qualities or characteristics do they embody? State that all of us must take stock of our own courage. Explain that courage is not necessarily what we see in action movies, but it is about taking action whenever there could be consequences. Courage is necessary for organizations because it means that people in the organization will be willing to challenge popular opinion, present dissenting opinions, and have challenging conversations. Explain that the following activity will allow people to reflect on their courage by giving participants quiet time to address questions on the handout. Tell participants they will not be asked to share the private details of their answers, but they will be asked to comment on what they have learned by answering the questions.

The Activity

1. Give each participant a handout to complete. You can encourage people to go to a private space if the area is conducive to such. Tell people to return in 30 minutes with a completed handout.

2. Ask participants to form groups of four to reflect on courage, including how courage can help benefit organizations. Each group is to produce some key lessons learned or truths members believe are important. Instruct them to write at least three key lessons learned from reflecting on their experiences with courage.

3. Ask a spokesperson from each group to tell the full group participants their key lessons learned. Point out similarities as well as differences among the groups.

4. Debrief the activity.

Key Debrief Questions

➤ How can courage help you as a leader?

➤ When someone is courageous, how do you feel when dealing with that person?

➤ Is it always possible to be courageous?

➤ Under what conditions is courage most difficult?

➤ What happens when you continually chose to avoid a situation?

➤ Does acting with courage have consequences? What are they?

Key Learning Points

The facilitator should help the participants arrive at the following conclusions:

➤ Courage will enable leaders to have more productive, successful teams and will increase their influence.

➤ Individuals, as well as organizations as a whole, benefit when courageous actions are encouraged, but it can be difficult to break down underlying fear in the organization to encourage those acts.

➤ Addressing conflict honestly and courageously requires skill.

Note to the Trainer: If you are working with an intact team, the key lessons learned that the small groups produce can be captured and circulated as an output from the session. These key learnings can form a moral and behavioral compass for the group. However, it's important to note that if working with an intact team, you will have to carefully assess the readiness factor for this activity, as it is high disclosure especially for an intact team.

Reflection on Courage Handout

1. Think about a time when you spoke up about something in the workplace. What was the issue? Why did you speak up about it? What did you say? What did others think?

2. Do you ever wish you had said something in a meeting or encounter but didn't? Why didn't you?

3. What did you do the last time someone blamed you for something at work that wasn't your fault?

4. Think about a time when you were right, and you knew you were right, but someone else (a boss, a coworker, a customer) didn't believe you. What did you do?

5. Think about a time when you realized a situation at work was unfair. What did you do?

6. Think about a time when you were told to do something that you knew wasn't a good idea. What did you do?

7. Think about a time when you and a peer were at odds about a particular decision or direction. What did you do?

8. Think about a time when your boss had a particular opinion that differed from yours. What did you do?

9. Think about a time when you disagreed with a goal that you were told to achieve. Did you still work toward the goal? How did that go? What other actions did you take?

10. For leaders: Describe a difficult performance discussion you had with an employee.

11. For leaders: Think about a time when you decided not to discuss an issue with an employee. Why did you make that decision?

12. When do you know you were courageous and acted that way?

13. When do you think you should have been more courageous?

14. What would you like to be more courageous about in the future?

EQ 43 Authenticity Explored

Self-Awareness and Control
Empathy
Social Expertness
Personal Infuence
Mastery of Purpose and Vision

Inward Inward Outward

EQ Area and Competency

Mastery of Purpose and Vision: Authenticity

How to Use This Activity

- To help people define authenticity.

- To help people know what behaviors they can exhibit as a team member that would promote authenticity.

- To help people know how to market themselves in an authentic way.

Use this activity in teamwork, career-development, personal-development, and leadership-development programs, as well as for new and aspiring leaders. Because authenticity is a valued attribute in the workplace, defining it is a useful exercise. Defining authenticity in terms of behaviors gives people concrete behaviors to practice to make them more authentic. In particular, people must decide every day how to be authentic teammates and how to promote themselves in ways that don't make them sound like spin doctors. This activity leaves participants with some clear behaviors that others define as authentic, as well as clear behaviors that are viewed as inauthentic.

Applicable Content Area

Multiple: Teamwork, Career Development, Leadership Development

Audience: Classroom, Web-Based

Estimated Time: 60 minutes

Level of Disclosure/Difficulty: Medium

Materials

Flip charts for each group of 4
Markers

Purpose/Why This Is Important

When the individual sets his or her personal direction and goals based on a strong personal philosophy and acts in a manner consistent with that personal philosophy, he or she is authentic. This inner compass also provides resilience and strength to overcome obstacles. When inconsistent, many individuals will feel stress and discomfort. (It is important to note, that a few people can be comfortable in their lies and duplicitous behavior, until they eventually reveal themselves.) However, aligning our actions and words to what we believe is the best way to demonstrate authenticity to others and to create a sense of inner peace.

Set the Stage

Ask what the term "authentic" means? Ask, "When we apply that term to a person, what does it mean?" Then, "Who would you rather have on your team, someone you would define as authentic, or not? Why?" Explain that most people want to work with people they trust. Authenticity promotes trust because people do not have hidden agendas. Also, they are motivated by the mission or task, rather than the power, ego, or position the task may bring. Explain that this activity will encourage you to think about what it means to be an authentic teammate. It will also help us recognize how we can market ourselves in an authentic way.

The Activity

1. Divide the participants into groups of four. Give each participant group flip-chart paper and markers.

2. Ask the group to divide the flip chart as such:

Teamwork

AUTHENTIC BEHAVIORS	INAUTHENTIC BEHAVIORS

3. Ask group members to list behaviors they think contribute to authenticity among teammates in Column 1. Ask them to list behaviors they consider to detract from authenticity among their teammates in Column 2. Coach the group to be as specific as possible.

4. Ask a spokesperson from each group to report to the full group. Point out similarities as well as differences among the groups.

5. Debrief this portion of the activity. (See the debrief questions, Part 1.)

6. Refocus the group on the subject of career development. Ask the group, "We are all responsible for our own careers. How can we market ourselves in a positive light and maintain our authenticity? Is it possible, or are these two ideas mutually exclusive?" This portion of the activity will ask you to define how you can market yourself in an authentic way.

7. Assign new groups of four. Give each participant group flip-chart paper and markers.

8. Ask the group to divide the flip chart as such:

Marketing Oneself

AUTHENTIC BEHAVIORS	INAUTHENTIC BEHAVIORS

9. Ask the group to list behaviors they think contribute to their authenticity when marketing themselves in Column 1. Ask the group to list behaviors they consider to detract from authenticity when marketing oneself in Column 2. Coach the group to be as specific as possible.

10. Ask a spokesperson from each group to report to the full group. Point out similarities as well as differences among the groups.

11. Debrief this portion of the activity. (See debrief questions Part 2.)

Key Debrief Questions

Part 1

➤ What is the benefit of being viewed as authentic by your teammates?

➤ Why is authenticity important to you?

➤ What is the risk if you are not viewed as authentic by others?

➤ What if others on the team do not reciprocate and model authenticity?

Part 2

➤ What is the risk of overmarketing yourself?

- What is the risk of not marketing yourself?

- How can authenticity benefit your marketing efforts?

- How can a lack of authenticity detract from your marketing efforts?

Key Learning Points

The facilitator should help the participants arrive at the following conclusions:

- As a teammate, when you conduct yourself in an authentic way, you will engender a sense of trust with your teammates.

- Trust builds strong bonds with others.

- If you have trusting relationships, you can approach difficult situations, concerns, and conflicts in a way that resolve the situations without destroying relationships.

- Your authentic behavior sets the tone for how others should behave.

- Not everyone will reciprocate by acting in an honorable and authentic way. However, you should define your behavior based on your internal compass and what you consider to be correct, not on how others behave.

- When we over sell ourselves we risk our reputation.

- Everyone is responsible for his or her own career. Therefore, it is important that we realize that marketing our strengths in an honest and straightforward way, with evidence to back it up, is the best route to career success.

- If we market ourselves at the expense of others, it cheapens our goods; and it engenders a sense of distrust.

EQ 44 — Advertisement

Self-Awareness
and Control
Empathy
Social
Expertness
Personal
Influence
Mastery of
Purpose and
Vision

Inward   Inward   Outward

EQ Area and Competency

Personal Influence: Creating a Positive Work Climate

How to Use This Activity

- To consider the impact of words/actions on the work climate.

- To encourage participants to examine the changes in productivity due to work climate.

Use this activity in leadership-development and teamwork sessions. It is particularly helpful for leaders and managers because creating a positive work climate can improve productivity in the workplace. Teams must also examine their actions on a regular basis to be sure they are creating a positive work climate to positively influence results, so this activity is particularly useful for new or intact teams.

Applicable Content Area

Multiple: Leadership Development, Teamwork, Communications

Audience: Classroom

Estimated Time: 60 minutes

Level of Disclosure/Difficulty: Low

Materials:

Large sheets of paper
Colored markers
Magazines
Scissors
Glue
Tape

Purpose/Why This Is Important

Creating a positive work climate is a critical emotional intelligence competency for organizations and teams to develop. A positive work climate will improve employee satisfaction, retention, creativity, and innovation, as well as decrease stress in the workforce.

In a team setting, individual contributors can greatly affect the team's success by ensuring that everyone's ideas are heard and that concerns are addressed. On the other hand, it is easy for an individual contributor to create a negative atmosphere on a team by complaining about assignments, not including all members, and not equally soliciting ideas or opinions.

Set the Stage

The instructor should ask the group members to think about today's class and how they would describe the class to someone who is not a participant. Explain that the following activity will allow the groups to create an advertisement that will describe the class to others and that it is important to capture the perspective of everyone on the team.

The Activity

1. Divide the group into teams of five.

2. Have each group count off in fives, and ask each "Number 3" to remember his or her number.

3. Give each group materials and supplies and instruct the groups to create an advertisement for the class. The advertisement should be something the group works together to con-

struct, should have an element from each group member, and should be something all members of the group can feel proud of. It is important that each member of the group contributes something to the advertisement. Ask Number 3s to not immediately participate.

4. While the groups are creating their advertisements, take the Number 3s out of the room and give them instructions so they understand their roles. Divide the Number 3s in half.

   a. Tell half of the Number 3s to take a pair of scissors and rearrange the picture to make improvements as they see fit. Each Number 3 must make changes to the advertisement. They are not to ask for input or suggestions.

   b. Tell the other half to ask the group questions about the advertisement, so they can fully understand and appreciate the group's perspective. These Number 3s should be coached to actively listen to participants, to validate their thoughts, and to affirm the advertisement. Then, each Number 3 should suggest a possible change to the picture and should attempt to influence the group to include the change.

5. Ask a spokesperson from each group to tell the full-group participants their key lessons learned. Point out similarities as well as differences among the groups.

6. Debrief the activity.

Note to Trainer: If you wish to tailor the activity to leadership development, have each team select a leader, and then pull the leaders aside to provide them instructions. The instructions would be the same as those given to the Number 3 team members above.

Key Debrief Questions

➤ How did you feel when the individual made changes to your advertisement?

➤ Why is there a difference of opinions in your reactions?

➤ What were some of the methods that the individual used to influence you to change the advertisement?

➤ How did you react to the individual's suggestions?

➤ For those individuals who asked questions and discussed the advertisement before making changes, what was the tone of the group? Were you okay with the changes suggested? How did you feel?

➤ For those individuals who simply made the changes, what was the tone of the group after that? Were you okay with the changes? How did you feel?

➤ How did the tone of the group change when the individual came back into the room?

➤ How did the tone of the group help/hinder your progress?

➤ Is it ever ok for a leader to make a change without consulting the team? When is it ok? What can the leader do to help the team?

Key Learning Points

The facilitator should help the participants arrive at the following conclusions:

➤ A positive work climate, demonstrated through listening, asking questions, making sure to understand, and then providing suggestions, makes the leader more influential with the group.

➤ When the leader practices influence, it creates fewer negative feelings in the followers. Negative feelings in the followers create negative performances.

➤ By creating a positive work environment and trying to understand the group's perspective—demonstrated by asking questions, validating the group's thinking, and asking the group members what they really like about the advertisement and what they dislike—the leader has a better chance of influencing the group.

➤ Typically the group will resent the leader who just changes the advertisement without any attempt to understand the perspective of the group. Therefore, his or her influence will be weak.

EQ 45 The Rebuttal

Self-Awareness and Control
Empathy
Social Expertness
Personal Infuence
Mastery of Purpose and Vision

EQ Area and Competency

Empathy: Respectful Listening
Social Expertness: Conflict Resolution

How to Use This Activity

- To raise awareness of the process of respectful listening.

- To demonstrate the advantages of listening respectfully instead of listening for the purpose of rebuttal.

- To learn how to catch oneself in the process of listening for the sake of rebuttal during conflict or differences of opinion.

    Use this activity to highlight the need, difficulty, and mental process required to respectfully listen to a point of view that is contrary to one's own. This activity is appropriate for the classroom. It can serve as a strong reminder that listening is a gateway to respectful relationships and can create a pathway for resolving differences and conflict. It also points out that, most often, our natural inclination during a conflict is to listen for the sake of rebuttal, which further exacerbates the conflict.

Applicable Content Area

Multiple: Leadership Development, Teamwork, Conflict Resolution, Communications, Interpersonal Skills

Audience: Classroom

Estimated Time: 40 minutes

Level of Disclosure/Difficulty: Medium

Materials

A list of legitimate workplace issues that are controversial for the group. For example, perhaps the organization is considering a new building, and some favor and others oppose the idea. Or perhaps a new compensation or performance system or change to an employee benefit is being considered. Select a few topics specific to the organization that are likely to stir differences of opinion, but avoid issues that are extremely contentious. If you are an outside consultant unfamiliar with the organization, talk to the people inside the organization who hired you to determine an appropriate list of topics.

Purpose/Why This Is Important

Listening respectfully, especially during a discussion where our opinions differ, is a critical and useful skill in the workplace and in our daily lives. Most often, when we find ourselves in a situation in which our opinion differs from another person's we listen to the opposing opinion and then form a rebuttal to make our point or prove the other person's point to be incorrect. This causes further disagreement and defensiveness for the other party. It serves to broaden instead of close the gap between opinions. Everywhere in our daily lives, including the workplace, we have multiple opportunities per day to find differences of opinion. Respectfully listening and seeking to understand the other's viewpoint serves the team, the organization, and oneself. Listening respectfully allows us to air issues completely without taking sides or defending one's point of view so that we can make the best decision for the organization.

Set the Stage

Tell the participants they are about to enter a discussion about organizational issues about which they have strong opinions. Tell them the objective of the activity is to persuade the group with the opposing viewpoint to change its mind.

The Activity

1. List the controversial organizational topics on a flip chart. Ask people to select a topic about which they have a strong opinion. (Some group members may not have a strong opinion about any of the topics. If so, they can be made observers. If however, you find a large number of the group doesn't have an opinion, you should ask the group to brainstorm another topic. Or, ask if they are familiar enough with the topic, that they could argue a point of view.)

2. Divide the group by topics. Then further divide it depending on which side of the issue people most support. For example, if the issue is to move the headquarters of the company, some will be in agreement and others will oppose this idea. Form teams of no more than four or five people on each side of the argument.

3. Instruct the individuals on each team to list the reasons they think their point of view is correct. Encourage them to list facts, use data, and other information to secure their points of view. Also, encourage them to create more intangible reasons they think their point of view is correct. This could include, for example, how a new headquarters building will create better collaborative spaces and allow for employees to express more creativity in their collaboration.

4. Individuals on like-minded teams should now share their reasons with the other team members who share their side of the argument.

5. Assign a few observers to each team. Take the observers out of the room for review and give observers a copy of the observer checklist.

6. Organize a debate between the teams with opposing views. (You can have several debates going on at the same time.)

7. Encourage the teams to make sure they express their points of view.

8. Debrief the activity.

Key Debrief Questions

➤ How many issues were decided? Or, how many groups came to agreement or changed the opposition's mind? How many issues still had ongoing debates? How many groups didn't come to agreement?

➤ Who won the argument by getting the opposing group to change its mind?

➤ What tactics were used to get the other group to concur with your opinion?

➤ Ask the group that conceded, "How do you feel about the decision?"

➤ For those groups that did not persuade the other group, what tactics did you use?

➤ What occurred when you applied the tactics?

➤ How many people felt their points of view were heard and respected?

➤ How many people felt that their points of view were heard and then met with rebuttal?

➤ What does rebuttal cause us to do with our arguments?

➤ How can listening respectfully reduce rebuttal and defensiveness?

➤ How can listening respectfully change the course of the discussion?

➤ Why do we rebut?

➤ How often do we use rebuttal listening in the workplace?

➤ What is the goal of rebuttal listening?

➤ What is the goal of respectful listening?

➤ How can respectful listening increase our influence?

- If we feel our points of view were heard, but a decision was made supporting an opposing viewpoint, how should we react?

- When is rebuttal appropriate?

Key Learning Points

The facilitator should help the participants arrive at the following conclusions:

- Listening is a powerful tool to gain insight into another person's perspective.

- When we listen to rebuttal, it generally causes defensive behavior which escalates the differences.

- When we listen to fully understand another's perspective and we respect the other party's perspective, the other party may be more open to listen to our opposing point of view.

- In an organization, listening respectfully is the best path to resolving organizational issues. The goal isn't to make everyone happy, but to ensure that people feel their points of view were considered.

- Rebuttal discounts people's points of view. It sets up win/lose thinking.

- Rebuttal can also cross the line of feeling like a personal attack versus an assault on the issue.

- To influence another person or faction, respectfully listening to that point of view increases your influence because the others feel heard.

- Listening respectfully doesn't mean that you agree with the other party's viewpoint, but it means that you have sincerely heard it and tried to see the validity of that person's perspective.

- In all areas of our life, including work, differences of opinion can be useful and healthy if they are heard and respected. At some point, however, a decision could be made that does not support our viewpoints. In this case, consider how you can support the decision. (If something is morally or ethically wrong, that's a different case, and you may have to take another action. However, many other issues are not morally or ethically wrong and, as team members, we have to decide to how we wish to go forward.)

- Making an opposing point is valuable in the workplace. The end goal of this discussion is not to suggest that disagreeing with another's point of view is wrong. In fact, disagreement is encouraged. However, in the discussion process, listening respectfully, then offering opposing thoughts and ideas generate a trusting, healthy debate where ideas are aired and evaluated while still honoring the other person and his right to express himself.

Note to Trainer: It is important to frame this discussion on work-related differences. Do not attempt to use political, religious or other societal issues as discussion topics because these types of values conflicts may divide the group along personal lines and serve no purpose for the activity.

The Rebuttal Handout

Observer's Sheet: Listening Skills

Listen to the discussion carefully. Watch for the following behaviors. Place a check mark in Column 2 each time you observe the listed behavior.

Genuine active listening for the sake of understanding.	
Listening and then following with a rebuttal.	
Asking clarifying questions for the sake of understanding.	
Asking clarifying questions for the sake of rebuttal.	
Interrupting people before they have finished their thought.	
Nodding in agreement or understanding when the opposing team was speaking.	
Shaking their heads or negative body language when the opposing team was speaking.	
Using the word "BUT" to begin an opposing thought.	
Using the word "NO" to begin an opposing thought.	
Validating the opposing group's idea by saying "That's a point I hadn't considered...."	

EQ 46 Confidence Builder

Self-Awareness
and Control

Empathy
Social
Expertness
Personal
Infuence
Mastery of
Purpose and
Vision

Inward   Inward   Outward

EQ Area and Competency

Personal Influence: Self-Confidence

How to Use This Activity

- To examine the importance of having and presenting ideas with confidence and the impact confidence will have on the message.

- To encourage participants to reflect on criticism and its impact on confidence.

Use this activity in career-development, leadership-development, and personal-development sessions. It is particularly helpful for new hires and those new in their leadership roles because acting with confidence when challenged is a key skill.

Note to Trainer: If you have fewer than 10 people in your session, you may wish to eschew groups and use this as an individual activity.

Applicable Content Area:

Multiple: Leadership Development, Career Development, Interpersonal skills

Audience: Classroom, Web-Based

Estimated Time: 40 minutes

Level of Disclosure/Difficulty: Medium

Materials:

Flip charts—at least two
Colored markers
Tape

Purpose/Why This Is Important

Self-confidence is a critical emotional intelligence competency because if you are self-confident you are more likely to take risks, overcome challenges, aspire to reach new heights, and work to grow and succeed. In addition, even if it is not necessarily fair, you will be judged on the level of confidence you display. During your career, you will need to be convincing in order to be taken seriously in your position. By showing confidence, you are more likely to be successful at influencing others. Self-confidence does not mean you must be gregarious and outgoing. It does mean, however, that you believe you can accomplish something, that you show that belief, and then deliver on it. That level of confidence will create a presence that people will be willing to follow. Further, a lack of confidence leads to the perception that the leader (or anyone aiming to convey a message) is questioning himself or herself, which will cause followers to question the leader, as well.

Criticism is also a fact of life. In most cases, criticism comes from a place of genuinely wanting the other person or task to be better, although at times, it is not delivered as constructively as it could be. Many people react poorly to criticism by becoming defensive or argumentative, or by just shutting down. However, by being confident in the face of criticism, you can shift your thinking away from defensiveness and look to the criticism as a learning opportunity rather than an affront or attack. The self-confident individual sees criticism as a way to become even better.

Set the Stage

The instructor should talk about how important it is for individuals and leaders to develop self-confidence. Explain that the following activity will ask groups to determine ways to increase confidence that each person can take away and use as part of his or her daily life. Explain that it is important to capture the perspective of everyone on the team and ask that within the groups, everyone contributes at least one idea.

The Activity

1. Divide the group into teams of three to five people.

2. Provide each team with a piece of flip chart paper and markers. Ask the teams to work together to create a list of top ways to build confidence. Ask each team to come up with at least five methods and to ensure that everyone's ideas are included.

3. Give the teams 10 minutes to work on their lists.

4. Ask the teams to present their lists to the larger group.

5. Ask the larger group members to identify three things they like about the list. Document those items on the second flip chart.

6. Ask the larger group members to identify three things they didn't like about the list presented. Document those items on the second flip chart.

7. Repeat this process (#4 thru #6) for each of the teams.

8. Debrief the activity.

Key Debrief Questions

➤ Did you feel like you came up with a good list?

➤ Do you think there are things on the list you'd like to work on?

➤ How did it feel when people pointed out positive things on your list?

➤ How did it feel when people pointed out negative things on your list?

➤ Did you question any of the items on your list after hearing the negative comments? Why/why not?

➤ What impact did the negative comments have on your self-confidence?

➤ Did you dismiss any of the criticism? Why?

➤ Did it matter who the criticism came from?

➤ Do you dismiss feedback from someone you don't like?

➤ How does this work in real life? Are you more or less accepting of criticism on certain items? From certain people? Why?

Key Learning Points

The facilitator should help the participants arrive at the following conclusions:

➤ Self-confidence is a key skill that allows us to influence ourselves and others.

➤ Self-confidence comes from many different sources and can be developed through deliberate effort.

➤ Being self-confident can help you accept criticism and use the criticism to strengthen your approach. A lack of confidence can destroy your ability to grow from criticism.

➤ Criticism from different sources is interpreted differently based on the relationship of the individuals. Criticism from certain individuals is harder to accept, but is still valid and not designed to destroy confidence.

EQ 47

Flying High

Self-Awareness
and Control
Empathy
Social
Expertness
Personal
Infuence
Mastery of
Purpose and
Vision

Inward   Inward   Outward

EQ Area and Competency

Personal Influence: Leading Others
Empathy: Feeling Impact on Others

How to Use This Activity

- To raise awareness about the types of behaviors that contribute to positively leading others.

- To observe the positive group dynamics and the effect on productivity that occurs when the leader uses positive-influence behaviors.

- To observe the negative group dynamics and the effect on productivity that occurs when the leader fails to positively influence the team.

Use this activity to highlight the effect of the leader on a work group. This activity produces a strong reaction in the participants. It clearly demonstrates how the leader can affect productivity. This activity is appropriate for the classroom. In order for this activity to be most beneficial, the group size should be at least 20 persons, so four teams can be formed.

Applicable Content Area

Multiple: Leadership Development, New/Aspiring Leadership Development

Audience: Classroom

Estimated Time: 45 minutes (minimum of 20 persons)

Level of Disclosure/Difficulty: Easy

Materials

8½ by 11 paper in multiple colors. Each team (group of five) will need a total of 100 sheets of paper in three different colors. For example, 33 sheets of blue paper, 33 sheets of white paper, and 34 sheets of yellow paper.

Purpose/Why This Is Important

The leader can strongly influence the team's output. Depending on the behaviors the leader displays, his team can either become engaged in and enthusiastic about the task at hand or resistant to it. The attitude and cooperation of the team and its productivity can be damaged if the leader does not provide a clear understanding of the task, clear specifications and criteria of quality, proper training, feedback, positive reinforcement, and coaching. In addition, team dynamics can turn negative when the team does not understand the leader's actions and motives.

Set the Stage

Tell the group members that they are being assigned to work in an airplane production factory. Output is critical and that the number of planes correctly produced will determine if they have jobs for the future or if their competitors (the other teams in the room) will instead be awarded the contract. Tell the group that this is a timed activity and that each group will have 10 minutes to produce the airplanes. The team that produces the most airplanes in line with the performance criteria will win. Each group will have a supervisor who will be responsible for accepting and inspecting the airplanes and ensuring that the proper standards have been met.

The Activity

1. Have each group select a leader. Hand out supplies to each group.

2. Meet in a private location with all of the leaders to discuss the criteria for accepting quality

aircraft given in the handout. The leader's role is to make sure that all production follows these exact criteria. If the leader receives a completed aircraft that does not match the criteria listed, the leader MUST destroy the aircraft by crumpling it in a ball and throwing it on the floor and stepping on it. The leader is NOT permitted to talk to the team during this entire activity and is NOT permitted to share the criteria with the team. Send the leaders back into the room to join their teams.

3. Start the clock and instruct the teams to begin making aircraft and when each is complete to hand it to the leader for inspection. Tell the team that the leader will accept it if it meets the standard.

4. After 10 minutes, call time. Ask the leader of each team to report how many aircraft the team has successfully produced.

5. Debrief the activity.

Key Debrief Questions

➤ What did the team members do when the leader rejected their aircraft?

➤ How did rejecting the aircraft affect the team?

➤ When the leader did not give feedback to the group, what impact did that have?

➤ What did the leader do or fail to do that affected the productivity of the team?

➤ How can a leader's actions affect the morale of the team?

➤ Why are quality standards and proper discussion and training useful when leading others?

Key Learning Points

The facilitator should help the participants arrive at the following conclusions:

➤ Productivity is affected when people do not understand quality standards, when they do not receive proper training, and when they do not receive feedback on the tasks they are performing.

➤ The leader's actions create the climate that can enhance productivity or destroy it.

➤ If the leader isn't mindful and doesn't practice basic leadership principles, the productivity of his unit and his ability to influence his team are greatly compromised.

➤ Feedback is an essential tool of leadership. Giving performance feedback helps to influence the team's output. Of course, the way in which the feedback is given is critical. One could argue that the leader gave feedback by rejecting and destroying the aircraft. Feedback given to coach, train and encourage team members is much more effective than feedback that only rejects the task.

➤ Group dynamics can turn negative, and group members can band together against a leader they view negatively. This can dramatically affect production.

➤ Group members can also turn on each other if some are perceived to be favorites of the leader.

Flying High Handout

The leader can only accept aircraft if ALL of the following criteria are met:

1. The aircraft must be handed to the leader by a different member of the team each time. If the same person hands you a second aircraft, you must reject it.

2. Aircraft must be accepted only if it is in a different color from the last aircraft you accepted. So, if you just accepted a blue aircraft, the next aircraft must be a color besides blue.

3. Aircraft must be accepted only if the aircraft is handed to you tail first. If someone hands you an aircraft nose first, you must reject it.

EQ 48 Shoe Switch

Self-Awareness
and Control

Empathy

Social
Expertness

Personal
Infuence

Mastery of
Purpose and
Vision

Inward   Inward   Outward

EQ Area and Competency

Empathy: Feeling Impact on Others

How to Use This Activity

- To examine a challenging situation from another viewpoint to build empathy.

- To encourage participants to reflect on how their actions are viewed by others and the emotional reactions caused by those actions.

Use this activity in teamwork, leadership-development, and personal-development sessions. It is particularly helpful for those new in their leadership roles and also with teams because feeling one's impact on others can help the leader build empathy and create more cohesive teams.

Applicable Content Area

Multiple: Leadership Development, Teamwork, Customer Service

Audience: Classroom, Web-Based, Coaching

Estimated Time: 40 minutes

Level of Disclosure/Difficulty: High

Materials: None

Purpose/Why This Is Important

When the leader is able to feel the impact he has on others, he can anticipate what a person's reaction to a situation may be. The leader can also read the emotional climate of a situation and react in a way that will best suit the situation, while still accomplishing goals. The individual who can master the skill of feeling his impact on others will be able to quickly pick up on a tense conversation and work to diffuse it. He will perceive that others may be stressed about a change in the organization and work to ease concerns. He will be able to anticipate how his words or actions may affect others and deliberately choose to deliver his message in a way that will have the most positive impact. He will also be able to react to undercurrents and moods that may derail the group's goals. As the leader becomes skilled in understanding his impact, he becomes skilled in delivering results through others.

Set the Stage

The instructor should talk about how important it is to look at situations that may not have gone well, or at least not as well as anticipated, and reflect on them to help determine what went wrong. Explain that the following activity will ask individuals to share with their partners a situation that did not go as anticipated and to think about how the situation may have been perceived by others.

The Activity

1. Split the group in to partnered pairs.

2. Ask one partner (Partner A) to explain to the other a situation that didn't go as anticipated in as much detail as possible. Provide five to seven minutes for the Partner As to discuss their situations.

3. Ask the other partner (Partner B) to try to figure out what the others in the situation described might have been thinking or feeling when they reacted in Partner A's scenario. Ask Partner B to share his thoughts with Partner A.

4. Switch partners, so Partner B talks about a situation that didn't go as anticipated and Partner A tries to understand the unanticipated reaction.

5. Debrief the activity.

Key Debrief Questions

➤ Was anyone surprised by the observations made about what actually happened in the situation?

➤ Do you think there was something else occurring, a thought or a feeling that caused the unanticipated reaction?

➤ Did anyone sense that something else was going on in the moment? What did you do or not do?

➤ How can reading the emotional climate help you succeed?

➤ What can you do to practice your skills at reading the emotional climate? Does talking through a situation after the fact with an impartial observer help? Why/why not?

Key Learning Points

The facilitator should help the participants arrive at the following conclusions:

➤ Being able to read the emotional climate of a situation and react appropriately will help you gain others' trust.

➤ Reading emotional climates and feeling and anticipating the impact of an action on others before proceeding can help us properly direct our actions to create better outcomes.

➤ Having a trusted impartial observer help us look at situations and determine the drivers of a reaction may help us better understand and anticipate those drivers in the future.

EQ 49 # What Have You Done?

Self-Awareness
and Control

Empathy

Social
Expertness

Personal
Infuence

Mastery of
Purpose and
Vision

Inward   Inward   Outward

EQ Area and Competency

Mastery of Purpose and Vision: Taking Action toward Purpose

How to Use This Activity

- To show that without taking actions participants may not be living their purposes and values.

- To encourage participants to reflect on how their actions will help them meet their purposes and values.

Use this activity in career and leadership development and in personal development sessions. It is particularly helpful for more experienced individuals who may need to focus on what actions to take next in order to meet their stated purposes and values.

Applicable Content Area

Multiple: Leadership Development, Career Development

Audience: Classroom, Coaching

Estimated Time: 60 minutes

Level of Disclosure/Difficulty: High

Materials: "What Have You Done?" handout

Purpose/Why This Is Important

Gaining an understanding of purpose and values is a key emotional intelligence competency because it provides clues as to what a person really loves, what he is passionate about, and what he will work wholeheartedly to achieve. However,
simply understanding purpose and values is not enough. Without taking actions toward that purpose, a person will not fulfill her purpose. That can cause extreme discontent. It is important to not just understand the purpose, but also to have a plan in place for action and to take action toward that purpose.

Set the Stage

The instructor should talk about how important it is for people to not just have an understanding of their purposes but also to begin taking actions toward those purposes. Explain that the following activity will ask individuals to reflect on the actions they have taken thus far to live out their purposes and values.

The Activity

1. Pass out the "What Have You Done?" handout and instruct the participants to complete it.

2. Provide 15 minutes for participants to complete the handout.

3. Ask the group members to share their responses to at least one of the questions.

4. Debrief the activity.

Key Debrief Questions

➤ Were you able to list concrete actions you've taken?

➤ Looking at what you've done so far, are you happy with the actions you've taken?

➤ What other actions would help you achieve your purpose?

➤ What actions are you taking right now that are not helping you achieve your purpose?

➤ How do you feel when you are taking actions toward your purpose?

➤ How do you feel when you are not taking actions toward your purpose?

Key Learning Points

The facilitator should help the participants arrive at the following conclusions:

➤ It is important to understand the actions we have taken and those we should still take that will help us achieve our purpose.

➤ Thinking about the actions we've taken in the past that have helped us get to where we are can help us identify further actions we can take.

➤ Taking action toward purpose can help us feel fulfilled; not taking action toward purpose can cause us to feel unsatisfied.

What Have You Done? Handout

1. How did you decide on your chosen field of endeavor, college major, or line of work? What influenced you? What actions did you take to end up in this field?

2. What do you like about your chosen field?

3. What do you dislike? What do you plan to do about it?

4. What actions have you taken related to your career that you are pleased you took? What pleases you about those actions?

5. Have you ever pursued a career-related goal, perhaps a credential or a specific job, only to discover when you achieved your goal that you were disappointed? What did you do?

Review of Emotional Intelligence Using Quotations

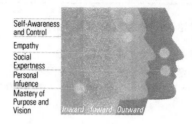

Self-Awareness and Control
Empathy
Social Expertness
Personal Infuence
Mastery of Purpose and Vision

Inward   Inward   Outward

EQ Area and Competency

Review of Several Areas of Emotional Intelligence

How to Use This Activity

- To determine participant understanding of emotional intelligence.

- To help people stay focused on their own development of emotional intelligence.

Use this activity in leadership-development training, teamwork, and personal development. This activity is best suited to a classroom setting. This activity is an excellent review or summary of emotional intelligence concepts. It can serve as a strong reminder of a particular emotional intelligence concept for participants. Use it to summarize content and to help participants determine how to turn the concept into action in their lives. It can be used as a final classroom activity or to select appropriate quotes at various points along the way in the curriculum to encourage participants to review and personalize the concepts.

Applicable Content Area

Multiple: Leadership Development, Teamwork, Personal Development

Audience: Classroom, Web-Based

Estimated Time: 30 minutes

Level of Disclosure/Difficulty: Medium

Materials

A basket with quotations written on slips of paper. (Use the quotations at the end of this activity or use your own to capture the same concept.)

As an alternative to the baskets: Have the quotations printed and stuffed into fortune cookies.

Purpose/Why This Is Important

Quotations can summarize key concepts quickly and succinctly. Quotations are also memorable. If participants can verbalize what key quotations related to emotional intelligence means to them, it is a good assurance that they are grasping the key concepts of emotional intelligence. Further, by having the participants talk about how the concept would be applied in their own lives, they can determine how they would act differently based on the concept. Grasping the key concepts and determining how they would influence our actions ensure learning.

Set the Stage

Share a favorite quotation with the class, explain what it means to you, and share a specific example or incident when you acted in a way that was consistent with the meaning conveyed in the quotation. Tell the class that the purpose of this activity is to review some key concepts of emotional intelligence and to have them think about how they can act on these key concepts. The trainer should select quotations based on content he wishes to review. For a list of content areas of emotional intelligence, please see Chapter 1, Figure 1-2. Explain that the quotations will be used as inspiration.

The Activity

1. Ask participants to select a quotation from the basket or give each person a fortune cookie. Ask them to summarize in their own words what the quotation means to them and to think about a time in their lives/careers when

they applied the concept or how they will apply it in the future.

2. Have participants take turns and stand before the class to read their quotations, summarize them, and talk about how they can apply them to their lives/careers.

3. Debrief the activity.

Key Debrief Questions

➤ How can quotations help us to stay focused?

➤ What other reminders can help us on our journey to greater emotional intelligence?

Key Learning Points

The facilitator should help the participants arrive at the following conclusions:

➤ Quotations succinctly convey important concepts and wisdom that can help us improve our emotional intelligence and serve as excellent reminders.

➤ Journaling, mentors, books, pictures, cartoons, tangible objects, and other mementoes can serve to keep us focused on the emotional intelligence concepts that we are trying to practice.

Review of Emotional Intelligence Using Quotations Handout

You can use your favorite quotations. However, here are a few that address key emotional intelligence concepts:

- I have striven not to laugh at human actions, not to weep at them, nor to hate them, but to understand them.—Baruch Spinoza.

- Habit is stronger than reason.—Santayana.

- Let's not forget that the little emotions are the great captains of our lives and we obey them without realizing it.—Vincent Van Gogh.

- To do good things in your life, first you must know who you are and what gives meaning to your life.—Paula Brownlee.

- Knowing others is wisdom, knowing yourself is enlightenment.—Lao Tzu.

- "Ah! If only there were two of me," she thought, "one who spoke and the other who listened, one who lived and the other who watched, how I would love myself! I'd envy no one."—Simone de Beauvoir.

- The key to understanding others is to understand oneself.—Helen Williams.

- When a man gains knowledge through the observation of his truth, the world changes.—Kilindi Iyi.

- The trick is to accept what makes you good.—James Baldwin.

- Always being in a hurry does not prevent death, neither does going slowly prevent living.—Ibo.

- The only thing that will stop you from fulfilling your dreams is you.—Tom Bradley.

- We need quiet time to examine our lives openly and honestly. . . spending quiet time alone gives your mind an opportunity to renew itself and create order.—Susan Taylor.

- Reflect upon your blessing of which every man has plenty, not on your past misfortunes of which all men have some.—Charles Dickens.

- It doesn't happen all at once. You become. It takes a long time.—Margery Williams.

- Real knowledge is to know the extent of one's ignorance.—Confucius.

- He who knows only his side of the case, knows little of that.—John Stuart Mill.

- No matter what accomplishments you make, somebody helps you.—Althea Gibson.

- The extent to which you are able to transform your "self-concern" into "other concern" will determine your effectiveness in getting others to follow along.—Anonymous.

- To attempt to climb—to achieve—without a firm objective in life is to attain nothing.—Mary Roebling.

TABLES OF RELATED ACTIVITIES

Activities by Competency

TABLE 6-1 Activities by Competency

Activity Number	Activity Name	Authenticity	Taking Actions Toward Purpose	Understanding Purpose and Values	Flexibility	Optimism	Goal Orientation	Initiative and Accountability	Self Confidence	Getting Results Through Others	Creating a Positive Work Climate	Leading Others	Organizational Savvy	Conflict Resolution	Collaboration	Building Relationships	Service Orientation	Feeling Impact on Others	Respectful Listening	Resilience	Courage	Emotional Expression	Accurate Self-Assessment	Emotional and Inner Awareness	Impact on Others
1	The Critic									X	X		X					X							
2	Know a Guy															X									
3	Cups and Ice				X			X																X	
4	Fifteen Minutes																			X				X	
5	The Invitation												X			X									
6	Doozie of a Disappointment																			X					
7	Facebook Feed																						X	X	X
8	Your TED Talk								X																
9	Hot Potato							X																	
10	Your Theme Song										X			X								X			
11	If I Had a Billion Dollars			X																					
12	Finish Line!						X																		
13	Selfie Listening																		X						
14	To Talk or Not to Talk—That Is the Question															X		X							X
15	Gumball														X							X			

#	Activity						
16	What Do You Assign to the Pictures of Your Life?	X				X	
17	Practice Assigning New Thoughts/Feelings to Something in Your Career	X		X		X	X
18	Puzzler			X	X		
19	Last Name				X		X
20	ROYGBIV				X		
21	Look Around				X		
22	States	X	X	X			
23	Good Enough					X	
24	Reflection Errors—Part 1	X					
25	Reflection Errors—Part 2	X					
26	Swing Set				X		
27	Restaurant Reviews	X		X			
28	Using Quotations to Anchor Purpose						X
29	Academy Award	X					
30	Judgment Day—Remote Teams	X		X			
31	Let's Go!			X	X		
32	A Wondering Mind or a Plan for the Future?		X				X
33	Actions Speak Louder Than Words		X				X
34	Shoots and Scores		X				
35	Blind Vote		X				

TABLE 6-1 *Continued*

Category	Competency	36 Are you Flexible? Let's Find Out	37 How Am I doing?	38 Authenticity—A Reflection	39 Better Method	40 Flexibility—A New Leader Exercise	41 Help Who?	42 Reflection on Courage	43 Authenticity Explored	44 Advertisement	45 The Rebuttal	46 Confidence Builder	47 Flying High	48 Shoe Switch	49 What Have You Done?	50 Review of Emotional Intelligence Using Quotations
MASTERY OF PURPOSE AND VISION	AUTHENTICITY			X					X							
	TAKING ACTIONS TOWARD PURPOSE														X	
	UNDERSTANDING PURPOSE AND VALUES															
PERSONAL INFLUENCE	FLEXIBILITY	X				X										
	OPTIMISM															
	GOAL ORIENTATION															
	INITIATIVE AND ACCOUNTABILITY															
	SELF CONFIDENCE											X				
	GETTING RESULTS THROUGH OTHERS															
	CREATING A POSITIVE WORK CLIMATE				X					X						
	LEADING OTHERS			X						X			X			
SOCIAL EXPERTNESS	ORGANIZATIONAL SAVVY															
	CONFLICT RESOLUTION										X					
	COLLABORATION															
	BUILDING RELATIONSHIPS															
EMPATHY	SERVICE ORIENTATION						X									
	FEELING IMPACT ON OTHERS												X	X		
	RESPECTFUL LISTENING										X					
SELF-AWARENESS AND CONTROL	RESILIENCE															
	COURAGE							X								
	EMOTIONAL EXPRESSION															
	ACCURATE SELF-ASSESSMENT	X														
	EMOTIONAL AND INNER AWARENESS															X
	IMPACT ON OTHERS															

Competency Breakdown

If a trainer or coach is specifically looking to improve a particular competency, these tables have been created to show which exercises specifically target each competency.

TABLE 6-2 Impact on Others

ACTIVITY NUMBER	ACTIVITY NAME	ALL COMPETENCIES EXHIBITED	PURPOSE	SUMMARY	LEVEL OF DISCLOSURE	PAGE NUMBER
7	Facebook Feed	Impact on Others, Emotional and Inner Awareness, Accurate Self-Assessment	Provides analysis of how we are always sending messages that others are interpreting.	Discussion to analyze the messages we send as if others are interpreting using Facebook as an example.	Low	44
14	To Talk or Not to Talk—That is the Question	Social Bonds, Impact on Others, Feeling Impact on Others, Building Relationships	Sensitize people to the impact of talking too much or not enough.	Role play "talkers" and "non-talkers" and discuss impact.	Medium	64
16	What Do You Assign to the Pictures of Your Life?	Impact on Others, Optimism	Recognize how thinking affects our view and how optimism and pessimism can be influenced by changing our view.	People assign meaning to pictures based on their initial assumptions and then are asked to change their view.	Low	71
27	Restaurant Reviews	Feeling Impact on Others, Impact on Others	Identify the reaction and impact that behaviors cause in others.	Role play specific behaviors when performing a group task and analyze group dynamic.	Low	104

TABLE 6-3 Self-Awareness and Control: Emotional and Inner Awareness

ACTIVITY NUMBER	ACTIVITY NAME	ALL COMPETENCIES EXHIBITED	PURPOSE	SUMMARY	LEVEL OF DISCLOSURE	PAGE NUMBER
3	Cups and Ice	Initiative and Accountability, Flexibility, Emotional and Inner Awareness	Explore one's attitude and approach to mundane tasks and recognize that others form opinions based on attitude.	Show videoclip and process specific questions.	Low	33
4	Fifteen Minutes	Emotional and Inner Awareness, Resilience	Explores perspective and resiliency related to one's skills and also one's failures.	Handout provides thought provoking questions around fame and failure in one's life.	Medium	35
7	Facebook Feed	Impact on Others, Emotional and Inner Awareness, Accurate Self-Assessment	Provides analysis of how we are always sending messages that others are interpreting.	Discussion to analyze the messages we send as if others are interpreting using Facebook as an example.	Low	44
17	Practice Assigning New Thoughts/Feelings to Something in Your Career	Emotional and Inner Awareness, Optimism, Flexibility, Feeling Impact on Others	Examine our thinking about situations or people and how it affects our behavior.	Analyze current thinking about a person or situation, challenge the thinking, and then predict different behavior.	High	74

22	States	Emotional and Inner Awareness, Emotional Expression, Collaboration	Identify emotional reactions—Use collaboration to perform task.	Alphabetize states as individuals and as a group.	Low	88
29	Academy Award	Emotional and Inner Awareness	Identify false rational beliefs that impact one's behavior.	An assigned actor and challenger role play to demonstrate the impact of irrational thinking on behavior.	Low	109
30	Judgment Day— Remote Teams	Emotional and Inner Awareness, Conflict Resolution	Examines judgments we make that interfere with our actions toward others.	Groups are given scenarios and asked to list assumptions that come to mind.	Low	113
50	Review of Emotional Intelligence Using Quotations	Review of Several Areas of Emotional Intelligence, Emotional and Inner Awareness	Reinforce concepts of emotional intelligence.	Use quotations as part of a review of concepts of emotional intelligence.	Medium	176

TABLE 6-4 Self-Awareness and Control: Accurate Self-Assessment

ACTIVITY NUMBER	ACTIVITY NAME	ALL COMPETENCIES EXHIBITED	PURPOSE	SUMMARY	LEVEL OF DISCLOSURE	PAGE NUMBER
7	Facebook Feed	Impact on Others, Emotional and Inner Awareness, Accurate Self-Assessment	Provides analysis of how we are always sending messages that others are interpreting.	Discussion to analyze the messages we send as if others are interpreting using Facebook as an example.	Low	44
24	Reflection Errors—Part 1	Accurate Self-Assessment	Identify reflection errors in thinking.	Interview regarding something that is problematic—Watch for reflection errors.	High	93
25	Reflection Errors—Part 2	Accurate Self-Assessment	Turn reflection errors into productive problem solving behavior.	Imagine different scenarios to problem situations.	Medium	98
36	Are You Flexible? Let's Find Out	Flexibility, Accurate Self-Assessment	Obtain feedback regarding flexibility.	Use 360-interview format to assess flexibility.	High	133

TABLE 6-5 Self-Awareness and Control: Emotional Expression

ACTIVITY NUMBER	ACTIVITY NAME	ALL COMPETENCIES EXHIBITED	PURPOSE	SUMMARY	LEVEL OF DISCLOSURE	PAGE NUMBER
10	Your Theme Song	Creating a Positive Work Climate, Conflict Resolution, Emotional Expression	Raise awareness about the tone that people set in their interactions.	Use music to identify and describe tone and how one comes across to others.	Medium	53
15	Gumball	Emotional Expression, Collaboration	Participants identify their typical M.O. related to stressful tasks.	Participants asks to complete a task with built in stressors.	Low	68
22	States	Emotional and Inner Awareness, Emotional Expression, Collaboration	Identify emotional reactions. Use collaboration to perform task.	Alphabetize states as individuals and as a group.	Low	88

TABLE 6-6 Self-Awareness and Control: Courage

ACTIVITY NUMBER	ACTIVITY NAME	ALL COMPETENCIES EXHIBITED	PURPOSE	SUMMARY	LEVEL OF DISCLOSURE	PAGE NUMBER
35	Blind Vote	Courage	Examine courage and its value to leadership positions and organizations.	Scenarios presented with various resolutions; group rates and discusses resolutions based on courage.	Medium	130
42	Reflection on Courage	Courage	Increase self-awareness related to one's courage.	Reflection handout to create thought and dialogue and goals related to courage.	High	154

TABLE 6-7 Self-Awareness and Control: Resilience

ACTIVITY NUMBER	ACTIVITY NAME	ALL COMPETENCIES EXHIBITED	PURPOSE	SUMMARY	LEVEL OF DISCLOSURE	PAGE NUMBER
4	Fifteen Minutes	Emotional and Inner Awareness, Resilience	Explores perspective and resiliency related to one's skills and also one's failures.	Handout worksheet provides thought-provoking questions around fame and failure in one's life.	Medium	35
6	Doozie of a Disappointment	Resilience	Encourages perspective and strength to overcome a disappointment by recalling past disappointing events.	Recall past disappointments and rate them as they occurred and then with the distance of time and perspective.	High	41
34	Shoots and Scores	Resilience	Examines emotion and resilience related to a difficult task.	Group is asked to perform a task that requires members to think differently and identify what is affecting their performance.	Low	128

TABLE 6-8 Empathy: Respectful Listening

ACTIVITY NUMBER	ACTIVITY NAME	ALL COMPETENCIES EXHIBITED	PURPOSE	SUMMARY	LEVEL OF DISCLOSURE	PAGE NUMBER
13	Selfie Listening	Respectful Listening	Learn listening and empathy skills and the impact they have on others.	Orchestrate listening and nonlistening behaviors and solicit discussion regarding impact as well as behavior.	Low	62
45	The Rebuttal	Respectful Listening, Conflict Resolution	Illustrates difference between respectful listening and rebuttal listening.	Orchestrated debate on contentious issues while observing listening behavior.	Medium	162

TABLE 6-9 Empathy: Feeling Impact on Others

ACTIVITY NUMBER	ACTIVITY NAME	ALL COMPETENCIES EXHIBITED	PURPOSE	SUMMARY	LEVEL OF DISCLOSURE	PAGE NUMBER
1	The Critic	Organizational Savvy, Feeling Impact on Others, Getting Results Through Others, Creating a Positive Work Environment	Read the climate and observe and respond to influencers in a group setting.	A group leader's behavior is deliberately showing favoritism toward one group member, and others must determine how to navigate.	Low	27
14	To Talk or Not to Talk—That Is the Question	Social Bonds, Impact on Others, Feeling Impact on Others, Building Relationships	Sensitize people to the impact of talking too much or not enough.	Role play "talkers" and "nontalkers" and discuss impact.	Medium	64
17	Practice Assigning New Thoughts/Feelings to Something in Your Career	Emotional and Inner Awareness, Optimism, Flexibility, Feeling Impact on Others	Examine our thinking about situations or people and how it affects our behavior.	Analyze current thinking about a person or situation, challenge the thinking, and then predict different behavior.	High	74
27	Restaurant Reviews	Feeling Impact on Others, Impact on Others	Identify the reaction and impact that behaviors cause in others.	Role play specific behaviors when performing a group task and analyze group dynamic.	Low	104
47	Flying High	Leading Others, Feeling Impact on Others	Demonstrates influence of the leader using influence tactics.	Group task of building airplanes is either enhanced or thwarted based on leader behavior.	Low	168
48	Shoe Switch	Feeling Impact on Others	Encourages empathy when reviewing situations in the workplace.	Work with a partner to review a situation that didn't go well to determine how the other party may have been reacting.	High	171

TABLE 6-10 Empathy: Service Orientation

ACTIVITY NUMBER	ACTIVITY NAME	ALL COMPETENCIES EXHIBITED	PURPOSE	SUMMARY	LEVEL OF DISCLOSURE	PAGE NUMBER
18	Puzzler	Service Orientation, Getting Results Through Others	Examine service orientation and leadership in a challenging group setting.	People are asked to build puzzles with incomplete pieces and without being able to communicate.	Low	76
41	Help Who?	Service Orientation	Explore importance and what service orientation looks like when dealing with peers.	Use scenarios with various options to select the best course of action and discuss reasons why.	Medium	151

TABLE 6-11 Social Expertness: Building Relationships

ACTIVITY NUMBER	ACTIVITY NAME	ALL COMPETENCIES EXHIBITED	PURPOSE	SUMMARY	LEVEL OF DISCLOSURE	PAGE NUMBER
2	Know a Guy	Building Relationships	Demonstrate the importance of building and nurturing relationships in the workplace.	Ask participants to search their network for access to particular skills or resources—discusses value of networks.	Low	30
5	The Invitation	Building Relationships, Organizational Savvy	Foster relationships, bridge generational differences, and transfer learning.	Send selected individuals (such as mentors) a printed invitation to meet and share wisdom.	Low	38
14	To Talk or Not to Talk—That Is the Question	Social Bonds, Impact on Others, Feeling Impact on Others, Building Relationships	Sensitize people to the impact of talking too much or not enough.	Role play "talkers" and "nontalkers" and discuss impact.	Medium	64
26	Swing Set	Building Relationships, Getting Results Through Others	Identify conflicting goals, assumptions and communication that interfere with success of task because of silo thinking.	Group works in department silos and must complete a simulated task.	Low	100

TABLE 6-12 Social Expertness: Collaboration

ACTIVITY NUMBER	ACTIVITY NAME	ALL COMPETENCIES EXHIBITED	PURPOSE	SUMMARY	LEVEL OF DISCLOSURE	PAGE NUMBER
22	States	Emotional and Inner Awareness, Emotional Expression, Collaboration	Identify emotional reactions—Use collaboration to perform task.	Alphabetize states as individuals and as a group.	Low	88
31	Let's Go!	Collaboration, Conflict Resolution	Gives participants a process to use in resolving conflict by focusing on interests.	Teams must resolve a conflict over where to go on vacation by using a process for conflict resolution.	Low	116

TABLE 6-13 Social Expertness: Conflict Resolution

ACTIVITY NUMBER	ACTIVITY NAME	ALL COMPETENCIES EXHIBITED	PURPOSE	SUMMARY	LEVEL OF DISCLOSURE	PAGE NUMBER
10	Your Theme Song	Creating a Positive Work Climate, Conflict Resolution, Emotional Expression	Raise awareness about the tone that people set in their interactions.	Use music to identify and describe tone and how one comes across to others.	Medium	53
30	Judgment Day—Remote Teams	Emotional and Inner Awareness, Conflict Resolution	Examines judgments we make that interfere with our actions toward others.	Groups are given scenarios and asked to list assumptions that come to mind.	Low	113
31	Let's Go!	Collaboration, Conflict Resolution	Gives participants a process to use in resolving conflict by focusing on interests.	Teams must resolve a conflict over where to go on vacation by using a process for conflict resolution.	Low	116
45	The Rebuttal	Respectful Listening, Conflict Resolution	Illustrates difference between respectful listening and rebuttal listening.	Orchestrated debate on contentious issues while observing listening behavior.	Medium	162

TABLE 6-14 Social Expertness: Organizational Savvy

ACTIVITY NUMBER	ACTIVITY NAME	ALL COMPETENCIES EXHIBITED	PURPOSE	SUMMARY	LEVEL OF DISCLOSURE	PAGE NUMBER
1	The Critic	Organizational Savvy, Feeling Impact on Others, Getting Results Through Others, Creating a Positive Work Climate	Read the climate and observe and respond to influencers in a group setting.	A group leader's behavior is deliberately showing favoritism toward one group member and others must determine how to navigate.	Low	27
5	The Invitation	Building Relationships, Organizational Savvy	Foster relationships, bridge generational differences and transfer learning.	Send selected individuals (such as mentors) a printed invitation to meet and share wisdom.	Low	38
21	Look Around	Organizational Savvy	Build observational skills in the moment to enhance one's ability to navigate organizational dynamics.	Participants complete handouts that enhance observation skills during an actual (or orchestrated) meeting.	Medium	86

TABLE 6-15 Personal Influence: Leading Others

ACTIVITY NUMBER	ACTIVITY NAME	ALL COMPETENCIES EXHIBITED	PURPOSE	SUMMARY	LEVEL OF DISCLOSURE	PAGE NUMBER
20	ROYGBIV	Leading Others	Explore and build skill around influence.	A leader must influence the group to align themselves in a particular order.	Low	81
37	How Am I Doing?	Leading Others	Gain direct feedback about one's leadership.	Use interview 360 structure to gain feedback about one's leadership.	High	137
47	Flying High	Leading Others, Feeling Impact on Others	Demonstrates influence of the leader using influence tactics.	Group task of building airplanes is either enhanced or thwarted based on leader behavior.	Low	168

TABLE 6-16 Personal Influence: Creating a Positive Work Climate

ACTIVITY NUMBER	ACTIVITY NAME	ALL COMPETENCIES EXHIBITED	PURPOSE	SUMMARY	LEVEL OF DISCLOSURE	PAGE NUMBER
1	The Critic	Organizational Savvy, Feeling Impact on Others, Getting Results Through Others, Creating a Positive Work Climate	Read the climate and observe and respond to influencers in a group setting.	A group leader's behavior is deliberately showing favoritism toward one group member and others must determine how to navigate.	Low	27
10	Your Theme Song	Creating a Positive Work Climate, Conflict Resolution, Emotional Expression	Raise awareness about the tone that people set in their interactions.	Use music to identify and describe tone and how one comes across to others.	Medium	53
39	Better Method	Creating a Positive Work Climate	Frame language that creates positive climate and tone in teamwork interactions.	Choices of language are given to address various situations and participants select and discuss best language to maintain teamwork.	Low	144
44	Advertisement	Creating a Positive Work Climate	Demonstrate how to create (and destroy) a positive work climate.	Group is asked to create a advertisement—one member either positively or negatively changes the climate of the group.	Low	160

TABLE 6-17 Personal Influence: Getting Results Through Others

ACTIVITY NUMBER	ACTIVITY NAME	ALL COMPETENCIES EXHIBITED	PURPOSE	SUMMARY	LEVEL OF DISCLOSURE	PAGE NUMBER
1	The Critic	Organizational Savvy, Feeling Impact on Others, Getting Results Through Others, Creating a Positive Work Climate	Read the climate and observe and respond to influencers in a group setting.	A group leader's behavior is deliberately showing favoritism toward one group member and others must determine how to navigate.	Low	27
18	Puzzler	Service Orientation, Getting Results Through Others	Examine service orientation and leadership in a challenging group setting.	People are asked to build puzzles with incomplete pieces and without being able to communicate.	Low	76
26	Swing Set	Building Relationships, Getting Results Through Others	Identify conflicting goals, assumptions, and communication that interfere with success of task because of silo thinking.	Group works in department silos and must complete a simulated task.	Low	100

TABLE 6-18 Personal Influence: Self-Confidence

ACTIVITY NUMBER	ACTIVITY NAME	ALL COMPETENCIES EXHIBITED	PURPOSE	SUMMARY	LEVEL OF DISCLOSURE	PAGE NUMBER
8	Your TED Talk	Self-Confidence	Build confidence and examine connection between confidence and influence.	Prepare, videotape, and playback a presentation and receive feedback about confidence.	High	47
46	Confidence Builder	Self-Confidence	Addresses criticism and confidence and the impact criticism can create in some individuals.	Small groups produce a list and the larger group offers criticism—focused discussion about criticism and confidence.	Medium	166

TABLE 6-19 Personal Influence: Initiative and Accountability

ACTIVITY NUMBER	ACTIVITY NAME	ALL COMPETENCIES EXHIBITED	PURPOSE	SUMMARY	LEVEL OF DISCLOSURE	PAGE NUMBER
3	Cups and Ice	Initiative and Accountability, Flexibility, Emotional and Inner Awareness	Explore one's attitude and approach to mundane tasks and recognize that others form opinions based on attitude.	Show videoclip and process specific questions.	Low	33
9	Hot Potato	Initiative and Accountability	Provide guidance and choices when dealing with conflicting priorities especially in team environment.	Simulation of multiple priorities in a team environment to generate discussion of stressors and solutions.	Low	51

FIGURE 7-20 Goal Orientation

ACTIVITY NUMBER	ACTIVITY NAME	ALL COMPETENCIES EXHIBITED	PURPOSE	SUMMARY	LEVEL OF DISCLOSURE	PAGE NUMBER
12	Finish Line!	Goal Orientation	Build awareness and move forward on goals by analyzing steps used to obtain past goals.	Use worksheet to move forward on a present goal.	Low	59
23	Good Enough	Goal Orientation	Provide insight on self-directed goal setting and task achievement.	Worksheet based analysis of one's goal orientation for insight and discussion.	High	90

TABLE 6-21 Personal influence: Optimism

ACTIVITY NUMBER	ACTIVITY NAME	ALL COMPETENCIES EXHIBITED	PURPOSE	SUMMARY	LEVEL OF DISCLOSURE	PAGE NUMBER
16	What Do You Assign to the Pictures of Your Life?	Impact on Others, Optimism	Recognize how thinking affects our view and how optimism and pessimism can be influenced by changing our view.	People assign meaning to pictures based on their initial assumptions and then are asked to change their view.	Low	71
17	Practice Assigning New Thoughts/ Feelings to Something in Your Career	Emotional and Inner Awareness, Optimism, Flexibility, Feeling Impact on Others	Examine our thinking about situations or people and how it affects our behavior.	Analyze current thinking about a person or situation, challenge the thinking, and then predict different behavior.	High	74

TABLE 6-22 Personal Influence: Flexibility

ACTIVITY NUMBER	ACTIVITY NAME	ALL COMPETENCIES EXHIBITED	PURPOSE	SUMMARY	LEVEL OF DISCLOSURE	PAGE NUMBER
3	Cups and Ice	Initiative and Accountability, Flexibility, Emotional and Inner Awareness	Explore one's attitude and approach to mundane tasks and recognize that others form opinions based on attitude.	Show videoclip and process specific questions.	Low	33
17	Practice Assigning New Thoughts/Feelings to Something in Your Career	Emotional and Inner Awareness, Optimism, Flexibility, Feeling Impact on Others	Examine our thinking about situations or people and how it affects our behavior.	Analyze current thinking about a person or situation, challenge the thinking, and then predict different behavior.	High	74
36	Are you Flexible? Let's Find Put	Flexibility, Accurate Self-Assessment	Obtain feedback regarding flexibility.	Use 360-interview format to assess flexibility.	High	133
40	Flexibility—A New Leader Exercise	Flexibility	Create internal guidelines for leaders for balancing fair and consistent actions with the desire to be flexible.	Reflection handout and discussion on leadership flexibility.	High	148

TABLE 6-23 **Mastery of Purpose and Vision: Understanding Purpose and Values**

ACTIVITY NUMBER	ACTIVITY NAME	ALL COMPETENCIES EXHIBITED	PURPOSE	SUMMARY	LEVEL OF DISCLOSURE	PAGE NUMBER
11	If I Had a Billion Dollars	Understanding Purpose and Values	Helps participants clarify and identify what they view as purposeful work.	Handout is used to structure thinking and discussion around purpose.	Low	56
19	Last Name	Understanding Purpose and Values	Reflection on individual purpose and passion.	Handout based reflection to stimulate thinking and discussion around purpose and passion.	Low	78
28	Using Quotations to Anchor Purpose	Understanding Purpose and Values	Clarify intentions using wisdom of others.	Select and discuss quotations that reflect a life or leadership philosophy.	Medium	107
32	A Wondering Mind or a Plan for the Future?	Understanding Purpose and Values	Help people understand and clarify their purpose.	Use daydreams as a source of data regarding purpose.	High	119

TABLE 6-24 Mastery of Purpose and Vision: Taking Actions Toward Purpose

ACTIVITY NUMBER	ACTIVITY NAME	ALL COMPETENCIES EXHIBITED	PURPOSE	SUMMARY	LEVEL OF DISCLOSURE	PAGE NUMBER
33	Actions Speak Louder Than Words	Taking Actions Toward Purpose	Encourage action toward purpose and dreams.	Using handout, define actions that could be taken to explore purpose or dreams.	High	126
49	What Have You Done?	Taking Actions Toward Purpose	Stress value of taking actions toward goals and one's purpose.	Review through a handout the actions one has taken to achieve a particular career path.	High	173

TABLE 6-25 Mastery of Purpose and Vision: Authenticity

ACTIVITY NUMBER	ACTIVITY NAME	ALL COMPETENCIES EXHIBITED	PURPOSE	SUMMARY	LEVEL OF DISCLOSURE	PAGE NUMBER
38	Authenticity —A Reflection	Authenticity	Build refection around authenticity for the purpose of improving it.	Reflection handout and guided discussion on behaviors that lead to authenticity.	High	141
43	Authenticity Explored	Authenticity	Examine actions that are viewed authentically in teamwork and in career advancement.	Capture group thinking and norms around behaviors that are viewed as authentic and inauthentic.	Medium	157

Audience Suitability

The following table provides a method for the trainer or coach to quickly determine if an exercise is suitable for a coaching or web-based learning engagement. All of the exercises were designed for classroom training with groups. You can select activities based on your preference and needs.

TABLE 6-26 Audience Suitability

ACTIVITY NUMBER	ACTIVITY NAME	CLASSROOM/ GROUPS	COACHING	WEB-BASED LEARNING
1	The Critic	X		
2	Know a Guy	X		X
3	Cups and Ice	X		X
4	Fifteen Minutes	X	X	X
5	The Invitation	X	X	
6	Doozie of a Disappointment	X	X	
7	Facebook Feed	X		X
8	Your TED Talk	X		
9	Hot Potato	X		
10	Your Theme Song	X	X	X
11	If I Had a Billion Dollars	X	X	X
12	Finish Line!	X	X	X
13	Selfie Listening	X		
14	To Talk or Not to Talk—That Is the Question	X		
15	Gumball	X		
16	What Do You Assign to the Pictures of Your Life?	X	X	X
17	Practice Assigning New Thoughts/Feelings to Something in Your Career	X	X	
18	Puzzler	X		
19	Last Name	X	X	X
20	ROYGBIV	X		
21	Look Around	X	X	X
22	States	X		
23	Good Enough	X	X	X

ACTIVITY NUMBER	ACTIVITY NAME	CLASSROOM/ GROUPS	COACHING	WEB-BASED LEARNING
24	Reflection Errors—Part 1	X	X	
25	Reflection Errors—Part 2	X	X	
26	Swing Set	X		
27	Restaurant Reviews	X		
28	Using Quotations to Anchor Purpose	X	X	X
29	Academy Award	X	X	
30	Judgment Day—Remote Teams	X		X
31	Let's Go!	X		X
32	A Wondering Mind or a Plan for the Future?	X	X	X
33	Actions Speak Louder Than Words	X	X	X
34	Shoots and Scores	X		
35	Blind Vote	X		X
36	Are You Flexible? Let's Find Out	X	X	
37	How Am I Doing?	X	X	
38	Authenticity—A Reflection	X	X	
39	Better Method	X	X	X
40	Flexibility—A New Leader Exercise	X	X	
41	Help Who?	X		X
42	Reflection on Courage	X	X	
43	Authenticity Explored	X		X
44	Advertisement	X		
45	The Rebuttal	X		
46	Confidence Builder	X		X
47	Flying High	X		
48	Shoe Switch	X		X
49	What have you done?	X	X	
50	Review of Emotional Intelligence Using Quotations	X		X

We have also provided the following tables breaking listing the exercises suitable for coaching and for web based training for quick reference.

Coaching Appropriate Exercises

ACTIVITY NUMBER	ACTIVITY NAME	ALL COMPETENCIES ADDRESSED	PURPOSE	SUMMARY	PAGE NUMBER
4	Fifteen Minutes	Emotional and Inner Awareness, Resilience	Explores perspective and resiliency related to one's skills and also one's failures.	Worksheet provides thought provoking questions around fame and failure in one's life.	35
5	The Invitation	Building Relationships, Organizational Savvy	Foster relationships, bridge generational differences and transfer learning.	Send selected individuals (such as mentors) a printed invitation to meet and share wisdom.	38
6	Doozie of a Disappointment	Resilience	Encourage perspective and strength to overcome a disappointment by recalling past disappointing events.	Recall past disappointments and rate them as they occurred and then with the distance of time and perspective.	41
10	Your Theme Song	Creating a Positive Work Climate, Conflict Resolution, Emotional Expression	Raise awareness about the tone that people set in their interactions.	Use music to identify and describe tone and how one comes across to others.	53
11	If I had a billion dollars...	Understanding Purpose and Values	Helps participants clarify and identify what they view as purposeful work.	Worksheet is used to structure thinking and discussion around purpose.	56
12	Finish Line!	Goal Orientation	Build awareness and move forward on goals by analyzing steps used to obtain past goals.	Use worksheet to move forward on a present goal.	59
16	What Do You Assign to the Pictures of Your Life?	Impact on Others, Optimism	Recognize how thinking affects our view and how optimism and pessimism can be influenced by changing our view.	People assign meaning to pictures based on their initial assumptions and then are asked to change their view.	71

No.	Title	Competency	Objective	Description	Page
17	Practice Assigning New Thoughts/Feelings to Something in Your Career	Emotional and Inner Awareness, Optimism, Flexibility, Feeling Impact on Others	Examine our thinking about situations or people and how it affects our behavior.	Analyze current thinking about a person or situation, challenge the thinking and then predict different behavior.	74
19	Last Name	Understanding Purpose and Values	Reflection on individual purpose and passion.	Worksheet based reflection to stimulate thinking and discussion around purpose and passion.	78
21	Look Around	Organizational Savvy	Build observational skills in the moment to enhance one's ability to navigate organizational dynamics.	Participants complete worksheets that enhance observation skills during an actual (or orchestrated) meeting.	86
23	Good Enough	Goal Orientation	Provide insight on self-directed goal setting and task achievement.	Worksheet based analysis of one's goal orientation for insight and discussion.	90
24	Reflection Errors—Part 1	Accurate Self-Assessment	Identify reflection errors in thinking.	Interview regarding something that is problematic—Watch for reflection errors.	93
25	Reflection Errors—Part 2	Accurate Self-Assessment	Turn reflection errors into productive problem solving behavior.	Imagine different scenarios to problem situations.	98
28	Using Quotations to Anchor Purpose	Understanding Purpose and Values	Clarify intentions using wisdom of others.	Select and discuss quotations that reflect a life or leadership philosophy.	107
32	A Wondering Mind or a Plan for the Future?	Understanding Purpose and Values	Help people understand and clarify their purpose.	Use daydreams as a source of data regarding purpose.	119

Coaching Appropriate Exercises (*Continued*)

ACTIVITY NUMBER	ACTIVITY NAME	ALL COMPETENCIES ADDRESSED	PURPOSE	SUMMARY	PAGE NUMBER
33	Actions Speak Louder Than Words	Taking Actions Toward Purpose	Encourage action toward purpose and dreams.	Using worksheet, define actions that could be taken to explore purpose or dreams.	126
36	Are you Flexible? Let's find out	Flexibility, Accurate Self-Assessment	Obtain feedback regarding flexibility.	Use 360 interview format to assess flexibility.	133
37	How am I doing?	Leading Others	Gain direct feedback about one's leadership.	Use interview 360 structure to gain feedback about one's leadership.	137
38	Authenticity—A Reflection	Authenticity	Build reflection around authenticity for the purpose of improving it.	Reflection worksheet and guided discussion on behaviors that lead to authenticity.	141
39	Better Method	Creating a Positive Work Climate	Frame language that creates positive climate and tone in teamwork interactions.	Choices of language are given to address various situations and participants select and discuss best language to maintain teamwork.	144
40	Flexibility—A New Leader Exercise	Flexibility	Create internal guidelines for leaders for balancing fair and consistent actions with the desire to be flexible.	Reflection worksheet and discussion on leadership flexibility.	148
42	Reflection on Courage	Courage	Increase self-awareness related to one's courage.	Reflection worksheet to create thought and dialogue and goals related to courage.	154
49	What have you done?	Taking Actions Toward Purpose	Stress value of taking actions toward goals and one's purpose.	Review through a worksheet the actions one has taken to achieve a particular career path.	173

Web Based Training Appropriate Exercises

ACTIVITY NUMBER	ACTIVITY NAME	ALL COMPETENCIES ADDRESSED	PURPOSE	SUMMARY	PAGE NUMBER
2	Know a Guy	Building Relationships	Demonstrate the importance of building and nurturing relationships in the workplace.	Ask participants to search their network for access to particular skills or resources—discusses value of networks.	30
3	Cups and Ice	Initiative and Accountability, Flexibility, Emotional and Inner Awareness	Explore one's attitude and approach to mundane tasks and recognize that others form opinions based on attitude.	Show video clip and process specific questions.	33
4	Fifteen Minutes	Emotional and Inner Awareness, Resilience	Explores perspective and resiliency related to one's skills and also one's failures.	Worksheet provides thought provoking questions around fame and failure in one's life.	35
7	Facebook Feed	Impact on Others, Emotional and Inner Awareness, Accurate Self-Assessment	Provides analysis of how we are always sending messages that others are interpreting.	Discussion to analyze the messages we send as if others are interpreting using Facebook as an example.	44
10	Your Theme Song	Creating a Positive Work Climate, Conflict Resolution, Emotional Expression	Raise awareness about the tone that people set in their interactions.	Use music to identify and describe tone and how one comes across to others.	53
11	If I had a billion dollars...	Understanding Purpose and Values	Helps participants clarify and identify what they view as purposeful work.	Worksheet is used to structure thinking and discussion around purpose.	56
12	Finish Line!	Goal Orientation	Build awareness and move forward on goals by analyzing steps used to obtain past goals.	Use worksheet to move forward on a present goal.	59

Web Based Training Appropriate Exercises (*Continued*)

ACTIVITY NUMBER	ACTIVITY NAME	ALL COMPETENCIES ADDRESSED	PURPOSE	SUMMARY	PAGE NUMBER
16	What Do You Assign to the Pictures of Your Life?	Impact on Others, Optimism	Recognize how thinking affects our view and how optimism and pessimism can be influenced by changing our view.	People assign meaning to pictures based on their initial assumptions and then are asked to change their view.	71
19	Last Name	Understanding Purpose and Values	Reflection on individual purpose and passion.	Worksheet based reflection to stimulate thinking and discussion around purpose and passion.	78
21	Look Around	Organizational Savvy	Build observational skills in the moment to enhance one's ability to navigate organizational dynamics.	Participants complete worksheets that enhance observation skills during an actual (or orchestrated) meeting.	86
23	Good Enough	Goal Orientation	Provide insight on self-directed goal setting and task achievement.	Worksheet based analysis of one's goal orientation for insight and discussion.	90
28	Using Quotations to Anchor Purpose	Understanding Purpose and Values	Clarify intentions using wisdom of others.	Select and discuss quotations that reflect a life or leadership philosophy.	107
30	Judgment Day—Remote Teams	Emotional and Inner Awareness, Conflict Resolution	Examines judgments we make that interfere with our actions toward others.	Groups are given scenarios and asked to list assumptions that come to mind.	113
31	Let's Go!	Collaboration, Conflict Resolution	Gives participants a process to use in resolving conflict by focusing on interests.	Teams must resolve a conflict over where to go on vacation by using a process for conflict resolution.	116
32	A Wondering Mind or a Plan for the Future?	Understanding Purpose and Values	Help people understand and clarify their purpose.	Use daydreams as a source of data regarding purpose.	119

33	Actions Speak Louder Than Words	Encourage action toward purpose and dreams.	Taking Actions Toward Purpose	Using worksheet, define actions that could be taken to explore purpose or dreams.	126
35	Blind Vote	Examine courage and its value to leadership positions and organizations.	Courage	Scenarios presented with various resolutions, group rates and discusses resolutions based on courage.	130
39	Better Method	Frame language that creates positive climate and tone in teamwork interactions.	Creating a Positive Work Climate	Choices of language are given to address various situations and participants select and discuss best language to maintain teamwork.	144
41	Help Who?	Explore importance and what service orientation looks like when dealing with peers.	Service Orientation	Use scenarios with various options to select the best course of action and discuss reasons why.	151
43	Authenticity Explored	Examine actions that are viewed authentically in teamwork and in career advancement.	Authenticity	Capture group thinking and norms around behaviors that are viewed as authentic and inauthentic.	157
46	Confidence Builder	Addresses criticism and confidence and the impact criticism can create in some individuals.	Self-Confidence	Small groups produce a list and the larger group offers criticism—focused discussion about criticism and confidence.	166
48	Shoe Switch	Encourages empathy when reviewing situations in the workplace.	Feeling Impact on Others	Work with a partner to review a situation that didn't go well to determine how the other party may have been reacting.	171
50	Review of Emotional Intelligence Using Quotations	Reinforce concepts of emotional intelligence.	Review of Several Areas of Emotional Intelligence, Emotional and Inner Awareness	Use quotations as part of a review of concepts of emotional intelligence.	176

Content Area Activities

Some exercises are most appropriate for certain content areas, for example, teamwork or conflict resolution. We have provided the following table to allow for a quick point of reference for each identified content area.

TABLE 6-27 Content Area Activities

ACTIVITY NUMBER	ACTIVITY NAME	LEADERSHIP DEVELOPMENT	TEAMWORK	COMMUNICATIONS	CONFLICT RESOLUTION	CUSTOMER SERVICE	INTERPERSONAL SKILLS	CAREER DEVELOPMENT
1	The Critic	X						
2	Know a Guy	X	X	X		X		
3	Cups and Ice		X					X
4	Fifteen Minutes	X	X				X	X
5	The Invitation	X	X	X	X			
6	Doozie of a Disappointment	X						X
7	Facebook Feed	X	X	X			X	
8	Your TED Talk	X		X			X	X
9	Hot Potato	X	X					
10	Your Theme Song	X	X	X	X	X		
11	If I Had a Billion Dollars	X						X
12	Finish Line!	X	X					X
13	Selfie Listening	X	X	X	X		X	
14	To Talk or Not to Talk—That Is the Question	X		X	X	X		X
15	Gumball	X	X	X	X			
16	What Do You Assign to the Pictures of Your Life?	X			X	X		X
17	Practice Assigning New Thoughts/ Feelings to Something in Your Career	X	X		X		X	X
18	Puzzler	X	X			X		
19	Last Name	X						X

ACTIVITY NUMBER	ACTIVITY NAME	LEADERSHIP DEVELOPMENT	TEAMWORK	COMMUNICATIONS	CONFLICT RESOLUTION	CUSTOMER SERVICE	INTERPERSONAL SKILLS	CAREER DEVELOPMENT
20	ROYGBIV	X			X		X	
21	Look Around	X	X		X		X	
22	States	X	X					
23	Good Enough	X	X					X
24	Reflection Errors—Part 1	X	X		X		X	
25	Reflection Errors—Part 2	X	X		X		X	
26	Swing Set	X	X	X			X	
27	Restaurant Reviews	X	X	X		X	X	
28	Using Quotations to Anchor Purpose	X	X		X		X	
29	Academy Award	X	X				X	
30	Judgment Day—Remote Teams	X	X		X		X	
31	Let's Go!	X	X		X		X	
32	A Wondering Mind or a Plan for the Future?	X						X
33	Actions Speak Louder Than Words	X						X
34	Shoots and Scores	X						X
35	Blind Vote	X	X		X			
36	Are You Flexible? Let's Find Out	X						X
37	How Am I Doing?	X						
38	Authenticity—A Reflection	X	X					X
39	Better Method	X	X	X	X		X	
40	Flexibility—A New Leader Exercise	X						
41	Help Who?			X		X		
42	Reflection on Courage	X			X			
43	Authenticity Explored	X	X					X

TABLE 6-27 *Continued*

ACTIVITY NUMBER	ACTIVITY NAME	LEADERSHIP DEVELOPMENT	TEAMWORK	COMMUNICATIONS	CONFLICT RESOLUTION	CUSTOMER SERVICE	INTERPERSONAL SKILLS	CAREER DEVELOPMENT
44	Advertisement	X	X	X				
45	The Rebuttal	X	X	X	X		X	
46	Confidence Builder	X					X	X
47	Flying High	X						
48	Shoe Switch	X	X			X		
49	What have you done?	X						X
50	Review of Emotional Intelligence Using Quotations	X	X					

TABLE 6.27A Leadership Development

ACTIVITY NUMBER	ACTIVITY NAME	PAGE NUMBER	ALL COMPETENCIES EXHIBITED	PURPOSE	SUMMARY
1	The Critic	27	Organizational Savvy, Feeling Impact on Others, Getting Results Through Others, Creating a Positive Work Climate	Read the climate and observe and respond to influencers in a group setting.	A group leader's behavior is deliberately showing favoritism toward one group member, and others must determine how to navigate.
2	Know a Guy	30	Building Relationships	Demonstrate the importance of building and nurturing relationships in the workplace.	Ask participants to search their network for access to particular skills or resources; discusses value of networks.
4	Fifteen Minutes	35	Emotional and Inner Awareness, Resilience	Explores perspective and resiliency related to one's skills and also one's failures.	Handout provides thought-provoking questions around fame and failure in one's life.
5	The Invitation	38	Building Relationships, Organizational Savvy	Foster relationships, bridge generational differences, and transfer learning.	Send selected individuals (such as mentors) a printed invitation to meet and share wisdom.
6	Doozie of a Disappointment	41	Resilience	Encourage perspective and strength to overcome a disappointment by recalling past disappointing events.	Recall past disappointments and rate them as they occurred and then with the distance of time and perspective.
7	Facebook Feed	44	Impact on Others, Emotional and Inner Awareness, Accurate Self-Assessment	Provides analysis of how we are always sending messages that others are interpreting.	Discussion to analyze the messages we send as if others are interpreting using Facebook as an example.

TABLE 6.27A *Continued*

ACTIVITY NUMBER	ACTIVITY NAME	PAGE NUMBER	ALL COMPETENCIES EXHIBITED	PURPOSE	SUMMARY
8	Your TED Talk	47	Self-Confidence	Build confidence and examine connection between confidence and influence.	Prepare, videotape, and playback a presentation and receive feedback about confidence.
9	Hot Potato	51	Initiative and Accountability	Provide guidance and choices when dealing with conflicting priorities especially in team environment.	Simulation of multiple priorities in a team environment to generate discussion of stressors and solutions.
10	Your Theme Song	53	Creating a Positive Work Climate, Conflict Resolution, Emotional Expression	Raise awareness about the tone that people set in their interactions.	Use music to identify and describe tone and how one comes across to others.
11	If I Had a Billion Dollars	56	Understanding Purpose and Values	Helps participants clarify and identify what they view as purposeful work.	Handout is used to structure thinking and discussion around purpose.
12	Finish Line!	59	Goal Orientation	Build awareness and move forward on goals by analyzing steps used to obtain past goals.	Use handout to move forward on a present goal.
13	Selfie Listening	62	Respectful Listening	Learn listening and empathy skills and the impact they have on others.	Orchestrate listening and nonlistening behaviors and solicit discussion regarding impact as well as behavior.
14	To Talk or Not to Talk—That Is the Question	64	Social Bonds, Impact on Others, Feeling Impact on Others, Building Relationships	Sensitize people to the impact of talking too much or not enough.	Role play "talkers" and "nontalkers" and discuss impact.
15	Gumball	68	Emotional Expression, Collaboration	Participants identify their typical M.O. related to stressful tasks.	Participants asks to complete a task with built in stressors.

#	Title	Competency	Purpose	Description
16	What Do You Assign to the Pictures of Your Life?	Impact on Others, Optimism	Recognize how thinking affects our view and how optimism and pessimism can be influenced by changing our view.	People assign meaning to pictures based on their initial assumptions and then are asked to change their view.
17	Practice Assigning New Thoughts/Feelings to Something in Your Career	Emotional and Inner Awareness, Optimism, Flexibility, Feeling Impact on Others	Examine our thinking about situations or people and how it affects our behavior.	Analyze current thinking about a person or situation, challenge the thinking, and then predict different behavior.
18	Puzzler	Service Orientation, Getting Results Through Others	Examine service orientation and leadership in a challenging group setting.	People are asked to build puzzles with incomplete pieces and without being able to communicate.
19	Last Name	Understanding Purpose and Values	Reflection on individual purpose and passion.	Handout-based reflection to stimulate thinking and discussion around purpose and passion.
20	ROYGBIV	Leading Others	Explore and build skill around influence.	A leader must influence the group to align themselves in a particular order.
21	Look Around	Organizational Savvy	Build observational skills in the moment to enhance one's ability to navigate organizational dynamics.	Participants complete handouts that enhance observation skills during an actual (or orchestrated) meeting.
22	States	Emotional and Inner Awareness, Emotional Expression, Collaboration	Identify emotional reactions. Use collaboration to perform task.	Recite alphabet backward as individuals and as a group.
23	Good Enough	Goal Orientation	Provide insight on self-directed goal setting and task achievement.	Handout-based analysis of one's goal orientation for insight and discussion.

TABLE 6.27A *Continued*

ACTIVITY NUMBER	ACTIVITY NAME	PAGE NUMBER	ALL COMPETENCIES EXHIBITED	PURPOSE	SUMMARY
24	Reflection Errors—Part 1	93	Accurate Self-Assessment	Identify reflection errors in thinking.	Interview regarding something that is problematic. Watch for reflection errors.
25	Reflection Errors—Part 2	98	Accurate Self-Assessment	Turn reflection errors into productive problem-solving behavior.	Imagine different scenarios to problem situations.
26	Swing Set	100	Building Relationships, Getting Results Through Others	Identify conflicting goals, assumptions, and communication that interfere with success of task because of silo thinking.	Group works in department silos and must complete a simulated task.
27	Restaurant Reviews	104	Feeling Impact on Others, Impact on Others	Identify the reaction and impact that behaviors cause in others.	Role play specific behaviors when performing a group task and analyze group dynamic.
28	Using Quotations to Anchor Purpose	107	Understanding Purpose and Values	Clarify intentions using wisdom of others.	Select and discuss quotations that reflect a life or leadership philosophy.
29	Academy Award	109	Emotional Inner Awareness	Identify false rational beliefs that impact one's behavior.	An assigned actor and challenger role play to demonstrate the impact of irrational thinking on behavior.
30	Judgment Day—Remote Teams	113	Emotional and Inner Awareness, Conflict Resolution	Examines judgments we make that interfere with our actions toward others.	Groups are given scenarios and asked to list assumptions that come to mind.
31	Let's Go!	116	Collaboration, Conflict Resolution	Gives participants a process to use in resolving conflict by focusing on interests.	Teams must resolve a conflict over where to go on vacation by using a process for conflict resolution.

#	Activity	Page	Topic	Objective	Description
32	A Wondering Mind or a Plan for the Future?	119	Understanding Purpose and Values	Help people understand and clarify their purpose.	Use daydreams as a source of data regarding purpose.
33	Actions Speak Louder Than Words	126	Taking Actions Toward Purpose	Encourage action toward purpose and dreams.	Using handout, define actions that could be taken to explore purpose or dreams.
34	Shoots and Scores	128	Resilience	Examine emotion and resilience related to a difficult task.	Group is asked to perform a task that requires them to think differently and identify what is affecting their performance.
35	Blind Vote	130	Courage	Examine courage and its value to leadership positions and organizations.	Scenarios presented with various resolutions; group rates and discusses resolutions based on courage.
36	Are You Flexible? Let's Find Out	133	Flexibility, Accurate Self-Assessment	Obtain feedback regarding flexibility.	Use 360-interview format to assess flexibility.
37	How Am I Doing?	137	Leading Others	Gain direct feedback about one's leadership.	Use interview 360 structure to gain feedback about one's leadership.
38	Authenticity—A Reflection	141	Authenticity	Build reflection around authenticity for the purpose of improving it.	Reflection handout and guided discussion on behaviors that lead to authenticity.
39	Better Method	144	Creating a Positive Work Climate	Frame language that creates positive climate and tone in teamwork interactions.	Choices of language are given to address various situations and participants select and discuss best language to maintain teamwork

TABLE 6.27A *Continued*

ACTIVITY NUMBER	ACTIVITY NAME	PAGE NUMBER	ALL COMPETENCIES EXHIBITED	PURPOSE	SUMMARY
40	Flexibility—A New Leader Exercise	148	Flexibility	Create internal guidelines for leaders for balancing fair and consistent actions with the desire to be flexible.	Reflection handout and discussion on leadership flexibility.
42	Reflection on Courage	154	Courage	Increase self-awareness related to one's courage.	Reflection handout to create thought and dialogue and goals related to courage.
43	Authenticity Explored	157	Authenticity	Examine actions that are viewed authentically in teamwork and in career advancement.	Capture group thinking and norms around behaviors that are viewed as authentic and inauthentic.
44	Advertisement	160	Creating a Positive Work Climate	Demonstrate how to create (and destroy) a positive work climate.	Group is asked to create an advertisement. One member either positively or negatively changes the climate of the group.
45	The Rebuttal	162	Respectful Listening, Conflict Resolution	Illustrates difference between respectful listening and rebuttal listening.	Orchestrated debate on contentious issues while observing listening behavior.
46	Confidence Builder	166	Self-Confidence	Addresses criticism and confidence and the impact criticism can create in some individuals.	Small groups produce a list and the larger group offers criticism. Focused discussion about criticism and confidence.
47	Flying High	168	Leading Others, Feeling Impact on Others	Demonstrates influence of the leader using influence tactics.	Group task of building airplanes is either enhanced or thwarted based on leader behavior.

		PAGE NUMBER		PURPOSE	SUMMARY
48	Shoe Switch	171	Feeling Impact on Others	Encourages empathy when reviewing situations in the workplace.	Work with a partner to review a situation that didn't go well to determine how the other party may have been reacting.
49	What Have You Done?	173	Taking Actions Toward Purpose	Stress value of taking actions toward goals and one's purpose.	Review through a handout the actions one has taken to achieve a particular career path.
50	Review of Emotional Intelligence Using Quotations	176	Review of Several Areas of Emotional Intelligence, Self-Awareness: Emotional and Inner Awareness	Reinforce concepts of emotional intelligence.	Use quotations as part of a review of concepts of emotional intelligence.

TABLE 6-27B Teamwork

ACTIVITY NUMBER	ACTIVITY NAME	PAGE NUMBER	ALL COMPETENCIES EXHIBITED	PURPOSE	SUMMARY
2	Know a Guy	30	Building Relationships	Demonstrate the importance of building and nurturing relationships in the workplace.	Ask participants to search their network for access to particular skills or resources. Discusses value of networks.
3	Cups and Ice	33	Initiative and Accountability, Flexibility, Emotional and Inner Awareness	Explore one's attitude and approach to mundane tasks and recognize that others form opinions based on attitude.	Show videoclip and process specific questions.
4	Fifteen Minutes	35	Emotional and Inner Awareness, Resilience	Explores perspective and resiliency related to one's skills and also one's failures.	Handout provides thought-provoking questions around fame and failure in one's life.
5	The Invitation	38	Building Relationships, Organizational Savvy	Foster relationships, bridge generational differences, and transfer learning.	Send selected individuals (such as mentors) a printed invitation to meet and share wisdom.

TABLE 6.27B *Continued*

ACTIVITY NUMBER	ACTIVITY NAME	PAGE NUMBER	ALL COMPETENCIES EXHIBITED	PURPOSE	SUMMARY
7	Facebook Feed	44	Impact on Others, Emotional and Inner Awareness, Accurate Self-Assessment	Provides analysis of how we are always sending messages that others are interpreting.	Discussion to analyze the messages we send as if others are interpreting using Facebook as an example.
9	Hot Potato	51	Initiative and Accountability	Provide guidance and choices when dealing with conflicting priorities especially in team environment.	Simulation of multiple priorities in a team environment to generate discussion of stressors and solutions.
10	Your Theme Song	53	Creating a Positive Work Climate, Conflict Resolution, Emotional Expression	Raise awareness about the tone that people set in their interactions.	Use music to identify and describe tone and how one comes across to others.
12	Finish Line!	59	Goal Orientation	Build awareness and move forward on goals by analyzing steps used to obtain past goals.	Use handout to move forward on a present goal.
13	Selfie Listening	62	Respectful Listening	Learn listening and empathy skills and the impact they have on others.	Orchestrate listening and nonlistening behaviors and solicit discussion regarding impact as well as behavior.
15	Gumball	68	Emotional Expression, Collaboration	Participants identify their typical M.O. related to stressful tasks	Participants asks to complete a task with built in stressors
17	Practice Assigning New Thoughts/ Feelings to Something in Your Career	74	Emotional and Inner Awareness, Optimism, Flexibility, Feeling Impact on Others	Examine our thinking about situations or people and how it affects our behavior.	Analyze current thinking about a person or situation, challenge the thinking, and then predict different behavior.

#	Name	Competencies	Objective	Activity
18	Puzzler	Service Orientation, Getting Results Through Others	Examine service orientation and leadership in a challenging group setting.	People are asked to build puzzles with incomplete pieces and without being able to communicate.
21	Look Around	Organizational Savvy	Build observational skills in the moment to enhance one's ability to navigate organizational dynamics.	Participants complete handouts that enhance observation skills during an actual (or orchestrated) meeting.
22	States	Emotional and Inner Awareness, Emotional Expression, Collaboration	Identify emotional reactions. Use collaboration to perform task.	Recite alphabet backward as individuals and as a group.
23	Good Enough	Goal Orientation	Provide insight on self-directed goal setting and task achievement.	Handout-based analysis of one's goal orientation for insight and discussion.
24	Reflection Errors—Part 1	Accurate Self-Assessment	Identify reflection errors in thinking.	Interview regarding something that is problematic. Watch for reflection errors.
25	Reflection Errors—Part 2	Accurate Self-Assessment	Turn reflection errors into productive problem-solving behavior.	Imagine different scenarios to problem situations.
26	Swing Set	Building Relationships, Getting Results Through Others	Identify conflicting goals, assumptions, and communication that interfere with success of task because of silo thinking.	Group works in department silos and must complete a simulated task.
27	Restaurant Reviews	Feeling Impact on Others, Impact on Others	Identify the reaction and impact that behaviors cause in others.	Role play specific behaviors when performing a group task and analyze group dynamic.

TABLE 6.27A *Continued*

ACTIVITY NUMBER	ACTIVITY NAME	PAGE NUMBER	ALL COMPETENCIES EXHIBITED	PURPOSE	SUMMARY
28	Using Quotations to Anchor Purpose	107	Understanding Purpose and Values	Clarify intentions using wisdom of others.	Select and discuss quotations that reflect a life or leadership philosophy.
29	Academy Award	109	Emotional Inner Awareness	Identify false rational beliefs that impact one's behavior.	An assigned actor and challenger role play to demonstrate the impact of irrational thinking on behavior.
30	Judgment Day—Remote Teams	113	Emotional and Inner Awareness, Conflict Resolution	Examines judgments we make that interfere with our actions toward others.	Groups are given scenarios and asked to list assumptions that come to mind.
31	Let's Go!	116	Collaboration, Conflict Resolution	Gives participants a process to use in resolving conflict by focusing on interests.	Teams must resolve a conflict over where to go on vacation by using a process for conflict resolution.
35	Blind Vote	130	Courage	Examine courage and its value to leadership positions and organizations.	Scenarios presented with various resolutions. Group rates and discusses resolutions based on courage.
38	Authenticity—A Reflection	141	Authenticity	Build reflection around authenticity for the purpose of improving it.	Reflection handout and guided discussion on behaviors that lead to authenticity.
39	Better Method	144	Creating a Positive Work Climate	Frame language that creates positive climate and tone in teamwork interactions.	Choices of language are given to address various situations and participants select and discuss best language to maintain teamwork.

41	Help Who?	Service Orientation	Explore importance and what service orientation looks like when dealing with peers.	Use scenarios with various options to select the best course of action and discuss reasons why.
43	Authenticity Explored	Authenticity	Examine actions that are viewed authentically in teamwork and in career advancement.	Capture group thinking and norms around behaviors that are viewed as authentic and inauthentic.
44	Advertisement	Creating a Positive Work Climate	Demonstrate how to create (and destroy) a positive work climate.	Group is asked to create a advertisement. One member either positively or negatively changes the climate of the group.
45	The Rebuttal	Respectful Listening, Conflict Resolution	Illustrates difference between respectful listening and rebuttal listening.	Orchestrated debate on contentious issues while observing listening behavior.
48	Shoe Switch	Feeling Impact on Others	Encourages empathy when reviewing situations in the workplace.	Work with a partner to review a situation that didn't go well to determine how the other party may have been reacting.
50	Review of Emotional Intelligence Using Quotations	Review of Several Areas of Emotional Intelligence, Emotional and Inner Awareness	Reinforce concepts of emotional intelligence.	Use quotations as part of a review of concepts of emotional intelligence.

TABLE 6-27c Communications

ACTIVITY NUMBER	ACTIVITY NAME	PAGE NUMBER	ALL COMPETENCIES EXHIBITED	PURPOSE	SUMMARY
2	Know a Guy	30	Building Relationships	Demonstrate the importance of building and nurturing relationships in the workplace.	Ask participants to search their network for access to particular skills or resources. Discusses value of networks.
5	The Invitation	38	Building Relationships, Organizational Savvy	Foster relationships, bridge generational differences, and transfer learning.	Send selected individuals (such as mentors) a printed invitation to meet and share wisdom.
7	Facebook Feed	44	Impact on Others, Emotional and Inner Awareness, Accurate Self-Assessment	Provides analysis of how we are always sending messages that others are interpreting.	Discussion to analyze the messages we send as if others are interpreting using Facebook as an example.
8	Your TED Talk	47	Self-Confidence	Build confidence and examine connection between confidence and influence.	Prepare, video tape, and playback a presentation and receive feedback about confidence.
10	Your Theme Song	53	Creating a Positive Work Climate, Conflict Resolution, Emotional Expression	Raise awareness about the tone that people set in their interactions.	Use music to identify and describe tone and how one comes across to others.
13	Selfie Listening	62	Respectful Listening	Learn listening and empathy skills and the impact they have on others.	Orchestrate listening and nonlistening behaviors and solicit discussion regarding impact as well as behavior.
14	To Talk or Not to Talk—That Is the Question	64	Social Bonds, Impact on Others, Feeling Impact on Others, Building Relationships	Sensitize people to the impact of talking too much or not enough.	Role play "talkers" and "nontalkers" and discuss impact.

15	Gumball	68	Emotional Expression, Collaboration	Participants identify their typical M.O. related to stressful tasks.	Participants asks to complete a task with built in stressors.
26	Swing Set	100	Building Relationships, Getting Results Through Others	Identify conflicting goals, assumptions, and communication that interfere with success of task because of silo thinking.	Group works in department silos and must complete a simulated task.
27	Restaurant Reviews	104	Feeling Impact on Others, Impact on Others	Identify the reaction and impact that behaviors cause in others.	Role play specific behaviors when performing a group task and analyze group dynamic.
39	Better Method	144	Creating a Positive Work Climate	Frame language that creates positive climate and tone in teamwork interactions.	Choices of language are given to address various situations and participants select and discuss best language to maintain teamwork.
44	Advertisement	160	Creating a Positive Work Climate	Demonstrate how to create (and destroy) a positive work climate.	Group is asked to create a advertisement. One member either positively or negatively changes the climate of the group.
45	The Rebuttal	162	Respectful Listening, Conflict Resolution	Illustrates difference between respectful listening and rebuttal listening.	Orchestrated debate on contentious issues while observing listening behavior.

TABLE 6-27D Conflict Resolution

ACTIVITY NUMBER	ACTIVITY NAME	PAGE NUMBER	ALL COMPETENCIES EXHIBITED	PURPOSE	SUMMARY
5	The Invitation	38	Building Relationships, Organizational Savvy	Foster relationships, bridge generational differences, and transfer learning.	Send selected individuals (such as mentors) a printed invitation to meet and share wisdom.
10	Your Theme Song	53	Creating a Positive Work Climate, Conflict Resolution, Emotional Expression	Raise awareness about the tone that people set in their interactions.	Use music to identify and describe tone and how one comes across to others.
13	Selfie Listening	62	Respectful Listening	Learn listening and empathy skills and the impact they have on others.	Orchestrate listening and nonlistening behaviors and solicit discussion regarding impact as well as behavior.
14	To Talk or Not to Talk—That Is the Question	64	Social Bonds, Impact on Others, Feeling Impact on Others, Building Relationships	Sensitize people to the impact of talking too much or not enough.	Role play "talkers" and "non-talkers" and discuss impact.
15	Gumball	68	Emotional Expression, Collaboration	Participants identify their typical M.O. related to stressful tasks.	Participants asks to complete a task with built in stressors.
16	What Do You Assign to the Pictures of Your Life?	71	Impact on Others, Optimism	Recognize how thinking affects our view and how optimism and pessimism can be influenced by changing our view.	People assign meaning to pictures based on their initial assumptions and then are asked to change their view.
17	Practice Assigning New Thoughts/ Feelings to Something in Your Career	74	Emotional and Inner Aware-ness, Optimism, Flexibility, Feeling Impact on Others	Examine our thinking about situations or people and how it affects our behavior.	Analyze current thinking about a person or situation, challenge the thinking , and then predict different behavior.

20	ROYGBIV	Leading Others	Explore and build skill around influence.	A leader must influence the group to align themselves in a particular order.
21	Look Around	Organizational Savvy	Build observational skills in the moment to enhance one's ability to navigate organizational dynamics.	Participants complete handouts that enhance observation skills during an actual (or orchestrated) meeting.
24	Reflection Errors—Part 1	Accurate Self-Assessment	Identify reflection errors in thinking.	Interview regarding something that is problematic. Watch for reflection errors.
25	Reflection Errors—Part 2	Accurate Self-Assessment	Turn reflection errors into productive problem-solving behavior.	Imagine different scenarios to problem situations.
28	Using Quotations to Anchor Purpose	Understanding Purpose and Values	Clarify intentions using wisdom of others.	Select and discuss quotations that reflect a life or leadership philosophy.
30	Judgment Day—Remote Teams	Emotional and Inner Awareness, Conflict Resolution	Examines judgments we make that interfere with our actions toward others.	Groups are given scenarios and asked to list assumptions that come to mind.
31	Let's Go!	Collaboration, Conflict Resolution	Gives participants a process to use in resolving conflict by focusing on interests.	Teams must resolve a conflict over where to go on vacation by using a process for conflict resolution.
35	Blind Vote	Courage	Examine courage and its value to leadership positions and organizations.	Scenarios presented with various resolutions. Group rates and discusses resolutions based on courage.

TABLE 6.27D *Continued*

ACTIVITY NUMBER	ACTIVITY NAME	PAGE NUMBER	ALL COMPETENCIES EXHIBITED	PURPOSE	SUMMARY
39	Better Method	144	Creating a Positive Work Climate	Frame language that creates positive climate and tone in teamwork interactions.	Choices of language are given to address various situations and participants select and discuss best language to maintain teamwork.
42	Reflection on Courage	154	Courage	Increase self-awareness related to one's courage.	Reflection handout to create thought and dialogue and goals related to courage.
45	The Rebuttal	162	Respectful Listening, Conflict Resolution	Illustrates difference between respectful listening and rebuttal listening.	Orchestrated debate on contentious issues while observing listening behavior.

TABLE 6-27E **Customer Service**

ACTIVITY NUMBER	ACTIVITY NAME	PAGE NUMBER	ALL COMPETENCIES EXHIBITED	PURPOSE	SUMMARY
2	Know a Guy	30	Building Relationships	Demonstrate the importance of building and nurturing relationships in the workplace.	Ask participants to search their network for access to particular skills or resources. Discusses value of networks.
10	Your Theme Song	53	Creating a Positive Work Climate, Conflict Resolution, Emotional Expression	Raise awareness about the tone that people set in their interactions.	Use music to identify and describe tone and how one comes across to others.
14	To Talk or Not to Talk—That Is the Question	64	Social Bonds, Impact on Others, Feeling Impact on Others, Building Relationships	Sensitize people to the impact of talking too much or not enough.	Role play "talkers" and "nontalkers" and discuss impact.
16	What Do You Assign to the Pictures of Your Life?	71	Impact on Others, Optimism	Recognize how thinking affects our view and how optimism and pessimism can be influenced by changing our view.	People assign meaning to pictures based on their initial assumptions and then are asked to change their view.

ACTIVITY NUMBER	ACTIVITY NAME	PAGE NUMBER	ALL COMPETENCIES EXHIBITED	PURPOSE	SUMMARY
18	Puzzler	76	Service Orientation, Getting Results Through Others	Examine service orientation and leadership in a challenging group setting.	People are asked to build puzzles with incomplete pieces and without being able to communicate.
27	Restaurant Reviews	104	Feeling Impact on Others, Impact on Others	Identify the reaction and impact that behaviors cause in others.	Role play specific behaviors when performing a group task and analyze group dynamic.
41	Help Who?	151	Service Orientation	Explore importance and what service orientation looks like when dealing with peers.	Use scenarios with various options to select the best course of action and discuss reasons why.
48	Shoe Switch	171	Feeling Impact on Others	Encourages empathy when reviewing situations in the workplace.	Work with a partner to review a situation that didn't go well to determine how the other party may have been reacting.

TABLE 6-27F Interpersonal Skills

ACTIVITY NUMBER	ACTIVITY NAME	PAGE NUMBER	ALL COMPETENCIES EXHIBITED	PURPOSE	SUMMARY
4	Fifteen Minutes	35	Emotional and Inner Awareness, Resilience	Explores perspective and resiliency related to one's skills and also one's failures.	Handout provides thought provoking questions around fame and failure in one's life.
7	Facebook Feed	44	Impact on Others, Emotional and Inner Awareness, Accurate Self-Assessment	Provides analysis of how we are always sending messages that others are interpreting.	Discussion to analyze the messages we send as if others are interpreting using Facebook as an example.
8	Your TED Talk	47	Self-Confidence	Build confidence and examine connection between confidence and influence.	Prepare, videotape, and playback a presentation and receive feedback about confidence.

TABLE 6.27F *Continued*

ACTIVITY NUMBER	ACTIVITY NAME	PAGE NUMBER	ALL COMPETENCIES EXHIBITED	PURPOSE	SUMMARY
13	Selfie Listening	62	Respectful Listening	Learn listening and empathy skills and the impact they have on others.	Orchestrate listening and nonlistening behaviors and solicit discussion regarding impact as well as behavior.
17	Practice Assigning New Thoughts/ Feelings to Something in Your Career	74	Emotional and Inner Awareness, Optimism, Flexibility, Feeling Impact on Others	Examine our thinking about situations or people and how it affects our behavior.	Analyze current thinking about a person or situation, challenge the thinking, and then predict different behavior.
20	ROYGBIV	81	Leading Others	Explore and build skill around influence.	A leader must influence the group to align themselves in a particular order.
21	Look Around	86	Organizational Savvy	Build observational skills in the moment to enhance one's ability to navigate organizational dynamics.	Participants complete hand-outs that enhance observation skills during an actual (or orchestrated) meeting.
24	Reflection Errors—Part 1	93	Accurate Self-Assessment	Identify reflection errors in thinking.	Interview regarding something that is problematic. Watch for reflection errors.
25	Reflection Errors—Part 2	98	Accurate Self-Assessment	Turn reflection errors into productive problem-solving behavior.	Imagine different scenarios to problem situations.
26	Swing Set	100	Building Relationships, Getting Results Through Others	Identify conflicting goals, assumptions, and communication that interfere with success of task because of silo thinking.	Group works in department silos and must complete a simulated task.
27	Restaurant Reviews	104	Feeling Impact on Others, Impact on Others	Identify the reaction and impact that behaviors cause in others.	Role play specific behaviors when performing a group task and analyze group dynamic.

#	Activity	Page	Skill	Description	Activity Detail
28	Using Quotations to Anchor Purpose	107	Understanding Purpose and Values	Clarify intentions using wisdom of others.	Select and discuss quotations that reflect a life or leadership philosophy.
29	Academy Award	109	Emotional Inner Awareness	Identify false rational beliefs that impact one's behavior.	An assigned actor and challenger role play to demonstrate the impact of irrational thinking on behavior.
30	Judgment Day—Remote Teams	113	Emotional and Inner Awareness, Conflict Resolution	Examines judgments we make that interfere with our actions toward others.	Groups are given scenarios and asked to list assumptions that come to mind.
31	Let's Go!	116	Collaboration, Conflict Resolution	Gives participants a process to use in resolving conflict by focusing on interests.	Teams must resolve a conflict over where to go on vacation by using a process for conflict resolution.
39	Better Method	144	Creating a Positive Work Climate	Frame language that creates positive climate and tone in teamwork interactions.	Choices of language are given to address various situations and participants select and discuss best language to maintain teamwork.
45	The Rebuttal	162	Respectful Listening, Conflict Resolution	Illustrates difference between respectful listening and rebuttal listening.	Orchestrated debate on contentious issues while observing listening behavior.
46	Confidence Builder	166	Self-Confidence	Addresses criticism and confidence and the impact criticism can create in some individuals.	Small groups produce a list and the larger group offers criticism. Focused discussion about criticism and confidence.

TABLE 6-27G Career Development

ACTIVITY NUMBER	ACTIVITY NAME	PAGE NUMBER	ALL COMPETENCIES EXHIBITED	PURPOSE	SUMMARY
3	Cups and Ice	33	Initiative and Accountability, Flexibility, Emotional and Inner Awareness	Explore one's attitude and approach to mundane tasks and recognize that others form opinions based on attitude.	Show videoclip and process specific questions.
4	Fifteen Minutes	35	Emotional and Inner Awareness, Resilience	Explores perspective and resiliency related to one's skills and also one's failures.	Handout provides thought provoking questions around fame and failure in one's life.
6	Doozie of a Disappointment	41	Resilience	Encourage perspective and strength to overcome a disappointment by recalling past disappointing events.	Recall past disappointments and rate them as they occurred and then with the distance of time and perspective.
8	Your TED Talk	47	Self-Confidence	Build confidence and examine connection between confidence and influence.	Prepare, videotape, and playback a presentation and receive feedback about confidence.
11	If I Had a Billion Dollars	56	Understanding Purpose and Values	Helps participants clarify and identify what they view as purposeful work.	Handout is used to structure thinking and discussion around purpose.
12	Finish Line!	59	Goal Orientation	Build awareness and move forward on goals by analyzing steps used to obtain past goals.	Use handout to move forward on a present goal.
14	To Talk or Not to Talk—That Is the Question	64	Social Bonds, Impact on Others, Feeling Impact on Others, Building Relationships	Sensitize people to the impact of talking too much or not enough.	Role play "talkers" and "nontalkers" and discuss impact.
16	What Do You Assign to the Pictures of Your Life?	71	Impact on Others, Optimism	Recognize how thinking affects our view and how optimism and pessimism can be influenced by changing our view.	People assign meaning to pictures based on their initial assumptions and then are asked to change their view.

#	Title	Page	Category	Purpose	Description
17	Practice Assigning New Thoughts/Feelings to Something in Your Career	74	Emotional and Inner Awareness, Optimism, Flexibility, Feeling Impact on Others	Examine our thinking about situations or people and how it affects our behavior.	Analyze current thinking about a person or situation, challenge the thinking, and then predict different behavior.
19	Last Name	78	Understanding Purpose and Values	Reflection on individual purpose and passion.	Handout-based reflection to stimulate thinking and discussion around purpose and passion.
23	Good Enough	90	Goal Orientation	Provide insight on self-directed goal setting and task achievement.	Handout based analysis of one's goal orientation for insight and discussion.
32	A Wondering Mind or a Plan for the Future?	119	Understanding Purpose and Values	Help people understand and clarify their purpose.	Use daydreams as a source of data regarding purpose.
33	Actions Speak Louder Than Words	126	Taking Actions toward Purpose	Encourage action toward purpose and dreams.	Using handout, define actions that could be taken to explore purpose or dreams.
34	Shoots and Scores	128	Resilience	Examine emotion and resilience related to a difficult task.	Group is asked to perform a task that requires them to think differently and identify what is affecting their performance.
36	Are You Flexible? Let's Find Out	133	Flexibility, Accurate Self-Assessment	Obtain feedback regarding flexibility.	Use 360-interview format to assess flexibility.
38	Authenticity—A Reflection	141	Authenticity	Build reflection around authenticity for the purpose of improving it.	Reflection handout and guided discussion on behaviors that lead to authenticity.

TABLE 6.27G *Continued*

ACTIVITY NUMBER	ACTIVITY NAME	PAGE NUMBER	ALL COMPETENCIES EXHIBITED	PURPOSE	SUMMARY
43	Authenticity Explored	157	Authenticity	Examine actions that are viewed authentically in teamwork and in career advancement.	Capture group thinking and norms around behaviors that are viewed as authentic and inauthentic.
46	Confidence Builder	166	Self-Confidence	Addresses criticism and confidence and the impact criticism can create in some individuals.	Small groups produce a list and the larger group offers criticism. Focused discussion about criticism and confidence.
49	What Have You Done?	173	Taking Actions Toward Purpose	Stress value of taking actions toward goals and one's purpose.	Review through a worksheet the actions one has taken to achieve a particular career path.

Disclosure Level

It is important to consider the disclosure level that the learner is able to accept at each point in the training. To quickly determine the disclosure level for each exercise, we have provided the following tables. We have also provided a reference chart for each of the content areas and which specific exercises that are supported by each content area.

TABLE 6-28 Disclosure Activities
TABLE 6-28A Low Disclosure Activities

ACTIVITY NUMBER	ACTIVITY NAME	PAGE NUMBER
1	The Critic	27
2	Know a Guy	30
3	Cups and Ice	33
5	The Invitation	38
7	Facebook Feed	44
9	Hot Potato	51
11	If I Had a Billion Dollars	56
12	Finish Line!	59
13	Selfie Listening	62
15	Gumball	68
16	What Do You Assign to the Pictures of Your Life?	71
18	Puzzler	76
19	Last Name	78
20	ROYGBIV	81
22	States	88
26	Swing Set	100
27	Restaurant Reviews	104
29	Academy Award	109
30	Judgment Day—Remote Teams	113
31	Let's Go!	116
34	Shoots and Scores	128
39	Better Method	144
44	Advertisement	160
47	Flying High	168

TABLE 6-28B   MEDIUM DISCLOSURE ACTIVITIES

TABLE 6-28C High Disclosure Activities

ACTIVITY NUMBER	ACTIVITY NAME	PAGE NUMBER
6	Doozie of a Disappointment	41
8	Your TED Talk	47
17	Practice Assigning New Thoughts/Feelings to Something in Your Career	74
23	Good Enough	90
24	Reflection Errors—Part 1	93
32	A Wondering Mind or a Plan for the Future?	119
33	Actions Speak Louder Than Words	126
36	Are you Flexible? Let's find out	133
37	How Am I Doing?	137
38	Authenticity—A Reflection	141
40	Flexibility—A New Leader Exercise	148
42	Reflection on Courage	154
48	Shoe Switch	171
49	What have you done?	173

Quick Activities

In some cases, it is important to be able to quickly reinforce a training concept and the trainer or coach needs to have at hand exercises that can be completed quickly. The activities in this table can be completed in 30 minutes.

TABLE 6-29 Quick Activities

ACTIVITY NUMBER	ACTIVITY NAME	PAGE NUMBER
1	The Critic	27
2	Know a Guy	30
3	Cups and Ice	33
7	Facebook Feed	44
11	If I Had a Billion Dollars	56
13	Selfie Listening	62
15	Gumball	68
17	Practice Assigning New Thoughts/Feelings to Something in Your Career	74
19	Last Name	78
22	States	88
23	Good Enough	90
30	Judgment Day—Remote Teams	113
39	Better Method	144
50	Review of Emotional Intelligence Using Quotations	176

As a reminder to trainers, activities can always be shortened by sharpening the focus of each activity. For example, you could concentrate on one of the key learning points. If you would like to make any of these exercises shorter, you can always select the debrief questions and discussion points that focus on the single key learning point you'd like to ensure is captured.

RECOMMENDED RESOURCES

Amdurer, Emily, Richard E. Boyatzis, Argun Saatcioglu, Melvin L. Smith, and Scott N. Taylor. "Long term impact of emotional, social and cognitive intelligence competencies and GMAT on career and life satisfaction and career success." *Frontiers in Psychology* **5** (2014).

Berger, Jennifer Garvey. *Changing on the Job: Developing Leaders for a Complex World* (Redwood City: Stanford University Press, 2013).

Boyatzis, Richard E. "Competencies as a behavioral approach to emotional intelligence." *Journal of Management Development* **28**, no. 9 (2009): 749–770.

Boyatzis, Richard E., James Gaskin, and Hongguo Wei. "Emotional and Social Intelligence and Behavior." In *Handbook of Intelligence*, pp. 243–262. New York: Springer Science+Business Media, 2015.

Brackett, Marc A., Susan E. Rivers, and Peter Salovey. "Emotional intelligence: Implications for personal, social, academic, and workplace success." *Social and Personality Psychology Compass* **5,** no. 1 (2011): 88–103.

Cooper, Robert K., and Ayman Sawaf. *Executive EQ Emotional Intelligence in Leadership and Organizations* (New York: The Berkley Publishing Group, 1997).

Côté, Stéphane, Paulo N. Lopes, Peter Salovey, and Christopher TH Miners. "Emotional intelligence and leadership emergence in small groups." *The Leadership Quarterly* **21,** no. 3 (2010): 496–508.

Cross, K. Patricia. *Adults as Learners: Increasing Participation and Facilitating Learning* (San Francisco: Jossey-Bass, 1973).

Dinh, Jessica E., Robert G. Lord, William L. Gardner, Jeremy D. Meuser, Robert C. Liden, and Jinyu Hu. "Leadership theory and research in the new millennium: Current theoretical trends and changing perspectives." *The Leadership Quarterly* **25,** no. 1 (2014): 36–62.

Freedman, Joshua. *The Business Case for Emotional Intelligence,* 3rd Ed. (San Mateo, CA: Six Seconds, 2010).

——— *Working With Emotional Intelligence* (New York: Bantam Doubleday Dell, 2000).

Gardner, Howard. *Art, Mind and Brain* (New York: Basic Books, 1982).

Gardner, Howard. *Frames of Mind: The Theory of Multiple Intelligences* (New York: Basic Books, 1983).

Goleman, Daniel. *Emotional Intelligence: Why It Can Matter More Than IQ* (New York: Bantam Books, 1995).

Goleman, Daniel, Richard Boyatzis, and Annie McKee. *Primal Leadership* (Boston: Harvard Business Press, 2002).

Harms, Peter D., and Marcus Credé. "Emotional intelligence and transformational and transactional leadership: A meta-analysis." *Journal of Leadership & Organizational Studies* **17,** no. 1 (2010): 5–17.

Kegan, Robert, and Lisa Laskow Lahey, *Immunity to Change: How to Overcome It and Unlock Potential in Yourself and Your Organization.* (Boston: Harvard Business Press, 2009).

Khalili, Ashkan. "The role of emotional intelligence in the workplace: A literature review." *International Journal of Management* **29,** no. 3 (2012): 355.

Klatt, B. *The Ultimate Training Workshop Handbook: A Comprehensive Guide to Leading Successful Workshops & Training Programs* (New York: McGraw-Hill, 1999).

Knowles, Malcom. S. *The Adult Learner: A Neglected Species,* 3rd Ed. (Houston:Gulf, 1984).

Kolb. D. A., and R,. Fry, "Toward an Applied Theory of Experiential Learning." In *Theories of Group Process,* ed. C. Cooper (London: John Wiley, 1975).

Lewis, Philip M. *The Discerning Heart: The Developmental Psychology of Robert Kegan* (Seattle: Amazon Digital Services, 2011).

Lynn, Adele B., *The EQ Difference: A Powerful Plan for Putting Emotional Intelligence to Work* (New York: AMACOM Books, 2005).

—— *The EQ Interview* (New York: AMACOM Books, 2008).

Nelson, Darwin B., and Gary R. Low. *Emotional Intelligence: Achieving Academic and Career Excellence in College and in Life",* 2nd Ed. (Upper Saddle River: Prentice Hall, 2011).

Pike, Robert. W. *Creative Training Techniques Handbook* (Minneapolis: Lakewood Books, 2003).

Sayeed, Omar Bin, and Meera Shanker. "Emotionally intelligent managers & transformational leadership styles." *Indian Journal of Industrial Relations* (2009): 593–610.

Seligman, Martin E. P. *Learned Optimism* (New York: Knopf, 1990).

Vidyarthi, Prajya R., Smriti Anand, and Robert C. Liden. "Do emotionally perceptive leaders motivate higher employee performance? The moderating role of task interdependence and power distance." *The Leadership Quarterly* **25,** no. 2 (2014): 232–244.

Wall, Bob. *Coaching for Emotional Intelligence: The Secret to Developing the Star Potential in Your Employees.* (New York: AMACOM Books, 2006).

Walter, Frank, Michael S. Cole, and Ronald H. Humphrey. "Emotional intelligence: sine qua non of leadership or folderol?." *The Academy of Management Perspectives* **25,** no. 1 (2011): 45–59.

Whitmore, John. *Coaching for Performance* (San Diago: Pfieffer, 1994).

INDEX

CPSIA information can be obtained
at www.ICGtesting.com
Printed in the USA
LVOW09s1826110618
580324LV00025B/393/P